SEX THERAPY TODAY

Sex Therapy Today

Patricia and Richard Gillan

Open Books

London

First published in 1976 by Open Books Publishing Ltd,
87–89 Shaftesbury Avenue, LONDON W1V 7AD

© Patricia and Richard Gillan 1976

ISBN 0 7291 0045 6

Set in 10/12pt Linotype Times and
printed in Great Britain by Northumberland Press Limited, Gateshead

Contents

We would like to pay tribute to the films which have helped to enrich our own fantasies and sex lives and those of others. We are particularly indebted to Buñuel, Borowczyk, Leopold Torre-Nilsson, Makevejev, Ken Russell, von Sternberg, Pasolini, Nagisa Oshima, Bertolucci, Fellini and Falcon Stuart.

1

Introduction

The problem of sexual dysfunction

Therapy versus medicine – therapists versus doctors
Modern sex therapy is a treatment for sexual problems, based on
scientific foundations. It is treatment in the sense that an attempt
is made to solve a problem, in this case a sexual problem, by
rational means.

In sex therapy the treatment takes the form of reassurance,
education and carefully designed recommendations. The treatment
has more in common with education than with medicine. It is
usually considered to be a type of psychotherapy. In the medical
situation at its simplest a patient who has a problem, an illness,
comes to a doctor who may be able to recommend a cure which
is then administered to the patient. Only the minimum intelligent
cooperation is required or expected from the patient. If the principles of the treatment are explained, it is more to indulge the
curiosity of the patient than to ensure the efficacy of the cure.
Antibiotics will work, even against the will of the patient. Within
the 'medical model', the wisdom, authority and knowledge of the
doctor are to be taken for granted, as being agreed, understood and
accepted by both the doctor and the patient. By the patient, who
offers passive cooperation in exchange for cure; and by the doctor,
who is relieved of the need to cajole and persuade.

While, in outline, this is the basis of the medical model, there are
of course educative aspects to many medical situations. The
physician will advise the overweight patient to slim and will increase
the effectiveness of the dietary advice by some simple theoretical
'back-up' explanations. The cardiac patient is advised to stop
smoking in order to relieve the heart of unnecessary load. The
prescription to slim or to stop smoking is rendered more effective

by the advice. The advice may allow the patient to make intelligent decisions to cover unforeseen contingencies. The advice may gratify the person's need to feel he is contributing to the resolution of the disorder. In part, some of the credit for his health accrues to himself. It could be said that the patient must work towards his cure.

In the therapy of sexual disorders there is no cure without work. The sex therapist offers himself as an educator: a person who is prepared to sit down with the sufferer and work out a solution which will not be effective unless understood and accepted. The patient is not asked to assume the cure in advance but only to try certain recommendations, the possible value of which has been explained.

The sex therapist, then, will devote much of the therapy time to discussion, a discussion in which the contributions of the patient are of equal importance to those of the therapist. Within a certain theoretical framework the sex therapist adjusts the recommendations in accordance with the personality and attitudes of the patient. To emphasise give and take, the mutual responsibility and the cooperation required, the therapy usually takes place in a comfortable setting which does not stress the authority of the therapist, and the therapist neither wears a white coat nor sits behind a desk.

Sexual dysfunction – a problem not an illness.
This book deals with sexual problems, not sexual illnesses. The particular complaint of sufferers may be that their performance is less than ideal, as, for example, with impotence; equally it may be that their enjoyment is insufficient. Both are sexual problems: the one of mental and physical function, the other, possibly one mainly of attitude. Where sexual enjoyment or activity are concerned, to believe one has a problem is to have a problem. Similarly, in the domain of appetites, to believe one has a deprivation is to have one. What the eye does not see the heart cannot grieve over.

Some problems may be solved speedily by a short informative discussion. These problems are often ones of ignorance. The question 'does masturbation damage the health?' may be quickly answered. The belief that a vagina may be too small or that a penis may be too large can be sources of worry and problems to some women, but again such beliefs may be dealt with by the simple act of providing information. Where the reassurance is not accepted, of course, one has a different problem.

A problem is a problem without reference to its severity. There is no natural division between minor problems and more serious ones. Sex therapists are usually to be found treating fairly well-defined problems, of which impotence is a well-known example. But a problem without a name, such as the failure to enjoy sex sufficiently or as much as is desired, is one which well illustrates the idea that something becomes a problem only when one has taken the step of saying 'this situation is wrong or unsatisfactory for me', 'this situation is a problem which may have a solution'. At any time, there will be many others for whom a similar situation is not seen as a problem. The person who does not enjoy sex a great deal may say 'that's me, I cannot change' or may not even say anything at all. The sufferer, on the other hand, wants the situation to change. He has a certain goal in mind: to become potent, for example, or to enjoy sex more.

Sexual problems – personal solutions

The natural response to the idea of a problem is to seek a solution. No one who believes he has a problem goes immediately to a sex therapist. This is partly because sex problems often start quite insidiously; but also, more importantly, because the sufferer will try first to help himself, then perhaps ask the advice of friends, and later the opinion of medical men not directly concerned with sex. To try out all the potential recommendations may take time. He may be distracted from the problem by some new event in life, a new job or a new house. Repeated failures may 'set up' a state of mind akin to defeat, in which the problem is seen as insoluble. His sex life may limp along in the form of a bad habit. In such a situation it is usually some outside event which precipitates the therapy. The spouse, who apparently has no problem, may insist on a consultation.

A sad way in which a sexual problem may be diverted might be classed as psychosomatic or partly concealed. The sufferer may begin to experience other symptoms which can be an expression of sexual discontent, whether he is aware of it or not. Vague aches in the back and lower abdomen are typical, though of course there are many other causes as well. In a less extreme situation is the person who is unable to speak openly of the problem, either from

3

embarrassment or from an expectation of a rebuff or ridicule. Such is the burden of work of many doctors that, even if such repression or shyness is perceived, they prefer a conspiracy of silence to confronting a problem which they see as potentially embarrassing or insoluble.

Emotions

The educational and persuasive role of the therapist towards the patient does not by any means complete the picture of therapy as problem solution. Sexual problems are attended by emotions which are difficult to control. The person with a sex problem often likes to conceal this fact, as he feels it is a shameful thing to admit. The problem reveals him as less successful than he wishes to appear. He may believe that people will treat him with less respect, should they learn of the sexual inadequacy.

Many people, having never openly discussed sex, find it quite embarrassing to discuss the intimate details of their sex lives – their masturbation habits, for example. One spouse may wish to conceal some fact from the other. It may be a 'guilty' secret. The secret may refer to behaviour which is clearly unusual. Guilt may pervade the whole sexuality of some people, particularly those brought up in an embarrassed and sexually repressive childhood milieu.

The sex therapist, unlike the doctor, has to respect such anxieties, not from politeness but from a belief that anxiety reduction, the diminution of guilt, shame and embarrassment, is an aim of treatment. Without it the treatment will fail. These disturbing emotions are nearly always present to some degree with sexual problems, although when the problem has existed for a long time the emotions may be very much in the background and may only appear when successful sexuality becomes a possibility.

The sex therapist, then, aims to remove such emotions and to replace them with emotions of pleasure, calm and sexual excitement, which will allow sexual behaviour to flourish.

New attitudes and new behaviours

Society and individuals

In attempting such a change the therapist is working towards the same goals that are seen to be desirable by society itself. There is nowadays a widespread expectation that sexual behaviour shall be a source of pleasure. The furtive and constrictive attitudes of the past have been identified and condemned. Sexual happiness and creativity is in demand. Today the imagination is being liberated from the puritanical burden which it has carried for so long. People are asking themselves whether they may be 'missing out'. They feel themselves beckoned into a hitherto forbidden land. In previous generations it was only necessary to have some sexual thoughts for one to believe that such an activity was wrong and should be suppressed at once. Thoughts revealing a part of one's nature which was animal and coarse. Thoughts which should be replaced with ideas more noble and less indulgent. This is not to say of course that people of the past have not enjoyed their sexually repressive attitudes. They were able to dwell on their virtue and their superiority in an orgy of earnest rectitude. Repressive and hidebound parents brought up guilty and inhibited children. Children who, in the course of time, began to experience their own sexuality with no other model to guide them than the embarrassed and secretive attitude of their parents. Naturally the sexual energy and enthusiasm of many people were able to surmount these restrictions, but for many the scope of their enjoyment must have been very much reduced. Ignorance of the existence and possibilities of the clitoris is still widespread. What wasteful neglect! Such was the selfishness of many men that female sexuality was lost in the myths of idealised purity.

In the last one hundred or so years, publicists such as Zola and Lawrence began to change the prettified stance of contemporary society, themselves reflecting the gradual deposition of man from pre-Darwinian times. Writers such as these made it quite clear that physical passion was a desirable thing in itself and that an attitude of sensuality naturally led to enhanced sexuality. At the same time science moved on from the world of things and of the interactions of matter to penetrate areas hitherto taboo. This began with speculative enquiry but then increased in vigour, and culminated in the detailed work of Masters and Johnson, who, not content with asking questions, observed people during sexual behaviour and supplemented this with detailed instrumental recordings. It is only in the last fifty years that novels, newspapers, films, and latterly T.V. have begun to influence people at all widely. Prior to this there was no general access to new ideas other than by word of mouth and by example. Human structures are very slow to change in the absence of some compelling force. The more tightly knit the society, the slower the pace of change, the more powerful the dictates of the past. Christianity placed massive emphasis on property and propriety. Property and its associate values demanded order; sexuality represented disorder and was thus subjected to the onerous restraints of a code of manners designed to emphasise the docility and compliance of the majority. Everyone was allotted a place and expected to keep it. Naturally even in the most constipated and rigid societies there have been liberated spirits, but because of the absence of the media and the acquiescence of the majority, these examples were easily muted.

This is now all changing. There is less and less talk of morality, of what is right and wrong. Ordinary people feel that they have the right to behave more or less as they please, especially in private, and within obvious limits.

Public behaviour and morality are changing also. The constant stream of new ideas are taken up by bolder spirits as a kind of experiment in living. Some of these ideas after a short while disappear. Others like, say, the Twist have influences which live on in a new style of dancing. Styles of behaviour and of sexuality, just as in fashion and in music, are subjects for experiment.

In the last fifty years premarital sexual relations have become the rule and there are many who feel that these experiments are essential in order to establish sexual compatibility. Marriage itself is no longer an inviolate institution. 'Swinging', the practice of swopping marital partners, is very fashionable especially in parts of the U.S.A., though it is too early to know whether it will become widely accepted.

The pace at which new ideas and experiments are introduced and tested owes a lot to the communications explosion. The ideals of sexuality are no longer concealed. The media speak openly of sexual behaviour and, despite censorship, sexuality pervades newspapers and films. It is only in the last twenty years that sexual intercourse has been shown in films, though even now more often than not cuts are made at crucial moments. The erect penis is rarely viewed, though with the present rate of change this common and exciting part of the human condition may be open to the interest and admiration it deserves. Happily the prudery and

6

prurience of previous generations is giving way to a new frankness.

Individual adjustment
Happily, those who do not obtain pleasure from their sexual behaviour can nowadays envisage the idea of therapy. It may be difficult, and expensive, to obtain; they may have only the vaguest idea of how it might help them – but the possibility is now there. The average person is quite likely to feel that he has a right to enjoyment just as he has a right to share in the general prosperity. The quality of life has become important, now that it is no longer a perpetual grind. The quality of relationships has begun to seem important since the leisure to enjoy them has appeared. At least as important is the demand for equality by women, who in the past have often had their needs and wishes ignored in a masculine dominated society.

Emotional and sexual harmony as a goal can clearly only be reached where the partners believe they must contribute equally, intelligently and continuously to its welfare. Selfishness and dominance can only engender rebellion or passive compliance, neither of which can lead to true harmony.

Sex as part of life – sexual versus ordinary behaviour
Ideally of course in order to be truly happy the individual must have a good adjustment in other areas of life, such as work and friendship, and where such adjustments are not good, they should if possible be improved. Nevertheless, for many people a permanent or semi-permanent relationship with a member of the opposite sex is a large ingredient of happiness. However long the relationship may last, the sexual interaction between the pair will be an important part of it; a part which will both mirror the quality of the bond and may well sustain it.

Separately, the sexual and the non-sexual interaction between the partners are of equal importance and one cannot speak of either as being prime. The special characteristic of sexual behaviour, however, is that it demands a certain abandon, a certain surrender, a suspension of our normal inhibitions. It is an activity in which one has no choice but to be sincere if real satisfaction, as distinct from mere orgiastic relief, is to be achieved. Furthermore, sexual behaviour between two people takes place in a private arena and because of this it is freed to some extent from the immediate external demands of society. In such privacy abandonment becomes possible.

So much of our social life depends on constant calculation, constant adjustment, constant vigilance, and frequent inhibition of our normal impulses, that the ability to relax and to surrender our inhibitions becomes extremely difficult. Because sexual expression demands abandon and sincerity it is particularly vulnerable to feelings of anxiety, guilt, and hostility, all of which can seriously disrupt it.

The free expression of natural sexual behaviour is often severely suppressed in childhood and at school. The outcome of this is that when sexual activity becomes more urgent and more competitive, difficulties may be encountered. Where expectations are so high, small failures can seem disastrous. Many people establish a reasonable adjustment only to lose it in middle life when a relationship has lasted a long while. Sex therapists frequently find, in such cases, that adequate sexual expression has never been truly achieved. Many people wait until their marriage is imperilled before seeking help.

Sex and personal relationships
Although the people who come to a sex therapist believe primarily that they have a sex problem they often experience some deterioration in their personal relationship as well. Indeed the fact that they are still together despite these twin difficulties is significant. Each partner may have weighed up the advantages of staying together as against the dangers of parting. A satisfactory new partner may not be easy to find. Security may be of paramount importance. Children may come into the situation – their welfare cannot be set aside. Many people are aware that society is reconsidering marriage as an institution, and here two ideas seem to conflict. The first demands that when a relationship goes sour it should be abandoned; the second, that any couple should maximise both their sexual and personal bond. The resolution of such a conflict may be achieved by asking two other questions. Firstly, are there powerful reasons to persist with the relationship? and secondly, have we sincerely tried to make the relationship, both personal and sexual, as successful as possible? The answer may point directly towards a fresh start, perhaps with the aid of a therapist.

It is a happy fact that even though the sex therapist may seem to devote all the attention to the sexual difficulty, the personal relationship often improves concurrently. This is not difficult to understand. Where the partner gives and is willing to give sexual pleasure, whatever quarrels and differences there may be in the background become easier to forgive. The new warmth may permit a new openness. Problems may be discussed with calm and not with rancour. Because of this and because of the simplicity of the method, sex therapy as described in this book is of value where sexual difficulties exist, whether or not there are other disturbances of personal relationship. These may well disappear if the sexual difficulties are resolved, as part of the increased love and affection released by the new satisfaction. Also, since therapy is a learning situation, the strategies that may have been suggested may well give rise to a new confidence in all areas of the relationship.

The person who has asked for help with a sexual problem may or may not have a permanent sexual partner. Indeed the sexual problem may have made the acquisition of a permanent partner a doubtful aim. In that case the therapist will perhaps take the first step of treatment with one person alone. Nevertheless, quite early in treatment, the patient will have to make a relationship in which the problem can be finally resolved. Where the patient finds such a relationship impossible to make, sex therapy is no longer the answer and the problem has to be dealt with differently.

Treatment

Analysis of the problem
Usually the therapist works with a couple. The treatment consists of a thorough analysis of the problem as a first step. The sexual history of the individuals is taken in considerable detail. The therapist will want to know, for example, when the patient began to masturbate and how. Was the masturbation pleasant or ridden with guilt? What sexual fantasies were conjured up to aid the act? Are the fantasies still a big part of the present sexual activity? What attitude is there towards such fantasies and so on? Intimate and detailed discussion of sexual intercourse, frequency, positions, time of day, oral sex behaviour and so on will take place, so that

9

in making an assessment of what treatment is required, the therapist is fully conversant with the facts and the patients may feel that no topic is concealed or beyond discussion.

Patients often get considerable relief from this 'giving' alone. In the case of partners with 'guilty secrets', long kept from the other for fear of rejection or contempt, the relief experienced is enhanced by the calmness with which these 'guilty secrets' are accepted. Accepted easily because so often the partner also has 'secrets', even if less lurid ones. To accept one's partner 'warts and all' is to imply that one's love and acceptance is not conditional upon perfection, but upon a certain mixture of qualities different in each relationship. To admit weaknesses and failures may place new burdens upon the relationship but it also shows the other partner how much he or she is needed – which is an essential ingredient in any relationship. Both men and women often choose partners partly because they feel they can help and complement them in some way. In short, because they feel needed.

While the patient is giving his or her story the therapist will be evolving ideas about the details of the treatment. Deciding on the emphasis to be given between, say, anxiety reduction and re-education. Where a couple is being treated, the therapist may decide that each partner has different needs, and the treatment will have to be adjusted accordingly. A tentative plan of treatment is evolved as the history proceeds and is considered in more detail when the session is over.

Individuals and couples
Much of this book concerns the problems of sexual adjustment between couples. However, the theory of behaviour therapy provides a general suggestion and guidance bank which can be drawn upon and applied to the problems of single people as well. An example of the type of problem is the young man suffering from premature ejaculation who has not yet chosen a settled partner. Here some preliminary sessions may be given before making an attempt to obtain a cooperative sexual partner with whom further treatment is usually given. While far more couples than single people are at present referred for sex therapy, sex clinics should make treatment for single people just as readily available.

The treatment plan

Where one is working with a couple, the manner of treating the problem by means of a graded series of tasks is first explained. The couple will be sent away to try out these first easy steps, and when they return their experiences are discussed. Where there have been difficulties, new strategies are evolved and incorporated into new exercises. Part of each discussion is devoted to reassurance and education. Education concerning the anatomy of the sexual parts, the mechanism of the sexual response, and some explanation of the principles and theory of behaviour therapy. The therapist hopes that by teaching new attitudes and new techniques in this way, the sensual and erotic life of the couple will be vastly expanded.

Treatment will progress by stages. The couple will attend the clinic on average for about ten sessions of one hour each. They will always have to attend together since the treatment is the treatment of a mutual difficulty and of a relationship; where there are also some difficulties in the non-sexual relationship these can be discussed alongside the sexual problem itself.

Although much of the time will be spent sitting talking to the therapist, the couple will also be asked to touch one another during the treatment in order to exemplify some of the exercises. However, no undressing or sexual activity need take place in the presence of the therapist.

Sex therapists – who are they?

The new sex therapy has been evolved and promoted mainly by psychologists. Medical and psychiatric attitudes have been on the whole less fruitful, perhaps because doctors are wedded to the idea of drug treatment and are of course often temperamentally unsuited to the patient psychotherapeutic attitudes required by the newer therapies. Furthermore, just as a couple who have sexual problems are stuck, so also the psychiatric and medical profession have been stuck, in the past, with a sense of helplessness and frustration engendered by a lack of effective therapeutic ideas. This pessimism still lingers.

Those best qualified to undertake the treatment of sexual problems are usually psychologists specialising in behaviour therapy, or medical workers, often psychiatrists, who have taken an interest in the treatment of marital and sexual problems. These therapists have often received training in handling psychotherapeutic inter-

11

actions and will have discovered during this time whether they have the patience and adjustment to continue with it. The advantages of specialist training in therapy are undoubted, though there are many non-specialists in other, related fields who could usefully be included in a' sex therapy team.

Once equipped with the general theoretical knowledge, the ideal therapist will have undertaken the treatment of patients under the supervision of a more experienced therapist. After a number of such cases he or she may have decided to specialise in one form of therapy, and from there have decided to concentrate on the treatment of sexual difficulties.

Recruitment of sex therapists

However, the actual number of psychologists and medical workers who are competent and willing to give therapy for sexual problems is very limited. With the result that the chances of a patient finding such therapy are also very limited, especially where the patient has no idea how to go about finding help. It is also, unfortunately, expensive.

However, there are numerous people who would with very little extra training be capable of undertaking this kind of therapy. Marriage guidance counsellors have much of the relevant experience, as have many psychiatric social workers. Family doctors and physicians are inhibited in this field mainly by a lack of time and/or interest. Though when a knowledge of the effectiveness of the new therapy becomes more widespread perhaps they will undertake it more frequently, especially where some of the more straightforward problems are involved.

In some European and American centres nurses are being encouraged to take training in this field. Many nurses have considerable ability in handling people and their problems, and they could usefully put this skill to much wider use were they not hamstrung by the role definitions of the past.

The advantages of introducing non-specialists into sex therapy are obvious; just as with marriage guidance, far more people could be helped. The problem of diagnosis, of sorting out those who will respond to sex therapy from those who need a different therapy, those who are psychiatrically ill from those who are essentially normal, can be readily overcome by including such non-specialist workers in a team supervised by trained psychiatrists and psychologists.

Personal qualities

Before anyone, qualified or not, undertakes this kind of therapy, they should ask themselves whether they have the personal qualities required. Clearly they must have first-hand experience of personal relationships with a successful sexual adjustment, otherwise the advice they give will be solely theoretical. They will not truly sympathise. Their sex life should be imaginative and full: they must be able to practise what they preach. In character, it is best if they relate easily to all types of people and have no serious problems in their own make-up. They must be able to deal equally with anxiety and hostility without draining themselves or becoming too involved.

This sounds demanding but the wrong person risks making matters worse and diverting patients from those who might genuinely be able to help them.

The training of therapists

The further training is best done in an established sex clinic. The trainees can join an experienced pair of co-therapists and attend during the treatment of a few couples as an observer. After a short while they are ready to have patients of their own, though they will still need to have an experienced therapist as their partner. In practice this system works very well. Besides treating the patients, many sex clinics have discussion groups and other teaching activities for the therapists in training. In such a setting, a therapist can usually be trained in two years, though naturally this will vary a little. During this time, they will experience a wide variety of problems and will learn to judge the treatment possibilities inherent in any given case. This is particularly important since sexual difficulties are often symptoms of other disorders such as personality distortions and depression, which are sent to medical centres for assessment by psychiatrists and psychologists. This vital experience of a wide range of problems is perhaps the hardest part of the training to acquire. The ability to handle people with tact and sympathy and the theoretical background of behaviour therapy can both be learnt readily if the trainee is reasonably well adjusted and intelligent.

Self-help

One important question should be examined here : can people help themselves? The answer is that they should try, but try only for a limited period. If they believe their problem is not serious, they should begin by reading some of the books recommended in the appendix and by understanding the methods and principles of treatment outlined in this book. The mode of procedure should be obvious, but any attempt should not go on too long. After three months, if difficulties persist, professional help should be sought.

The trouble with self-help is that one has usually already made some attempts at solving the problem and become pessimistic through failure. An attitude of mind is established which constipates thinking constructively on the problem. Trying out new solutions becomes an effort of will. Where there are quarrels and unsolved personal issues at stake it is very difficult to abandon these attitudes, because of pride and the danger of loss of face. Human beings also tend to fear any new situations, often feeling that the old situation, even though faulty, is preferable to a new one with perhaps new insecurities.

This is really where a therapist, as mediator and educator, comes in. The therapist can evolve tactics for bypassing confrontations; can overcome the reluctance to face the unknown by giving the reassurance of continued help; and most important of all can enhance the motivation towards change without which treatment will fail. Thus, you should think twice before attempting any self cure. Even a small amount of professional help may make all the difference.

The quality of outside help

At the moment, unless they are unusually well-informed, most people have to accept whatever treatment they are offered. Once the decision to seek treatment is made, most people will visit a local doctor and what happens next will depend on that doctor. Commonly the patients will find themselves referred to another doctor, usually a psychiatrist, who will make the next decision. What is decided depends partly on the nature of the problem, and partly on the training and theoretical outlook of the psychiatrist, and partly on the ideas of the patient.

This book is concerned with altering this situation. The most pressing problem of today is the treatment of difficulties experienced within relationships both by the married and the unmarried. Modern psychological theory provides an effective tool for this treatment. The particular system which is the subject of this book is the treatment evolved by Masters and Johnson, with some alterations and additions. This type of treatment is designed mainly for couples, but since the theory upon which it is based, that is behavioural theory, may be applied successfully to many other sexual disorders, the next section attempts, briefly, to relate the whole range of sexual disorders to the various treatments available.

The range of sexual problems

Some sexual problems are produced by deeper disturbances in the personality; for example, serious difficulties in making relationships with other people, or perhaps an overriding and unnecessary concern with dirt and germs. (There are of course many others.) There are also sexual difficulties which are part of depression and more serious disorders of the mind, such as schizophrenia. However, it is unusual in such cases for the sexual difficulties to be seen as anything but secondary to the underlying disorder and hence such sexual difficulties almost never come before a sex therapist. In any case the treatment indicated is the treatment of the main disorder.

Perversion versus deviation

There is a second group of sexual disorders which used to be called 'perversions'. This word is a condemnation and is no longer appropriate. To some extent modern thinking considers that people are not wholly responsible for their style of behaviour and thus should not be blamed for what they do. Equally, many people now believe that others should be allowed to indulge in whatever activities they please, unless these are seriously harmful either to themselves or others. Either way the word 'perversion' has become unsuitable, and the favoured alternative is 'deviation'.

The idea behind 'deviation' is this: the majority of people will behave in a certain manner. For example, the majority prefer heterosexual intercourse in the male superior position. However, in any large group there will be a number of people who behave in unusual ways. Small numbers of people in such a group

15

will behave in very unusual ways. Behaviour that is very rare would be called extremely deviant; for example, people who obtain sexual pleasure while tied up are very deviant, but in saying this one is not taking a moral attitude.

To give some further examples, homosexual behaviour is considered a deviation, as is also transvestism (the desire to 'dress up' in the clothes of the opposite sex, for sexual purposes), and various forms of fetishism (a fetish is usually an inanimate material or object, the possession and handling of which increases sexual excitement. Many fetishists are, for example, very attached to rubber; others prefer women's handbags or underwear).

Some deviants commonly come to doctors from the courts; a good example of this being male exhibitionism (the exposure of the erect penis usually to single or small groups of women or girls).

These deviations are usually considered to be due to quite fundamental personality disorders often reaching back into childhood. Probably the majority of people who could be called deviants have no desire to change their behaviour and never dream of consulting a therapist. As far as the therapist is concerned deviations are important for three reasons. Firstly, the deviants may wish to increase their sexual options: the homosexual may wish to marry. Secondly, minor degrees of deviant sexual interest are common among people who would call themselves 'normal'. This deviance may be a source of shame and conflict. It may be concealed from the partner and may divert sexual energy from the relationship. Where the other partner can accept the deviation the problem usually disappears, as do many other unnecessary worries when brought out into the open. Thirdly, the deviation may be difficult to displace as the preferred mode of sexual expression.

Where a deviation is found in one of the marital partners the therapist does not usually attempt to eradicate it. Most therapists now prefer to increase the satisfaction derived from alternative and more cooperative sexual behaviour. Where this is accomplished the deviant behaviour may fade. Deviance which is unwanted may be treated similarly. The therapists will attempt to teach the patient a new manner of behaviour and to teach it in such a way as to establish it as the main source of satisfaction, or at least a pleasurable alternative.

Dysfunctions of normal behaviour
A further group of patients consists of those who have had sexual difficulties from the outset of the usual period of increased sexual activity – during the time of life when heterosexual behaviour is being learned. Such people find that they cannot respond in some way they know to be desirable. For example, the woman who becomes very tense at the moment when the penis enters, or the younger man with impotence or premature ejaculation. Unfortunately, such people often do not come for treatment until years after the establishment of their trouble. Often they have married and it is only the complaints of their spouse which lead them to seek advice. Their difficulties are often readily improved by the application of behavioural techniques.

Couples with sexual difficulties form the final group. From the point of view of the sex therapist they are the largest group. This may be because the demand for treatment and for improvement is most urgent. After all, the difficulties may begin right at the outset, even on the honeymoon if full sexual relations have not taken place before. Such difficulties usually arise from problems which were apparent before the contract was arranged. Many others begin well with a satisfactory sex life which as the years go by gradually fails. For the man the typical difficulty might be impotence of gradual onset; for the woman, a loss of pleasure perhaps. The treatment of Masters and Johnson was specifically evolved for couples who have either kind of difficulty.

The range of treatments

The type of treatment given will depend on the treatment favoured by the therapist to whom the patient has been sent. We shall be describing the method of sex therapy which is based on behaviour theory, and in particular the method of Masters and Johnson, together with additional behavioural methods more recently evolved. However, before the advent of behaviourism other methods were evolved and disseminated, and while these methods are likely to be superseded, it is best to be armed with the facts, and for this reason some other therapies will also be described.

Psychotherapy – Freud
Among the psychological methods of sex therapy the first evolved is associated with the name of Freud. Of course his treatment methods were able to cover almost any psychological disorder and were not specifically designed for sexual disorders. Nevertheless, Freud promoted the idea that sexual difficulties were deep-seated distortions of the early childhood development. His proposed solution was the radical restructuring of the personality by means of analysis. A fuller insight into the patient's nature is sought by means of discussion in which the therapist gives little direction but encourages the patient to draw the conclusions. The patient is encouraged to relive with the therapist the unsatisfactory parental relationship and by such means to experience and analyse his distorted emotional development.

Freud's followers have shortened, elaborated and altered his methods in an attempt to accommodate new ideas and new exigencies. But such treatments remain very lengthy and are for most people quite impractical. They are very time-consuming and expensive, there is no proof of their efficacy, and since the demand for sex therapy will for some time to come exceed the number of therapists available, the employment of such radical and time-consuming methods effectively reduces the chances of patients receiving adequate sex therapy still further. However, there are a number of other methods of treatment available which do not derive from the ideas of Freud.

Other types of psychotherapy
Directive and supportive psychotherapy is widely given. Here the psychiatrist treats the patient at a common-sense level. He gives advice in a direct manner: 'I would do x if I were you.' x here might be, 'go out more often' or perhaps 'don't work so hard'. In any case, a persistent attempt may be made to offer sensible 'easy-to-follow' advice to the patient. At the same time, the doctor offers the patient moral support and encouragement which may help him over difficult times. Commonly such methods are backed up with the use of simple tranquillisers to relieve anxiety.

This rather general kind of treatment varies a good deal in its application and method. It cannot be said to be well defined and partly because of this it is impossible to discover how effective it may be. Sex therapists feel that it would be better replaced by treatment which is more specific and probably more effective.

Conjoint therapy
Where the physician or psychiatrist is familiar with conjoint therapy and where the sexual problem exists within a relationship, the options for effective treatment widen. Conjoint here means that the couple are treated as a couple, and the problem is seen as a problem of their relationship, not one peculiar to either partner. There are many varieties of conjoint therapy. What they have in common is that the couple sit down together with a therapist, with whom and in front of whom they discuss their problem. Sometimes the therapist will give the couple tasks to do at home as part of the treatment. Sometimes contractual exchanges are arranged on the lines of, 'If you will consult me on the family budget I will show you more affection', or, 'If you agree to turn off the television early, I will show more enthusiasm during love-making.'

Some form of conjoint therapy is probably the treatment of choice for purely marital problems. In a marriage with problems both of the relationship and of sex, it is sometimes argued that the marital problem, a relationship problem, is the cause of the sexual problem and hence should be treated first and most importantly. No one can pronounce on this dilemma, and the therapist must judge whether to concentrate on the one or the other or both; where the therapist is uncertain, trial and error will help.

Behaviourism – learning theory – Masters and Johnson
Masters and Johnson Therapy is a type of conjoint therapy based on modern lines of behaviour modification. The theory behind such treatment is called Behaviour Theory, Behaviourism or Learning Theory. These terms are used rather loosely but this is not important. Three important ideas underlie behaviourism and learning theory. Firstly, that a substantial part of sexual behaviour is learned. That is, sexual behaviour in part has to be taught, or discovered by trial and error, or invented. In any event the individual learns to behave in a certain manner, and the learning takes place piecemeal and comes from diverse sources: friends, films, gossip, newspapers, magazines, and, increasingly, from sex education. The idea that much of sexual behaviour is learned suggests that ignorance of sexual behaviour is also a possibility. Indeed,

ignorance of sexual matters is widespread, together with prejudice and a mass of misinformation.

Reward and punishment The second main idea of learning theory is that rewards and punishments will determine what behaviour is learned. Behaviour which is rewarded will be established in the behavioural repertoire of the individual. Conversely, behaviour which is punished will be discarded.

The words 'reward' and 'punishment' are used in a rather general sense. However, in learning theory, as applied to human beings, a reward is that which gives pleasure. It may be a sweet, it may be money, it may be a smile or it may be a sexual favour. The word 'punishment' has a similar latitude. Punishment may be a scowl, a blow, or a fine, for example.

Drive The third main idea of learning theory is the idea of drive. A human being has many drives, one of which is the sex drive. A drive is a state of readiness or otherwise to behave in a certain way. A person in a high state of sexual drive wants to behave sexually. After sexual behaviour which is satisfactorily completed and has led to orgasm, the sexual drive is reduced for a variable time. All human beings vary from day to day in their sexual drive, and some people have more sex drive than others. Young people have more sex drive than older people.

Behaviour therapy uses all these ideas in the treatment of sexual problems, which are essentially problems of behaviour, and which respond well to these methods.

The theory applied The behaviour therapist, then, applies these three main ideas to teach a new pattern of behaviour. The theory behind the treatment is easily learned and readily explained to the patients.

The first behaviourists to evolve a systematic method of treating the common sexual problems were Masters and Johnson, working in the United States. The elements of their method are quite few: they restrict themselves to treating couples who have a sexual problem. The treatment which they give is intensive. All patients are treated by two therapists, a female and a male. The therapists aim to educate the couple, to make sure they understand the basic anatomy of the sexual organs. They introduce them to sexual techniques which will give increased pleasure to their love-making. To assist with the relearning of new habits and with the unlearning of the undesired behaviour, the clients are given a series of graded tasks which they perform at home together and then report on the results. At each visit the difficulties are discussed and new tasks given, depending on the progress achieved. The couple goes from simple undemanding tasks all the way to normal and satisfactory sexual relations.

Newer ideas in sex therapy

While the Masters and Johnson approach is probably the best known and the most widely practised, there are also other distinctive methods in use. All these methods are behavioural and educative, and many are used in combination with the basic Masters and Johnson treatment structure.

SAR: Sexual Attitude Restructuring

At the National Sex Forum in San Francisco in the United States there is the SAR school, designed principally to educate professional workers and sex therapists about sexual matters, but also used therapeutically with patients. Clients sit round a room on deep cushions watching films projected all over the surrounding walls. These films, eight to twelve at a time, portray every conceivable unharmful human sexual activity over a period of about one hour. The idea of this is partly educative. The clients may watch how other people behave and they learn the range of possible sexual behaviours. They gain new ideas of how their own and others' sex lives may be expanded. It is also hoped that such films will remove prejudices and 'hang-ups'. The fact that the clients see normal-looking people doing things with enjoyment that they have never done, let alone spoken about, gives some of them a feeling that such behaviour is generally permissible, and the possibility of behaving in new ways is in itself exciting. The programme goes on to other films and discussions but usually with the emphasis more upon the individuals and their especial needs. A similar kind of programme has also been used in France and in the United Kingdom.

Surrogates

The use of surrogate partners was also started in the United States.

By a surrogate partner one means a person specifically employed to help the client by engaging in sexual behaviour with him or her. There are both male and female surrogate partners. Therapists in the United States use them fairly openly and with success. Detractors of surrogate partners claim that it is little more than prostitution. However, the seriousness and pride with which such surrogates help their clients puts such detractors to shame. Surrogates always work with a sex therapist and regularly accompany the client to the therapist in order to join in, and help with, the cure. They do so in a genuinely informed and knowledgeable manner.

In the United Kingdom the method is only used in one centre, in Birmingham. Legal difficulties and newspaper sensationalism make it very difficult elsewhere.

Desensitisation in the imagination

In the U.S.A., United Kingdom, Netherlands and Germany a method known as desensitisation is used. The aim here is the reduction of anxiety. Many patients experience anxiety during some particular piece of sexual behaviour, and this anxiety inhibits performance.

The essence of the method is to teach the patient to relax both the mind and body and while in this state to imagine the feared situation. If the patient can be taught to remain calm (mentally relaxed) while thinking of the feared situation, then it becomes easier to face the feared situation in real life.

In practice the therapist teaches the relaxation first and when this skill is well established will make a graded list of the patient's fears and will suggest to the patient that he or she imagine one of the minor feared situations and try to remain relaxed and calm while he does so. If the patient can remain relaxed while imagining the minor fear then he can go on to work gradually through the list until eventually he is able to imagine the most serious, panic-making fears and still remain calm.

This imaginative progression can be seen as a rehearsal for real life, and the next step in therapy can be for the patient to apply what he has learnt to reality, beginning again with the least feared behaviour first.

The term 'desensitisation' is usually used to describe the process taking place in the imagination but some people use it to mean a process of desensitisation taking place in real life.

The 'phone in'
Two centres in the United States and one British centre have also experimented with an excellent and valuable telephone information service. Anybody may ring in for information of any kind, and the anonymity of the phone may help people to say things otherwise unsayable. It usefully allows single questions to be put and answered without formality, and furthermore, it allows teenagers to obtain information in a manner at once easy and private. One remarkable thing about such phone-ins is the ignorance they reveal in the general public.

Of course the system has also been abused. However, the organisers admirably extend their offers of help to the abusers as well as to genuine callers.

Stimulation therapy – pornography
In addition to the basic densensitising and educative approach of Masters and Johnson, their book also emphasises the value of stimulation therapy. Of the three basic concepts of learning theory, stimulation therapy rests upon the idea of drive and its manipulation. Some patients with sexual problems appear to be suffering from a state of low drive: their sexual appetite and desire seem to be too low.

Stimulation therapy tries to increase the sexual drive, and education in sexual techniques and activities, whether through films or in direct discussion, may increase sexual drive. However, it may also be desirable to attempt to change a patient's whole attitude towards sexuality – to encourage him to actively seek out sexual and erotic stimulation in a manner which may never have occurred to him or in a manner which he has felt too inhibited to follow. Stimulation therapy uses all kinds of erotic and pornographic material – books, films, tapes and illustrations. It encourages the patient to use this material to obtain pleasure – it attempts to free him from the guilt which he may have felt with such material in the past.

Many elements within society see pornography as dangerous. On the face of it this might seem quite reasonable. It is an admission of the power of new ideas in representational form. The possibility exists that pornography may change the behaviour of those exposed to it for the worse, and it has been suggested that pornography might encourage crime or lead to deviant behaviour. There is however very little evidence that any of these fears are justified, and there is good evidence of the therapeutic and educative value of this material.

Pornography is used to expand the sexual repertoire and to increase the sexual drive. This drive increase certainly takes place in the patients who seem to be of low drive, and the effect of treatment is to bring the sex drive up to a level where they are happier and have fewer sex problems. It is believed that each person has a level of sexual drive at which they will feel most comfortable. In patients, there is no danger of overstimulation, neither is there any evidence of overstimulation in 'normal' people who are probably functioning at their own optimal level in any case. People who are exposed to a lot of pornographic material soon become bored.

The effects of pornography are looked at in more detail in the next chapter.

Fantasy

A large proportion of normal people have sexual fantasies. They imagine sexual behaviour in which they may or may not be involved. These fantasies are sometimes called up for pleasure and sometimes in order to rehearse some behaviour which is likely to happen. It is the first reason, that of pleasure, which is important in stimulation therapy. Many clients with sexual problems have a poor fantasy life. That is, they do not frequently use sexual fantasies to increase their enjoyment of sexual activity. For some people it is a matter of relieving them of guilt – of indicating that fantasies are good and normal – but for others it is necessary to suggest ideas upon which they can fantasise. These ideas may be obtained from pornography or films which the therapist will choose and recommend. Patients who have great difficulty may be asked to invent and write down some fantasies which can be used as a basis for fantasy development. In stimulation therapy the therapist will suggest uses to which these fantasies may be put. They may be used during solitary or mutual masturbation, or during intercourse, and may be shared with the partner. Thus, fantasies can become a vital and pleasurable part of a new style of life.

The advantages of the behavioural approach

Behaviour therapy need not be restricted to the treatment of couples but may be equally applied to undesired deviations and to other individual sexual problems. One great advantage of behavioural methods over analytical psychotherapy is the emphasis on the treatment of the complaint. Freud believed that to remove the symptom one requires a radical restructuring of the personality. Behaviourism on the contrary believes that, regardless of the cause of a given complaint or symptom, it can be eradicated and replaced by more desired behaviour.

Most psychologists believe that behaviour therapy is the best method of treatment of sexual problems today, and further, that for couples with sexual problems the system of Masters and Johnson with some additions offers the best practical hope of cure. Therapists are gaining confidence in the field as successful results are achieved, and because of its pre-eminently practical approach the general public is being made aware of its advantages and is thereby being given new hope.

However, the type of treatment recommended will finally depend on the patients' demands. Anybody with a sexual problem would be advised to become as well informed about the alternatives as possible. This is not to say that they will be able to arrange their own treatment but it will mean that they are in a position of greater strength and will not, like so many others, be passed off with ineffective advice or useless treatment.

The therapeutic goal

What, then, does the sex therapist seek to achieve? Certainly to remove the problem, but also to establish a situation in which the problem will not recur. Having been through a course of treatment the clients will have been taught that in order to avoid the problem in the future, it is necessary to have a permanently altered attitude towards their sex life. It is no longer a function that can be allowed to take care of itself. Its maintenance requires thought, adventure, calculation and care. No longer can sex take second place, to be harried, hurried or snatched. Between a couple, each has equal responsibility in these respects.

What is true of their sex life is also true of their relationship

25

in a wider sense. This too will have been discussed during therapy and suggestions made for its improvement. The improvements should not stop where therapy itself ceases.

The manner in which both the relationship and the sexuality of a couple develop after therapy is of course a matter for the people concerned – they must develop in their own characteristic way, develop their own style. During therapy they should have collected ideas for this development along the way. The development of sexuality demands a new awareness of the responses of the partner. These responses may be only slowly learned, but having learned them, the pleasure one can give, the excitement one can produce, will have much increased.

The therapist may spend time building a new responsiveness to sensation itself, a new sensuality. A new sensuality extending maybe to other relationships, to food, to films, to movement, and to music. The therapist's aims are that these ideas should become part of a new life style, extending well beyond the cessation of therapy.

The therapy can be seen as a first step, the solution of the problem itself, the re-establishment of a satisfactory sexual interaction which will then remain on a permanent basis. The therapist also hopes that the benefits of this change will pervade the whole life of the people concerned. That they will be happier and more relaxed, better able to deal with the irritations and trials that are part of life, better able to deal with a partner who may become fed up, tired or quarrelsome. In short that they will become equipped to evolve as society changes and to enjoy the changes rather than to resist them.

2

Facts and fallacies

Sex organs

Female sex organs
Many women are ignorant about their own genitalia. Many men are even more ignorant about their partner's sex organs. This can sometimes make an initial sex experience with a man quite a traumatic experience for a woman, especially if he fails to arouse her sufficiently and initiates her before she is ready. However, when couples begin to understand where the female genitalia are and what can be done to stimulate them, then love-making begins to be successful and enjoyable for both partners.

1 *The vulva* The external female sex organs or genitalia are contained in an area called the *vulva*. The vulva is situated between the thighs and is bounded by the anus behind and the mons pubis in front.

The *mons pubis* is the area which is covered by pubic hair. The amount of pubic hair varies in women, as in men. There can also be a wide range of colour and texture. Pubic hair usually grows at puberty.

The opening of the vagina lies between the labia minora, or lesser lips of the vulva. It is divided into left and right halves by a cleft. The outer lips of the vagina are called the labia majora. The skin in this outer surface is coarse and bears hair (their male counterpart is the scrotum).

2 *The labia minora* The inner lips or *labia minora* are composed of smooth, inner surface skin. They can best be seen when the legs are parted. They vary in colour, ranging from pinkish to deep red.

Many women worry about the size of their labia minora, but there is no standard size and a wide range of differences; often one lip may be larger than the other. Both lips usually swell during sexual excitement and deepen in colour. This is more obvious in women who have had children. The labia minora join above the clitoris.

3 *The clitoris*   The *clitoris* technically and anatomically corresponds to the penis in the man, and like the penis it becomes erect when sexually aroused. However, the clitoris is of course far smaller than the penis; nor does it have a passage for urine. Its size and positioning vary considerably in women. The size can vary from $\frac{1}{8}$ of an inch to $\frac{1}{2}$ an inch, but it must be stressed that the size is not related to capacity for sexual enjoyment.

The clitoris lies between the front parts of the labia minora. Unlike the penis it does not hang freely from a base but is attached throughout its length. It consists of a *shaft* and a *glans*, the glans being the slightly bulbous end part. Anatomically the shaft and glans correspond to these parts of the penis. The glans is often extremely sensitive and even touching it fairly lightly can cause pain in some women as it contains nerve endings. Like the penis the clitoris becomes engorged with blood and erect when excited. Direct stimulation need not be necessary to produce such arousal. Stroking the vulva around the clitoris and the labia minora will often affect the clitoris and cause it to become distended with swollen blood vessels. At this stage of excitement the clitoris can greatly increase in size.

When masturbation takes place the clitoris is usually stimulated directly or fairly directly for some of the time. Women vary in their technique. Some women get pleasure from rubbing the shaft, but others prefer to stimulate the glans directly.

During sexual intercourse the clitoris is often stimulated indirectly by the penis pushing and pulling the area of the vulva. This can be very exciting for many women and often the best positions for this type of stimulation are the 'woman above' position or the 'lateral' position. Some women cannot obtain enough stimulation to reach an orgasm by this method and prefer direct manual stimulation of the clitoris, either by self-stimulation during intercourse, or with the manual help of their partner.

4 *The vagina*   Below the clitoris is the opening of the urethra or

urinary passage and below this again is the *vaginal opening*. The vaginal entrance is called the *introitus* and the intact hymen of a virgin covers this entrance. Hymens vary greatly, and there is too much importance attached to the myth of the hymen. It is a symbol of virtue but if it is not intact it is no proof that the girl is not a virgin. Some virgins have quite a large opening to the vagina, where the hymen has perhaps been stretched or perforated by horse riding, athletics, inserting sanitary tampons or her own finger. Other virgins have a thick and tough hymen which make it impossible for the man to penetrate. A minor operation is often called for if this is the case. If the hymen is suddenly torn or stretched there is usually bleeding. Some cultures attach great importance to the hymen, but it is not valued as greatly by Western society.

The vagina could be described as the path between the uterus and the vulva, the path from the womb to the outside world. Traditionally and anatomically the function of the vagina is to contain the erect penis and permit it to deposit the semen near the mouth of the womb from whence the sperm may swim to the womb and fertilise an egg. Besides this function, the vagina also gives pleasure and although this has always been known it has not been much discussed. Masters and Johnson, during their research on the human sexual response, have shown that stimulation of the vagina plays a large part in the production of female excitement and orgasm.

The space within the vagina is like the space within a bed. When the bed is not in use the space does not exist. It is only a potential space. When a person climbs between the sheets the space opens up to admit them and to enclose them comfortably. So it is with the vagina. When not in use the front and back walls of the vagina lie against one another obliterating the space. The walls of the vagina are capable of very considerable stretching and are capable of fitting penises of any size. The vagina is, after all, designed to accommodate a baby's head during childbirth. When a woman becomes excited the vagina lubricates itself by secreting a fluid from glands similar to sweat glands in the skin. During sexual excitement the vaginal walls become swollen with engorged blood vessels. When the penis enters, the space opens up according to the penile size. Besides dilating to take the penile girth, the vagina can also elongate to accommodate the penile length. The woman who complains that her partner's penis is too large may be saying that he enters her when she is insufficiently lubricated. She can be re-

29

assured that the penis can do no harm on account of its size.

Vaginal lubrication need not necessarily be produced by direct sexual contact – many women can get moist by thinking or reading about sex. Other women become moist when they look at an attractive man.

During sexual excitement and also in the resting condition the vagina produces secretions which have a sexual odour. Unfortunately, many women have been conditioned to find this odour unpleasant or to believe that others may find it unpleasant. Cosmetic manufacturers have capitalised on this fear by selling vaginal deodorants and scented applications. These preparations not only have the bad effect of disguising the naturally exciting odours of the woman but may also cause local inflammation or itching.

If either partner does find the odour unpleasant, this attitude can usually be changed during treatment.

The *vaginal wall* is composed of two layers – the inner lining which is soft and moist, and the outer layer which is thicker, consisting of muscle fibres. During orgasm the outer one-third of the vagina undergoes a series of strong rhythmic contractions. This muscle which surrounds the orifice of the vagina and also covers the whole floor and surrounds the anus is called the *pubo-coccygeal muscle*. The PC muscle can also be contracted voluntarily and during sexual intercourse can be made to grasp the penis more tightly and cause the male partner additional excitement.

One worker who experimented with PC muscle training for urinary incontinence found that this training also increased the intensity and pleasure of orgasm. This training consequently became an important part of the retraining of women experiencing difficulty with orgasm and, indeed, of any woman who wishes to increase her sexual pleasure.

Male sex organs
More is usually known about the male organs than about female sex organs; this is probably due to the fact that the male genitalia are more accessible and prominent.

1 The scrotum The *scrotum* or ball bag lies below the penis and contains the balls or testes. When the man stands up the scrotum hangs behind the penis. It consists of a wrinkled bag of darkish skin and is sensitive to touch.

Temperature can affect the size of the scrotum. When a man is cold or anxious the scrotum contracts considerably into a tight pouch. When it is warm the scrotum hangs low and expands to form a loose pouch. This can happen during or after a hot bath. Too high a temperature can interfere with sperm production, and these conditions may be produced by thick, tight underwear and trousers which enclose the scrotum too warmly.

2 *The testes*   Inside the scrotum there is a division, and on each side lie the *testes* or testicles. In most men the left testicle hangs a little lower than the right. They are an ovoid shape and can be felt through the scrotal wall.

The function of the testes is to produce the sperms. The testes also produce the male sex hormone called testosterone which causes the various bodily changes that occur in puberty. If the testes are removed before puberty the boy does not develop fully. Such a person is called a 'eunuch'. He is often fat and flabby. During the Renaissance boys were often castrated to prevent the voice breaking, as the high tones that they were able to produce were much sought after. This practice has now ceased since castration causes loss of virility and sexual potency.

Each testis is divided into small compartments which contain *seminiferous tubules*. This very fine sperm-producing tubing produces sperms continuously, and not just at the moment of orgasm when they are ejaculated through the penis. All the tubules eventually discharge into the *epididymis*, which is a long structure, tightly coiled and lying closely applied to the testis. The epididymis and testes store the sperm.

Leading from the epididymis is a long tube called the *vas deferens* which is about eighteen inches long and surrounded by thick muscular walls. Together with blood vessels and nerves the vas deferens forms the spermatic cord which eventually leads from the testis to the penis via the abdomen. It is the vas deferens which may be cut in the small operation to sterilise the male. *Seminal vesicles* connect to the vas deferens. They produce and store a yellowish fluid which forms the bulk of the ejaculation in which the sperm are able to swim and thrive.

The second secretion necessary for the sperms to be fully active is produced by the prostate. The prostate lies below the bladder and opens into the urethra. The urethra leads from the bladder to the

31

tip of the penis. The prostate produces a thin acidic fluid which gives semen its special odour and viscosity. Sometimes older men tend to have hard and enlarged prostates which interfere with the passage of urine. Where such enlargement is considerable the gland may have to be removed surgically. This does not interfere with virility and many men need reassurance that they will not become impotent after this operation.

Just below the prostate there are two other small glands called *Cowper's glands* which produce the third special secretion, which is a mucous substance.

All the above secretions produced by the 'accessory glands' are important to activate, nourish and carry the sperm along when they are ejaculated, eventually to impregnate the woman.

3 The penis   Psychologically the *penis* is the most important male sex organ. Its dual role is to enter the female's vagina and deposit semen there, and to pass urine. Apart from the deposition of semen and the voiding of urine it is a provider of psychological pleasure for both men and women.

The bulbous end of the penis is called the *glans*. In the un-circumcised male the glans is invested by a retractable covering, the foreskin or prepuce. During sexual excitation, together with the shaft of the penis, the glans becomes swollen and turgid. In this condition the foreskin is usually retracted, during or before sexual intercourse, usually before. Often the foreskin is removed at birth or later by an operation called circumcision.

One of the most sensitive parts of the penis is called the *frenulum*. The frenulum is to be found on the underside of the glans, bridging the furrow between the glans and the shaft. This delicate strip of tissue is sensitive in most males.

When the male becomes sexually aroused the penis becomes engorged with blood and then becomes large and stiff. It is then erect enough to be inserted in the vagina. When the penis is not in an excited state it is flaccid and floppy. It is easier to urinate when it is in this flaccid state.

4 The size of the penis   Many myths are associated with penile size. The penis has been a symbol of virility and potency since ancient days. Many early religions encouraged the use of fertility symbols and often these consisted of a small stone statue of a man with a penis as long as his torso. It is hardly surprising that men and women associated potency with a giant phallus. In some ancient religions the penis or lingam is worshipped in its own right.

Men who have small flaccid penises observe other men with large flaccid penises and immediately imagine that during sexual excitement the increase in size will be proportional. That is, that a large flaccid penis will become a giant erect one and a small flaccid penis, a small erect one. In fact small flaccid penises increase in size proportionately more than large flaccid ones. Thus, the variation in size among flaccid penises is greater than among penises in a state of erection. The erect penis length is probably fairly constant, though the dimensions of the erect penis have not yet been fully researched, so perhaps the last word on this matter has not yet been said.

Another fallacy associated with penile size is the belief that the longer the penis the more sexual satisfaction it will produce for the woman. Masters and Johnson's research ended this fallacy when they reported that as only the outer one-third of the vagina possesses the sensitive nerves associated with orgasm, length is quite unimportant. The remaining deeper two-thirds of the vagina are not sensitive. As some women say, 'It's not what you've got but what you do with it that is important.' Many women comment that if they had to choose between a man with a large penis and a man who could skilfully use his finger to stimulate the clitoris they would choose the lover with the latter skill.

Probably the girth of the penis is more important than the length. When the penis is inserted in the vagina it pulls on the labia minora of the woman, and these lips pull the clitoral hood to and fro over the glans as thrusting takes place. It is this mechanism that is associated with the female orgasm, and it may be that the penis with the wider girth is more effective and vigorous in producing this movement. More research needs to be carried out on this topic as well.

5 *Circumcision* Circumcision is the removal of the foreskin. The surgical techniques used in its removal vary from one culture to another. Some more primitive methods can damage the glans, but this happens only rarely in civilised countries. The usual technique is to slit the foreskin from tip to base then snip it away around the

collar between the glans and the shaft. Some small stitches are inserted. The operation leaves the glans exposed, the skin of which becomes somewhat less sensitive.

The operation is carried out in many cultures as a mark of manhood or as a religious necessity. The advantages claimed for the circumcised over the natural state are four-fold. Firstly, hygiene is more readily maintained. There may be an element of truth in this, since if the foreskin is not retracted and the glans washed regularly a secretion called smegma which is normally formed around the base of the glans may collect and cause an odour which is found to be objectionable. The odour of smegma is one of the sexual odours which is of natural occurrence like vaginal odours, but the offensive smell of the unwashed glans is probably due to the bacterial decomposition of the collected smegma. Provided the glans is washed regularly this is all that is required.

The second advantage is revealed by research. Cancer of the penis is more frequent in the uncircumcised. This has been shown by comparing the Hindus, who are not circumcised, with the Muslims, who are. A curious additional piece of research has found that among Jews, all of whom are circumcised, it is the orthodox who have the lower rate of this cancer. Defective hygiene may underlie these findings but other explanations have been offered. It is best as yet to be somewhat sceptical.

The third argument in favour of the removal of the foreskin is that to do so causes the skin of the glans to become less sensitive, which advantageously delays the male orgasm. This is probably a fallacy or of very slight effect since the other factors which determine the time to orgasm are more influential. It could be equally true that to retain this sensitivity is worthwhile.

The fourth argument is more certainly fallacious. It is claimed that women find the circumcised penis more beautiful. In fact women differ in their aesthetic preferences, and are probably more influenced by what they are familiar with: the appearance of their father or brothers, or that of the penis which gave them their first or the greatest satisfaction.

6 Erection A common fallacy is that there is a bone inside the penis which makes it stand up. This is not so. The penis actually consists of three cylinders or columns running along the whole length of the organ. Two of these columns, the *corpora cavernosa*,

lie side by side forming the uppermost part of the penis, and are attached at their base to the pelvic bones. The third column, the *corpus spongiosum*, carries within it the urethra, the passage for urine and semen, and lies centrally placed underneath the other two columns, continuing beyond them to form a bulbous end-piece which fits over the ends of the corpora cavernosa. This end-piece is the *glans penis*. From its tip the urethra opens. During sexual excitation cellular spaces within each of the three columns engorge with blood to produce the stiffness of the erect organ which increases in both girth and length.

There are two controlling mechanisms of erection. One may be called *psychogenic* since psychic events powerfully influence this mechanism. The actual nerve impulses travel through the sympathetic nervous system, and the psychic events which engender this mechanism may arise from the imagination, as in a sexual fantasy, or from the senses, as in the presence of an attractive woman. Guilt or anxiety may effect the erection by inhibiting this mechanism.

The other main controlling mechanism is a *reflex*, which operates through the parasympathetic nervous system at the base of the spinal cord. This reflex is brought about by the stimulation of the penis and genital region. The reflex can be initiated in the absence of psychic stimulation.

Erections are mainly produced in the presence of sexually exciting women or other erotic stimuli. Thus it is probably the sympathetic controlling mechanism which produces the erection initially, but once local stimulation of the penis occurs the reflex mechanism will operate in addition.

Erections often appear many times during an average night's sleep and may be associated with sexual dreams. Ejaculation sometimes occurs at the culmination of a particularly powerful erotic dream. In popular language this is called a wet dream; in the jargon of science a nocturnal emission. These are very common and most men experience them at some time, more frequently during adolescence but to a lesser extent during adult life. They are harmless, and men who are guilty and ashamed need to be reassured that this is a normal, 'natural' and pleasant thing to happen.

Many men have erections when they awake in the morning. The exact mechanism of this is unknown. It may be that a sexual dream wakes them up. In this case the erection is mainly psychic/sympathetic. It is possible, however, that nervous impulses arising from a distended bladder may operate this reflex, since the para-sympathetic centres in the lower spinal cord may confuse the source of these impulses.

During sexual excitement the glans may be moistened by a clear secretion appearing at its tip. This secretion has a lubricating effect.

7 Ejaculation and orgasm 'Intromission' is the insertion of the penis into the vagina. The man is then ready to enjoy sexual inter-course. Signals from the glans, caused by rubbing the penis inside the vagina, enhance the state of excitement which leads to orgasm when accumulated sexual tension is relieved.

For most men there is a sensation of orgasm about three seconds before ejaculation starts. During this stage the involuntary nerve signals cause the muscles around the vas deferens, seminal vesicles and prostate to contract. The sperm together with the liquid contri-butions of the accessory glands are together called the *ejaculate* or *semen*. This ejaculate is pumped along the urethra by muscular action under considerable pressure; it appears at the tip of the glans penis as a series of spurts at intervals of less than one second. Such spurts can cause semen to travel several feet if the penis is outside the vagina. While the semen is being pumped outwards the passage backward is closed off by muscles in the base of the bladder, preventing the semen from going the wrong way.

Orgasms vary in intensity but most men would describe them as pleasurable and as a relief of sexual tension. Ejaculation is not necessary for orgasm. Many young boys have experienced orgasm with no ejaculation.

Sexual response

In *Human Sexual Response* Masters and Johnson provided im-portant facts about the different stages of sexual response. They described four phases: the *excitement phase* which is initiated by whatever an individual finds sexually arousing; leading to the *plateau phase*, which is the goal that has to be reached before orgasm can take place; the *orgasmic phase*, which is an intense few seconds during which the individual climaxes; the *resolution phase*, which is the period of recovery during which the couple feel relaxed and loving. In the male there is a further period known as the refractory phase which follows the orgasmic phase and is a time during which a further orgasm is impossible. This refractory time varies for individuals from a few minutes to a whole night.

The Excitement Phase Many different types of stimuli can excite. The most obvious type of stimulus is that of stroking or touching the genitalia. Every person has of course their own particular 'switch-on'. For some it is heterosexual, for some homosexual and for others self-stimulation alone. For many it is variety that counts. The actual sexual response may be initiated through any or all of the senses: touch, sight, sound or smell.

Sexual response can be affected by many external factors such as health, fatigue, the menstrual cycle, pregnancy and drugs. One of the most important factors in sexual arousal is that of conditioning – what has the individual learned to be aroused by and respond to?

The body manifests sexual excitement in various ways. Most people show an increase in the pulse rate which is associated with faster and perhaps irregular breathing. There is often an increase in sweating, which may be visible on the forehead, for example, or felt on the hands. Muscular activity may change in states of sexual excitement. There may be restlessness, tension of the muscles or trembling. The blood vessels of various parts of the body become dilated and carry more blood than usual. This may produce a visible flush of the upper parts of the body and particularly the face, though this flush affects women more than men. The dilation and engorgement of the blood vessels of the genital region is a special part of the general sexual response and is responsible, as excitement increases, for the enlargement of both the female and more obviously the male parts. These bodily changes are accompanied by a whole variety of feelings. There is a feeling of general excitement and of sexual arousal, some elements of which seem to affect specific parts of the body, and others to be too vague or general to be located. The dilation and engorgement of the blood vessels produces a feeling of warmth; the increase in the pulse rate and blood pressure may produce palpitations or vague feelings in the chest, as well as the symptoms associated with rapid or irregular breathing. In very reactive people the feelings may border upon suffocation. Where sexual feelings are very intense, there may be a slight dizziness as well as a multitude of idiosyncratic and other indescribable reactions, all adding to the total experience. In addition, the experience is often complicated by the demands of social propriety:

37

in a formal social situation it may be necessary to suppress or disguise these feelings either out of a fear of showing responses which one has been taught to suppress, or as a matter of tactics in a sexually competitive situation. Here the effort of suppression may itself produce physical and mental feelings which confuse the originally purely sexual response. Also, sexual feelings may be quite naturally associated with some anxiety, as for instance when one makes sexual advances to a person for the first time. There are many other situations in life where the excitement is rendered more intense by some associated fear and this is probably also the case with sexual feelings.

Under ideal circumstances it is during the phase of excitement that foreplay will start. Under these conditions the woman and the man become erect due to vasocongestion. The scrotum becomes tense and thick. The testes are raised within the scrotum. Direct stimulation of the penis and clitoris may increase their turgidity. The labia minora swell and deepen in colour to a rich rugose plum. The labia majora draw back so as to permit penile entry.

The vagina responds to stimulation by becoming moistened by a lubricating fluid which is produced by a sweating reaction of the vaginal walls and occurs within ten to thirty seconds of the onset of sexual stimulation. Blood also enters the tissues around the vagina, producing vasocongestion. The inner two-thirds of the vagina behave independently of the outer third. During the phase of increasing excitement the inner part shows waves of expansion followed by slow relaxation progressively leading to an expanded state. When the vagina becomes moist it also begins to swell and the woman becomes aroused enough for the man to enter her vagina. If there was no lubrication it would be both difficult and painful for the man to enter.

The female breasts change during this stage. The nipples become erect and late in the excitement phase the actual breasts increase in size. This is more noticeable in women who have not breast-fed their babies. The veins of the breasts may become more prominent as blood is pumped into this area.

The Plateau Phase This phase is not clearly separated from the excitement phase and should be thought of as a continuation of, or levelling out of the excitement phase. In both sexes the rate of breathing increases, as does pulse rate and blood pressure. The sex flush becomes more noticeable. There is further activity of both voluntary and involuntary muscles. The sphincter muscle which holds the rectum closed may tighten up.

During this phase the ballooning of the inner two-thirds of the vagina may continue. The outer third changes in a different way. Here the vaginal walls and the surrounding tissues become so engorged with blood that the passage becomes much reduced. This tightens the contact between the vaginal walls and the thrusting penis to the mutual satisfaction of both parts.

During the plateau phase the clitoris is progressively drawn upwards towards the bony parts behind the mons pubis; that is, away from the vaginal opening. The clitoral shaft decreases in length – a process called the retraction of the clitoris – and at its most extreme this retraction can conceal the organ completely. Despite this, it is not difficult during manual stimulation to seek out the excited parts whose sensitivity is much increased. This increase in sensitivity can make rough stimulation unbearable.

During both the excitement and the plateau phase the penis produces a variable amount of clear fluid which probably has a lubricating effect. This fluid has been called the 'distillation'.

The Orgasmic Phase   At this stage blood pressure, pulse rate and respiration reach a peak. The sex flush is most pronounced. Muscles of the neck, arms, legs and feet may contract in a spasm. Muscles of the hands may clench or grasp vigorously, often resulting in tight gripping of the partner.

Women respond in orgasm by a series of powerful rhythmic contractions of the orgasmic platform or outer-third of the vagina. These are muscular contractions which occur at intervals of four-fifths of a second and are between three and twelve in number. It is impossible for a woman to contract these muscles voluntarily at this speed. Then the intensity decreases and the intervals tend to become longer. The uterus also contracts rhythmically, and these uterine contractions have been described as similar to but milder than labour contractions.

The male experience of orgasm has two phases. The first phase might be called the assembly phase. During this phase are assembled and mingled the various liquid components. These liquids are introduced into the male urethra in a part known as the prostatic bulb and consist of contributions from the seminal vesicles, and

39

from the testes via the epididymis and vas deferens, besides other minor additions. It is during this phase of assembly that the male experiences the first intimations of orgasm. The feeling has been called a feeling of orgasmic inevitability – a feeling that a process has been started over which the subject has no further control. This is indeed the case, for soon afterwards the second phase swings into action: the delivery phase. The collected material – the semen – is expelled by three to four muscular contractions, occurring every four-fifths of a second, down the male urethra, to emerge with force at the meatus. To accomplish this, one sphincter has relaxed to ensure delivery to the exterior, and one has contracted to prevent escape of urine. The experience of this expulsion is the most obvious and ecstatic part of the orgasm. Although the feeling of orgasm is mainly centred in the genitals, in reality the orgasm may involve the whole body; muscular jerking, arching and grasping figure in the total response, as do groans, gulps and gasps.

The Resolution Phase　In this phase the sexual excitement dies away and the bodily changes reverse. The muscles relax, the pulse and blood pressure fall, the breathing reassumes its regularity. The mental excitement and urgency are replaced by calm contentment and grateful love. During this phase relaxation may often lead to sleep.

During the resolution phase the penis shrinks in size and returns to near its unstimulated state – a complete return usually takes rather longer. After the resolution phase men enter the refractory phase, during which they are unable to achieve another orgasm for a period that varies from only a few minutes in some men to hours or days in others. During the refractory phase an erection may appear but orgasm is, by definition, impossible.

Women vary in their capacity to go on to further orgasms immediately after one has been experienced. There are some women who have one orgasm and no amount of stimulation can bring them to another. There are other, so-called multi-orgasmic women, who can go straight on to further orgasms with the appropriate stimulation. Some women can experience six or seven orgasms in a series, though it is more usual to have a more limited capacity. Some multi-orgasmic women report that the second or third orgasm is the most intense; others find, like men, that the first is the one of greatest intensity.

The changes of resolution are also seen in the clitoris, which slowly resumes its normal size and again takes up the position nearer the vagina from whence during the plateau phase it was retracted. The ballooning of the inner two-thirds of the vagina decreases and the vascular engorgement of the whole area disappears. This resolution phase may take a long time in the woman who has not achieved orgasm, but where orgasm has occurred resolution will be complete in under one hour. Resolution is faster in males than females.

Clitoral versus vaginal orgasm

There was a time when it was thought that there were two kinds of female orgasm. One of these orgasms was produced by clitoral stimulation and the other by vaginal stimulation. Freud, the father of this fallacy, equated vaginal orgasm with maturity and the clitoral orgasm with immaturity. Freud believed that the vaginal orgasm was produced during sexual intercourse by the friction of the penis against the vagina. Clitoral stimulation, characteristically produced by manual or oral stimulation, he saw as a kind of masturbation. Masturbation he judged to be wrong, perhaps because no man was required.

Masters and Johnson showed in a painstaking series of experiments that there is only one type of orgasm and that it had both clitoral and vaginal components. The orgasm is mainly triggered by clitoral stimulation, while it is experienced especially in and around the vagina. When sexual intercourse takes place the penis is thrust in and out. When the penis is thrust inwards a pull is transmitted to the labia minora which in turn pulls the clitoral hood over the clitoral glans. When the penis is withdrawn the pull relaxes and the clitoral glans is uncovered. It is this movement of the clitoral hood over the clitoral glans which produces the clitoral stimulation. Additional stimulation takes place in some positions of intercourse where the male parts immediately above the penile base, the hair-covered parts, come into pressure contact with the general clitoral area during repetitive thrusting.

Orgasm can also be produced by non-genital stimulation. For instance by fantasy, breast stimulation or by tickling. Although here the clitoris and vagina are not directly stimulated, they show the same changes but at a slower rate. One can say then that the orgasm is the same no matter how it is produced.

41

In one investigation, two hundred women were asked whether they preferred an orgasm produced during vaginal intercourse or by direct clitoral stimulation. The latter was chosen by sixty-four per cent. On questioning all the women, it was found that they took a different attitude towards the orgasm experienced during vaginal intercourse than towards the orgasm of clitoral stimulation. The clitoral orgasm was experienced as ecstatic but superficial, whereas the orgasm of intercourse was deeper, more emotional and more satisfying. The investigator found a lot of variation in the preferences which his female sample showed.

At the moment of orgasm the woman is in the plateau phase of the sexual cycle which is described earlier in the chapter. The woman becomes aware that orgasm is imminent. Masters and Johnson described the moment as a feeling of suspension or stoppage. The orgasm then follows. In most women there is some kind of cry or groan together with jerking movements and tension of the muscles, a facial grimace and gasping. An intense sensation originates in the clitoral-vaginal area with a series of contractions around the outer-third of the vagina and the area around the opening. These muscular spasms take place at 0.8 second intervals. In an intense orgasm there are between eight and twelve contractions, in an ordinary one between three and eight. These sensations seem to spread into the pelvis from the genital area and then envelop the body in a feeling of warmth. A feeling of throbbing may be experienced in the vaginal area.

During orgasm the womb contracts somewhat. However, when the orgasm is over there is some evidence that the internal pressure in the womb drops, which might have the effect of sucking in any available sperm.

People have speculated that the woman or man may absorb natural substance during intercourse which contributes to their general well-being and behaviour; there is as yet no evidence that this is so, though the semen contains a substance which is absorbed from the vagina and is capable of causing contractions of the womb.

Menstruation

There have been some extraordinary taboos and myths associated with menstrual flow. Before the physiological causes of the phenomenon were known no rational explanation was able to account for this apparently wanton issue. In all other circumstances blood was associated with injuries, violence and death. Contact with this blood was frequently taboo. The menstruating woman was often segregated in a special hut.

During the first century it was believed that menstrual women could cause grass and plants to wither and fruit to fall from trees if they sat underneath them. They could even turn wine sour. This souring effect was still believed during the last century when a debate appeared in a medical journal on the supposed effect of menstruating women upon pork, which was supposed to go sour in their presence. During the same century menstruating women were excluded from sugar refineries as it was believed that they would blacken the sugar. In some parts of India even today women are not allowed to cook at this time. Among orthodox Jews sexual intercourse is forbidden during menstruation, after which the women are expected to purify themselves of their 'uncleanliness' by a special bath.

What are the facts about menstruation? Is it unclean? Menstruation is the visible part of a complex cycle of interactions between the internal glands, the pituitary, the ovaries and the womb. The pituitary, which is part of the brain, lies in the skull. The two ovaries lie on either side of the womb. The pituitary produces hormones – chemical messengers – which influence the ovaries. The ovaries produce both eggs and hormones. In a normally functioning woman of child-bearing age one egg is produced each month, enters the womb via the fallopian tubes, and if sperm are present is fertilised, so that a sperm and an egg unite. The fertilised egg then embeds itself in the specially prepared lining of the womb and proceeds to develop there. This special lining is prepared afresh each month under the influence of the ovarian hormones, oestrogen and progesterone. If a fertilised egg is not available for embedding, the freshly prepared lining is not required. The shedding of this lining, when it becomes detached, causes the bleeding. This blood and detached and semi-liquid lining flows out of the womb and into the vagina. This is the menstrual flow. There is nothing unclean about this tissue or blood. In fact, the average volume of blood normally only amounts to one or two ounces; the remainder of the flow consisting of cells and tissues from the unwanted lining.

Facts and fallacies

A woman's menstrual cycles begin at puberty, last throughout the childbearing years and only end with the menopause. Each cycle is approximately a month long. The egg is produced about half-way between two monthly periods, and it is around this time that the woman is most fertile.

The menstrual cycle is associated with variations in bodily and mental feelings. There is considerable variation in the intensity of such feelings. During several days before a period many women become tense and depressed. This is called pre-menstrual tension and may be associated with a bloated or swollen feeling, and additional sensitivity or even pain in the breasts. Some women feel more highly sexed at this time, others less. It is only when the feelings of tension and depression are severe that medical aid is required. Where the sexual appetite is decreased it is sensible to have less sex; where it is increased, to have more.

Many women feel worried about having sexual intercourse when they are actually menstruating: a hangover from the previously mentioned taboos. In fact there is no harm in having sex during menstruation. Many women find it very enjoyable at this time, especially if they have fears associated with pregnancy, as it is not possible to get pregnant when one is menstruating. Another bonus associated with menstruation is that there is more lubrication of the vagina. The women who worry about being too dry during intercourse and dislike using a jelly to help with this can enjoy this side-effect of menstruation. It is also the experience of many women that intercourse can relieve the cramps from which some women suffer at this time.

Some women worry about the presence of blood if they want intercourse when they are menstruating. A useful way of containing the blood can be to wear a contraceptive diaphragm or cap. There are many family planning clinics which would fit a suitable appliance to wear during this time. This type of appliance will hold back the small quantity of blood until the woman takes it out after intercourse.

Other women worry that menstruation prevents them from douching after intercourse. This is not necessary, and a tampon will absorb the semen.

Drugs

So-called aphrodisiacs
Vegetable aphrodisiacs have been used for centuries. *Bella donna* (deadly nightshade) and *mandrake* (another poisonous plant, with knobbly and tenacious roots) have been the two most popular. In Africa and in the Orient the belief in the aphrodisiac potency of rhinoceros horn has reduced the creature almost to extinction. The primitive thinking behind this belief is nowadays difficult to credit. Neither rhinoceros horn nor the foregoing vegetable poisons are in the least way effective, though any substance may have a placebo effect.

Cantharides (Spanish Fly) and *amyl nitrite* have both been used as an aphrodisiac. Spanish Fly has been known for centuries. It produces its effect by causing an inflammation and burning of the mucosal surfaces of the body. This prurient effect extends to the genital mucosal surfaces and may be stimulating in some. Unfortunately it is usually males who use it on unwilling or ignorant girls, upon whom the worst effect can be death.

Amyl nitrite, which is used to relieve angina pectoris, may also have some aphrodisiac effect by virtue of the increased blood flow which it promotes. But again it is a potentially dangerous substance.

1 Hallucinogens The hallucinogen L.S.D. has been suggested as an aphrodisiac. So great are the varieties of reaction to this drug that it is improbable that someone has not been stimulated thereby. Sexual stimulation is not, however, reliable or common. The danger of a 'bad trip' has also to be reckoned.

Cannabis probably has a certain aphrodisiac quality but not one which is reliable or impressive. It may enhance erotic situations for some, and has been reported to increase eroticism in some women who have a degree of orgasm difficulty by enhancing effects on muscle contractions. More properly controlled research is required before any definite statement on its uses can be made.

However, because of its sedative and tranquillising properties the drug also produces a state of mind in which everything, even sex, seems too much trouble, which rather defeats its purpose as an aphrodisiac.

2 Amphetimines Substances containing amphetimines and also cocaine can be stimulating in small doses initially, but where addiction occurs sex drive will eventually be reduced. These drugs are too dangerous for casual use.

3 Alcohol and barbiturates Alcohol and barbiturates (which are a large class of drugs for insomnia) can in small doses both enhance and alter sexual feelings. Both possess an ability to disinhibit users and this may make sexual behaviour more exciting and unusual. This effect is probably greater in unrelaxed and anxious people. Where too much of either drug is consumed various effects will occur which militate against successful sexual behaviour. Muscular movements become uncoordinated and the orgastic response may be impaired. This happens both in women and men.

4 Hormones Male hormones (androgens) are reputed, without much evidence, to increase libido and performance where there is some deficiency. Because of this and because of their central effect in the establishment of male sexual behaviour, it has long been hoped that even where no deficiency exists, the prescription of an excess would increase sexual desire and performance. However, their prescription where no deficiency exists is probably useless. One very poorly reported trial claims success in impotent males, and it is likely that androgens will continue to be promoted for this purpose even though it has been well established that normal sexual behaviour can occur with blood levels of androgens much below the normal. It remains an area in which considerable research is required.

5 Other drugs L-dopa was originally prescribed for Parkinsonism (a disease of the brain causing tremulous muscles), but it was noticed that the sex drive was also increased. However, the unpleasant side effects probably preclude its use in sex therapy.

The female sex hormone *oestrogen* probably does not affect the woman's sex drive where adequate quantities are already circulating. After the menopause, when there may be a relative lack of oestrogen, hormone replacement therapy may relieve some women of the hot flushes, depression and other symptoms which can make the menopause a very real burden. The general improvement in well-being which may follow may include an enhanced feeling of sexual responsiveness, and the therapy will also reverse the thinning and dryness of the vaginal mucosa which sometimes makes intercourse less satisfactory or even painful. It may possibly also help to retain a youthful appearance.

The female sex hormone progesterone has no effect on sexual performance or interest.

Drugs which may decrease sexual function
1 Anti-anxiety drugs Sedation may reduce sexual drive.

2 Anti-depressants are reputed to affect sexual responses in one of two ways. Some members of the anti-depressant family could cause erectile difficulties and others delay the ejaculation.

Unfortunately depression itself has similar effects and it is not easy to tell which cause is operating. A large effect on sexual functioning is probably only likely with the higher doses. A patient who is taking such drugs, of which there are many varieties, should talk to the doctor who has prescribed the drug if the sexual difficulty has not been adequately discussed.

3 Tranquillisers The major tranquillisers which are used mainly in the treatment of schizophrenia are also capable of producing side effects in sexual functioning. They are capable of impairing the erection and interfering with the delivery of the ejaculate.

4 Heroin Hard drugs like heroin and related substances when taken in addictive quantities eventually produce a reduction in sexual drive.

5 Other drugs There remain various potent drugs which are used for hypertension and which may both reduce the erectile capacity and delay ejaculation. Some of the drugs used in peptic ulceration may also affect the erection.

Where a drug which is being taken does not come into any of the categories mentioned and sexual difficulties are being encountered, it is best to ask the physician whether there could be any connection.

Sex aids

Sex aids are by no means a recent invention. The earliest aids date back certainly to the fifteenth century B.C. What is new is the use of electricity which relieves some of the hard work. Electricity has revolutionised housework; perhaps it will revolutionise sex.

Sex aids are available both for use alone, perhaps as a substitute for a partner, and for mutual pleasure and amusement. Very little research has been done on the part these sexual gewgaws play in the overall satisfaction of their users, but they do at least satisfy the appetite of the curious and embellish the shelves of the 'love' shops. Sex aids have something of the dangerous beauty of tropical fungi and of the fetishistic satisfaction of surgical prostheses.

Sex aids mainly for women

Historically the oldest sex aid is the dildo, an artificial penis. One could say that it was but a short step from an artificial leg to an artificial penis. Babylonian figurines show them in the hands of women. The women of Ancient Greece obtained leather-covered dildoes from the local cobbler, but these were so expensive that many were shared. In the seventeenth century dildoes were made of glass and velvet.

Dildoes are still made and used, but are being superseded by the vibrator. Most vibrators are made in a phallic form and are operated either by batteries or from the mains. Research has established that the best frequency is about eighty cycles per second, and battery-operated ones may not be sufficiently powerful.

Vibrators may of course be used on any part of the body. Many women have found that while the phallic configuration suggests vaginal insertion, the most stimulating application is to the clitoral area, so some vibrators now have a vibrating element of a size better matched to the clitoral terminal. An electric toothbrush stripped of its bristles makes a good substitute.

Sex therapists recommend the use of vibrators. It has been found by various therapists in the U.S.A., including Masters and Johnson, that some women who have been unable to reach orgasm have been taught to do so by this means and have gone on to orgasm by more conventional means, either manually or during intercourse. Even for those who do not require it for this reason the vibrator provides a new and interesting experience, so why not use it?

Some sex aids are worn by the male during sexual intercourse to increase the stimulation of the woman. There are two types: one aims to increase clitoral stimulation and the other to increase the internal vaginal pleasure.

Clitoral stimulators come in two types. The first is a ring or collar which is worn around the base of the penis. Both the ring and the sheath are equipped with small latex protruberances which come into position over the clitoral area when intercourse takes place in the missionary position. The friction and extra stimulation provided demand some skill and cooperation. Clumsily used, soreness can result, and a good lubricant is necessary.

Vaginal stimulators can be divided into rings and sheaths. This time the ring is worn around the penis in the groove between the glans and shaft, and around it are a variety of soft projections which are designed to provide extra stimulation to the vaginal canal during the sexual thrust. Sheaths are similarly embellished. Some people may find these goods pleasurable. Many won't.

Sex aids for men

Vibrators can help many men achieve orgasm when they do not have an available partner. Again eighty cycles per second is the preferred frequency, and again, battery-driven vibrators may not always prove sufficiently powerful. The best site of application is often in the region of the frenum with a to-and-fro movement.

Greater verisimilitude is provided by the artificial vagina. These were first manufactured for sailors in the nineteenth century. Early varieties were made of animal bladders or gut stuffed with some soft substance. No doubt they were also lubricated with oil or fat. Today there is a variety of models made usually of plastic: some are hand-held, others are designed to remain static. Inflatable torsos or whole figures with artificial vaginas are also available, the odd one even equipped with a vibrating option. But they are usually very expensive; a do-it-yourself man of skill and ingenuity could have a field day.

Sex aids to help with impotence are also available, but regrettably none has been found to be truly effective. The vibrator, of course, can help during foreplay, but during intercourse itself it is difficult to provide vibrations other than natural ones.

The penile ring, marketed as the Penile Energiser Ring, is also sold. This sits around the base of the penis and scrotum, and the theory is that a small current generated by the interaction of metal plates in the device and the body's sweat is supposed to maintain the erection. However, a group of men with impotence did just as well whether the ring was fitted or not, and interestingly, the ring alone without the metal plates seemed to give some help.

None of the other mechanical devices available has been shown to be effective in the treatment of erectile failure.

Sex aids are worth experimenting with for pleasure or fun. Sex aids for dysfunction are on the whole very poor value, and sex therapy is infinitely more likely to be effective.

Sex education

Only by improved sex education can the facts about sex be learned and sexual fallacies be discarded. Sex education has been a neg-lected topic, but gradually educators are becoming aware that ignorance can result in problems. More seems to have been written about abnormal sex and deviations than about normal sexual development. Before Masters and Johnson we knew more about foot fetishists than about female sexuality.

It is never too early to begin sex education and it should be included in the curriculum from nursery school to university level. It should also be discussed freely at home from the earliest moment that a child shows interest in the subject.

In general sex education is very poor in the u.k. One investigator found that after a sex education lesson many children did not realise that they had received a lesson on sex at all. Even less did they realise that pollination in flowers and sexual intercourse in humans had biological similarities. Ideally, verbal information should be supplemented with films and books which may then be discussed between the teacher and the children. At some progressive schools the parents have been encouraged to take part. There are also a number of excellent books and films available today. Some of these are suitable for younger children and others for adolescents.

It is important to include the topic of contraception as well. Adolescents should know how to obtain contraceptive devices and the pill in the area in which they live, with or without the active support of their parents. An unwanted pregnancy, especially where much blame and recrimination is deployed, can be a traumatic ex-perience all round, and can have a serious effect on later sexual attitudes and experiences.

It would be an excellent thing if colleges and other centres of education, schools included, offered evening instruction to adults too. There has been some improvement in the sex education training for medical students but not nearly enough, with the result that few general practitioners are of much help when faced with a sexual dysfunction.

In America sex education is more advanced than in Europe. There are comprehensive courses for medical students on human sexuality in many American universities, with an especially good course at Yale University Medical School.

The most advanced sex education programme comes from the National Sex Forum in San Francisco (formerly the Glide Foundation). The sex education programme is called the SAR, short for Sexual Attitude Restructuring. It was founded in 1964 and sponsored by the United Methodist Church and other Protestant denominations. Its aim is both to help patients through re-education, and also to educate professional workers and sex therapists about sexual matters and problems so that they can better understand their own sexuality and the sexuality of others.

The bulk of the material comes in the form of films, slides and tapes. A course is programmed to cover twelve to fourteen hours and includes: reproductive biology, masturbation, homosexuality, female sexuality and the women's liberation movement, special problems related to medical, religious, and cultural matters, and sex therapy. The material is designed to desensitise clients to taboo areas and then to resensitise them with suggestions for improving and enriching their own sex life and that of those whom they help and counsel. The films are planned to educate people to feel as well as to think.

Groups of professional workers, doctors, social workers, counsellors, psychologists, nurses, ministers then discuss the presentation and use of the material.

There is a similar programme at Minnesota University inspired by the National Sex Forum.

Pornography

The word 'pornography' is probably impossible to define to everyone's satisfaction. It used to mean writings about prostitutes and their clients. Nowadays it is not limited in this way, and one talks about pornographic pictures, films and writings. There are even pornographic tapes. There are two things which can certainly be said about pornography: it is a representation of sex in some medium, and it is intended to be sexually arousing. Of course pornography can be either blatant and obvious, or subtle and low-key.

There seem to be good biological reasons for some social control of sexual behaviour, but the severity and pervasiveness of such control will probably always be a matter of contention in all but the most authoritarian societies. Those who favour strict regulation of human sexuality see pornography as an incitement to excess.

The availability of pornography at any time will reflect a state of balance between the often commercial attitude of those who promote it and the consensus of attitudes exhibited by the major pressure groups within society. In late Victorian England there was admittedly plenty of pornography but compared with today it was the merest trickle, whose distribution was clandestine. What was private and pornographic was for men who, as often as not, probably maintained a double standard of largely conscious hypocrisy. Where sexuality was allowed to be public, the erotic quality was both inhibited and romanticised. Of naked women there were plenty, as nymphs and other mythological cheesecake, but of pubic hair there was none. More often than not some chance of gesture or foliage served to conceal the penis.

Since the last world war the amount of easily available pornography has increased enormously. Symbolism, now unnecessary, has largely disappeared and the explicit sexual content of pornography has gradually increased. Generally available pornography is now, in the mid 'seventies, able to display activity which is nearly certainly intercourse and a penis which is nearly certainly erect.

It seems likely that pornography will become more accessible and probably more explicit, so there remain questions which should be answered: is pornography dangerous and could it be useful?

Is pornography dangerous?
Hard core pornography is now fairly readily available in large cities in the Netherlands, Denmark, West Germany, Sweden and some large cities in the U.S.A. Most of the other countries in Western Europe, including Norway, Spain, Italy, Eire and the U.K.,

make it difficult or impossible for the average citizen to buy it. Presumably it is believed by the authorities in these states that harm will result from the dissemination of hard core pornography and that they have the right and duty to prevent it.

The authorities who suppress pornography do not do so without some support from the people, and here two attitudes are visible. Many people – who usually have no experience of it – are nervous of pornography without knowing quite why. Another fairly large group of people, some of whom have experience of pornography, believe that it will corrupt, deprave or incite people to commit sexual crimes.

One should say at the outset that there is a great lack of solid evidence here. But such evidence as has been collected does not show that pornography causes sexual crimes, or that people are corrupted or depraved by it.

One study performed in the U.S. examined the amount of aggression shown after viewing either a pornographic or a 'neutral' film. Those who were sexually aroused were not more aggressive than those who were not when told they would need to show aggression in order to see a second film. But it was found that men with severe consciences and high sexual guilt were more aggressive than those of low sexual guilt consciences. This study does not obviously touch on 'real life', but perhaps suggests that pornography does not give rise to immediate post-exposure aggression.

A common problem that arises in the scientific evaluation of any data is whether the phenomenon (in this case pornography) is cause or effect. For example, there is evidence that people who show sexual deviance have had a greater exposure to pornography than those who do not show sexual deviance. Has the pornography caused the deviance, or do the qualities which lead to the deviance also cause a greater interest in pornography? Similarly, sexual offenders are often reported to have looked at pornography before going out to seek a victim, and in one study, four out of ten claim that pornography had something to do with the criminal act. But their exposure to pornography during the twenty-four hours before the crime has been found to be no greater than that of people who commit a non-sexual offence. So is it the pornography that incited the sexual crime, or is the sexual maladjustment manifest in these personalities responsible both for the crime and the interest in pornography?

In both cases it would seem to be the latter. Many perfectly normal sexually adventurous people have an equally great exposure to pornography, which may enhance their sex life but certainly does not lead to sexual offences of a criminal nature. And in countries where pornography is freely available there is evidence that sexual crimes have diminished. Nor is there any evidence in these countries that any other social disturbances or revolutionary tendencies have been exacerbated.

What about the people – ordinary, decent, respectable people – who have a slight fear of pornography? This could arise for several reasons : the repressive attitude of society towards sex produces guilt and fear; sexual conduct abounds with 'thou shalt nots'; fear of the unknown. From all these, pornography snatches away the covers. Those who are most afraid are probably the ones who have no experience of pornography, for people who have been exposed to recent pornography seldom see it as harmful. Exposure to pornography is in fact reassuring.

Is pornography useful?
It is now a fairly widespread ideal that children and later adolescents should be as well informed about sex as possible. To accomplish this, sexually explicit pictures and films are required. Simulated sex would easily be detected and rightly derided. Genital contact, erections and sexual pleasure have to be shown. The material which should be shown to adolescents is indistinguishable from hard pornography except possibly with respect to the intention of the publisher, and in the fact that the educational material is sometimes better presented.

In which case why not pornography? The fact that it is sexually exciting is inevitable and should not obscure the fact that it is informative. There must be few other social skills or accomplishments in which such representational aids would not be used. The method of presentation of such sexually explicit material, and the age at which it is presented, are of course important, but these are details.

Pornographic material is undoubtedly useful in treatment. Firstly in the treatment of sexual offenders, many of whom are inexperienced in mutual sex. Perhaps more than most, they require education so that they can find satisfaction from normal, instead of abnormal sources. Fetishists, paedophiliacs and sexual sadists have been successfully treated in this way.

Secondly, there is no better way of giving sexual deviants information about normal heterosexual behaviour, and homosexuals who wish to learn heterosexual behaviour have been much helped by means of pornographic films and illustrations.

Thirdly, several scientific studies have now shown how useful pornography can be in ordinary sex therapy. As this book explains elsewhere, the pornographic material is used to educate, to redirect and to stimulate. People suffering from sexual dysfunction can learn more about normal sexual functioning in sixty minutes of film viewing than in a whole lifetime of other forms of vicarious experience. People do not just require information on mechanical couplings, but want to know something about the techniques of foreplay, of genital stimulation, of how to 'read' the sexual arousal of their partner, and something about the intensity of sexual feeling and orgasm. Where such pornographic films are combined with discussion and reading the value of the experience is unrivalled.

Normal people are curious about almost everything. They want to be informed. They want if possible to share as many experiences as possible, whether it be the rigours of exploration, the joys of goal-scoring or the experience of disasters. The fact that some of these experiences can be served up vicariously – second-hand – is, if anything, an advantage. People also want to know about sex in this way. They believe that their lives could be enhanced by the judicious application of new ideas and they are probably right. Curiosity is really information-hunger.

So, to sum up: pornography can cause sexual excitement in those exposed to it; the evidence that it directly causes sexually criminal behaviour is poor; there is no evidence that it corrupts or depraves; it has been proved to be valuable in both sex education and sex therapy, and in therapy both of sexual dysfunction and of sexual offences.

So certain questions remain. Have the authorities the right to suppress pornography? Have they any real hope of doing so in the long run? Should any limits be observed at all?

It is our opinion that pornography is less harmful than alcohol and less dangerous than cars. Because a limited number of people become alcoholics there is no reason why the pleasures of drink should be denied to the rest. Because some people drive dangerously there is no reason for dispensing with cars. People must be allowed to think for themselves. They have to accept the responsibility for their own behaviour.

But should there be any limits? The majority will wish to see a few, perhaps with respect to depicting young children and perhaps apropos of animals.

Similar male and female responses to pornography

Kinsey's survey, which is now two decades old, contained among the wealth of interesting data the idea that women do not respond to pornography with the same enthusiasm as do men. Kinsey was referring here to pornographic pictures of sexual activity and pornographic stories. On the other hand, he found that both sexes responded to love stories or non-pornographic literature concerning sexuality.

Of course in Kinsey's day women were much less liberated than they are today, though the change towards liberation had begun. Had it not, the survey itself would have been impossible. Kinsey and his collaborators were very well aware at the time that many women would give answers which were cautious, partial and sometimes untrue. Furthermore, to obtain an absolutely representative sample of American women was, of course, nearly impossible. Those women who responded were more likely to be liberated than those who held back. Despite all this Kinsey did valuable work in opening up the subject of sexuality to enquiry, even if one should be cautious about certain conclusions.

To the idea that women do not respond to pornography with the same enthusiasm as men, Kinsey gave a new statistical respectability. But statistics are there to be refuted, and those who wish to promote the general idea of sexual liberation have now provided some contrary evidence.

In small surveys of fairly unrepresentative groups, women have been shown to respond to pornographic material with interest and arousal. Methods exist which allow laboratory investigators to measure the genital changes which accompany pornographic viewing or hearing. In women, a probe is inserted into the vagina, which detects the increased blood flow and engorgement of the vaginal walls. Erection is measured in men by wearing a small cuff around the base of the penis; this cuff is sensitive to stretching. It has been shown by the use of these devices that both women and men respond to pornography with genital changes.

Other small groups of both women and men have been tested without these measuring devices in an attempt to discern male/female differences. In general, they have been shown a variety of pornographic material and then asked how they feel. Some have been asked, in addition, what their sexual activity has been in the ensuing day or two. Women have reported sexual interest and arousal to this pornography and have shown increased sexual activity in the following forty-eight hours.

As for differences between men and women, men respond more to 'pin-ups', more to oral sex and more to different sexual activity. Such differences may well not exist much longer since female preferences may also change; indeed, may have changed already, as further investigations and published results may show. It should be borne in mind that since Kinsey no general coast-to-coast survey has been attempted, and any recent results are based on very small samples of the population.

Some uncertainty remains, but the myth that women do not respond to pornography has certainly been exploded, and the response is probably increasing.

Varieties of sexual behaviour – what is normal?

Many people are over-concerned with what is normal and consider that there is something wrong with behaviour that is not average practice. People still associate deviant behaviour with something 'perverted' or wrong. But 'average' behaviour, 'average' morality, may not be right for everyone, and after all, only fifty years ago there were many who believed masturbation to be both sinful and harmful; nowadays most people believe it to be both pleasurable and 'normal'.

Sexuality is such an individual matter that it is not surprising that when two people come together in a permanent relationship there may be considerable differences in behaviour and preferences. Unfortunately, too, such preferences are often not revealed until after the marriage, or are only discovered by accident. Transvestities and fetishists are often discovered in this way and such discoveries may cause much hurt and resentment. Minor differences are usually ironed out in the early part of a relationship but where one partner baulks at joining in some activity that is important for the other, it makes for resentment and conflict, and the sad outcome may be that the couple drift apart, each to his or her own, often lonely, sexual scene. Sex therapists may spend a lot of time persuading couples to share activities and fantasies.

Moral and self-righteous objections, of course, are only one reason why a partner may refuse to cooperate in some sexual behaviour. The refusal may also be a form of spoken or unspoken protest, such as: 'Your approach to sex is so impersonal and unloving; you treat me like an object; therefore I won't join in.' Or it may just leave the other partner bored and unaroused.

In practice couples who have agreed to cooperate in a partnership might as well agree to cooperate in their sexuality as well, and where the difficulty is caused by rigid application of old-fashioned standards it is well to remember that standards of behaviour do change from generation to generation. At the present time we are living in an era of increasing sexual liberality which many people welcome. In the last thirty years male homosexuality between consenting adults has become both legal and fairly acceptable in many countries. Exhibitionists and transvestites are probably regarded with less fear than by previous generations; perhaps people are beginning to think of them as being more sick than dangerous. The general public has never known much about fetishism but preferences that are known about, such as that for rubber, are regarded with indulgence. It will be fascinating to see what will be considered 'normal' in the future.

Transvestism, which is the dressing up in the clothes of the opposite sex in order to obtain sexual pleasure, is usually a quite harmless activity. It can, however, upset the public when transvestites are discovered in public lavatories of the other sex, though again no real public harm usually results.

On the other hand, transvestism is one of those secret sexual behaviours which are usually only discovered by accident; the wife may find female clothes among her husband's possessions. The husband sometimes has quite a good sexual relationship with his wife but has lacked the courage to tell her of his other interest, and where therapists become involved they usually attempt to improve the sexual relationship of the couple and if necessary to introduce transvestite behaviour as a joint activity. This is sometimes successful. In any case, where the wife can be persuaded to be more accepting and where the couple can improve their sexual cooperation, the transvestism often wanes in attraction.

Fetishists are people who seek out and use certain objects or materials to enhance their sexual pleasure. The material or object is called the fetish or fetishistic object. Fetishistic objects usually have strong female associations such as shoes or handbags. The materials usually chosen are either shiny, smooth or glistening on the one hand, or fluffy and soft on the other. In use the fetish may just be handled during solitary sexual activity, or the fetishist may want to dress or to dress his wife up in a certain way, as for instance in rubber clothing. Fetishistic objects and materials can be seen as very strong preferences. When it is pointed out that we all have preferences for certain materials, objects and styles of dress, and that these preferences can be quite powerful and important to us, it is often made easier to tolerate extremes of fetishism when they come to our notice.

The fetishistic preferences of one partner are often known to the other, and frequently both accepted and integrated into their sexuality. However, if this is not so, sex therapists will try to persuade the couple to attempt such an inclusion as part of a general increase in tolerance and flexibility. There is no reason why such strong preferences be rejected because they seem somewhat bizarre.

The association of sexual behaviour with pain used to enjoy widespread execration. Here, too, the public may perhaps be changing to a more tolerant attitude. Fewer people anyway would be likely to condemn the association on the grounds that it was not sanctioned by some holy writ or that it was not biologically relevant. Pain and sex are often written about under the title of *sado-masochism* (SM). The sadist being the one who inflicts the pain – the masochist the one who enjoys receiving it.

Sado-masochistic behaviour is yet another example of an extreme. Lesser degrees of these tendencies are normal. Many people enjoy minor degrees of violence and pain during the sexual act, either giving or receiving. During intercourse either the man or the woman may be the one who does the thrusting while the other lies inert. Either the woman or the man may enjoy the feeling of dominance and power, either may like to act with some force – to embrace with strength, to kiss or bite with such power as to inflict pain and minor damage. Either may enjoy this pain, especially if sexually excited beforehand, and may enjoy the feeling of being used, humiliated or controlled – enjoy the feeling of passivity or servitude.

Such minor degrees of sado-masochism are common. Slightly greater degrees, which involve the deliberate infliction of pain, the use of whips and bondage and so on, can only be judged individually. Where people are seriously hurt or forced to act against their will, the behaviour becomes abhorrent. But as in so many other situations the existence of black does not condemn all shades of grey.

Society believes that sexual activity with children is immoral. Bestial activity is likewise condemned.

In summary, society is approaching the view that people should have the opportunity to do what they please, provided no physical or mental harm ensues, provided the freedom and dignity of the individual is not impaired, and provided the activity does not impinge upon other activities of society or groups within society in any harmful way.

There remains a further option – that is, *no sex at all*. Individuals who have no sexual inclinations are rare and it must be said that there is no reason why a condition of no sex or nearly no sex should not be a perfectly happy one, especially when the individual is no longer youthful and has other satisfying pursuits in life.

Frequency of intercourse

Many people are obsessed with how frequently they should have sexual intercourse. When the Kinsey report was published, showing that on average young married couples have coitus two to three times a week, many believed that this should be the standard for everyone. This type of statistical 'average' is confusing for a lot of people as it does not reveal that it includes the whole 'range', from people who have intercourse once a day to those who have it once a year. It is better to let couples work out their own pattern and to discourage them from comparing their frequency with Kinsey subjects. The difficulties associated with frequency are often the result of one partner being more interested in sex and more active than the other.

The main point to emphasise here is that couples vary considerably and there is no 'ideal' frequency for sexual intercourse. Some couples might like sex every night of the week and others once a fortnight. Surveys have emphasised the wide variations between couples. And there seems to be no correlation or agreement between the number of times a couple have intercourse and how satisfactory it is for them. In other words there is no connection between quality and quantity.

Sometimes frequency of intercourse between partners can be affected by the woman's menstrual cycle. She may feel aroused at the middle of her cycle, when ovulation takes place, and maybe a week before her period feel rather low. Many women report that they suffer from pre-menstrual tension at this time and do not feel like sexual contact; on the other hand, others feel at their peak at this time. Menstruation can also affect frequency in that many women feel embarrassed about making love when they have a period. This is often related to superstition, or may be for aesthetic reasons. Some women patients even believe that taking a bath at this time is harmful. But neither making love nor taking a bath during menstruation ever did anyone any harm.

Pregnancy can also affect frequency of intercourse and can lead to much sexual frustration for both partners. But during a normal pregnancy the foetus is in no danger and abstaining from sexual intercourse is unnecessary. Certain positions may be found to be more comfortable during the later months of pregnancy, and here is a further reason for learning different positions. Only if miscarriage is threatened may the obstetrician occasionally veto intercourse for a period of time.

Satisfaction / fatigue

It has long been believed that after orgasm there will be a fatigue and depression. As early as the second century A.D. Galen wrote: *Triste est omne animal post coitum, praeter mulierem gallumque* (Every animal is sad after coitus except the human female and the rooster). But there are no facts to support this myth, nor for the Victorian belief that orgasm causes a loss of energy.

Sexual abstinence is sometimes recommended by sports clubs and trainers who believe that the performance of their charges will deteriorate if they spend their energy in sexual activity. It would be equally valid to argue that a state of sexual frustration and tension will impair their finer skills and judgement.

Masters and Johnson consider that sexual intercourse takes up as much energy as running fifty yards and that in a healthy person this energy is available many times per day. Where the sexual act has been satisfactory the ensuing feelings should be those of relaxation and calm.

Where the sexual act is prolonged or associated with difficulty or anxiety there may be a much greater expenditure of energy. If the sexual act was unsatisfactory for one of the partners, because it was insufficiently loving or exciting, again the post-coital feeling may be of some depression, and depressed people complain of tiredness. There are occasions of course when people are tired before they start; they will naturally still be tired afterwards, though they may well feel more relaxed. Those people who are 'run down', overweight, or physically unfit should get their companion to do most of the work and adjust the positions accordingly.

Masturbation

Masturbation guilt is a common problem because of the numerous fallacies and myths associated with it. Historically, biblically and socially masturbation has been associated with sin. Probably more misery has been caused by these beliefs than by any other sexual myth.

Many people still feel afraid and guilty about discussing this topic. In the past the Church inveighed against it and medical men believed that masturbation produced various debilitating mental and physical effects ranging from tiredness and poor memory to emaciation and insanity. In the nineteenth century the practice was called self-abuse.

Nowadays it is no longer believed that physical harm results. Most doctors today would probably regard masturbation as an important part of development and growing up. It is quite natural for children to be interested in their genitals; if their parents smack them or reprimand them for exploring themselves and they are told it is wrong and dirty they are bound to be guilty about their genital organs. If children are observed masturbating in unsuitable circumstances it is better simply to divert them skilfully to another activity. Otherwise they should be left alone.

If adults who have full opportunity to have sexual intercourse regularly prefer to masturbate, then there is a problem and they may need help. Perhaps they are afraid of penetration or coitus. However, surveys show that married people, both men and women, do continue to masturbate occasionally after marriage even when sexual intercourse is readily available, and mutual masturbation after marriage is quite a normal way of obtaining sexual pleasure as an alternative to intercourse. There is no reason why it should cease entirely upon marriage.

There is also no reason why masturbation should be associated with fatigue. If this happens it is probably due to the guilt the person feels afterwards; the guilt is obviously causing tension and this is tiring. If he or she just relaxed afterwards there would be a pleasant sense of well-being and no fatigue.

Nowadays the medical profession regards it as a harmless practice and a healthy way of relieving tension. If patients have sex problems and have never masturbated before, sex therapists recommend them to try it; it is described to them as a treatment task to attempt at home. Masters and Johnson mentioned that masturbation during menstruation relieved the associated pains and cramps in some women, and so was worth trying for this reason as well.

Oral sex

Oral–genital contact between men and women had long been known as a source of sexual pleasure. When the male kisses and licks the female genitalia this is called cunnilingus. When the female kisses, licks or takes the penis into her mouth, the activity is called fellatio or fellation, the verb being to fellate. There have been strong moral objections to this behaviour in the past and there are many objectors even today.

Many people disapprove of oral–genital contact on obscure moral grounds and the practice is illegal in some American states. Kinsey found that oral sex was a rare occurrence for women born before 1900. Cunnilingus was accepted, however, by forty-six per cent of younger women who had coitus. There was not this marked contrast for fellation. As oral sex is receiving much pornographic publicity, it is likely to become a commoner practice. Most sex therapists would regard it as being as natural and normal as masturbation. Some degree of oral–genital contact is common among animals.

A common anxiety for both sexes associated with oral sex is that of the penile and vaginal odours. Genital odours probably have the biological function of attracting the opposite sex and causing stimulation but unfortunately many people have been taught that these odours are disgusting and should be removed or obscured at all costs. The secretions which arise from the genitalia are certainly subject to bacterial fermentation which may change their smell if they are allowed to collect. But washing once a day between the labia, around the clitoris and the vaginal opening is quite sufficient for women. Men should also retract the foreskin and wash the glans every day. Whether to wash the genitals immediately before oral sex is simply a matter of preference for the couple concerned. It should be stressed that there is no need on the grounds of hygiene.

Ejaculation often takes place during fellation. Some men enjoy ejaculating into their partner's mouth but others feel more inhibited. Some women like the taste of semen and swallow it, some prefer to use a handkerchief to put the sperm in. No harm can result for the woman or the man if the ejaculation takes place in the mouth and the semen is swallowed. When talking to the very young or ignorant it is important to add that pregnancy cannot result.

Pain

Pain as a deliberate sexual stimulus is probably not much used. Nor is it generally acceptable, perhaps because pain is usually associated with fear, displeasure and injury and as a result the idea of linking it with sex is repugnant.

Consider, however, that normal sex has a variable amount of violence as an enjoyable concomitant. Passionate kissing can cause violent stimulation of the lips with pain, which because of the general sexual arousal becomes exciting rather than unpleasant. Kissing and biting the skin are natural expressions of sexual passion. Clawing and scratching of the back during the sexual act would, if taken alone, be regarded as painful, but in a sexual context is exciting. The arms and legs are employed in violent embraces sufficient to produce pain. The thrusting of the sexual act may cause pain which, though appreciable, is accepted with pleasure.

It is only when one mentions whips, and perhaps pinching or bondage, that the question of pain becomes a moral issue. Bondage refers to a group of activities in which a person is physically constrained. These bonds may be ropes, straps, chains, harnesses or manacles, depending on the inclinations of those involved. The victim is often bound at the wrists or ankles and may wear a collar or gag. She or he is often forced into some humiliation or another for the sado-masochistic pleasure of one of the parties involved, who may brandish a whip or some other goad. Sexual acts of all kinds accompany these rather serious and sometimes dangerous games. People must only be gagged with great care and never left. It is also wise not to get involved in bondage with people whom one does not trust, lest they go much further than ever envisaged, even in fantasy.

While bondage is not everyone's cup of tea, there is no doubt that for some people pain will enhance their sexual arousal. This pain may be administered before the sexual act or as part of it, but in either case it has the effect of increasing the arousal of the person receiving it, unless they are receiving it solely to accommodate a partner who, for a variety of reasons, usually felt to be unhealthy, may be excited by the act of giving pain.

People who have not included pain in one form or another in their normal repertoire of sexual behaviour and who wish to have an adventure should try it. Where the initial tentative experiments please both, a new source of pleasure may have been found.

Anal sex

Anal sex between men and women is illegal in the United Kingdom and some American states, but it is legal between consenting males above the age of twenty-one in the U.K., except in Scotland and Northern Ireland.

Many people find anal sex disgusting mainly because of its association with intensive toilet training and handwashing during childhood. It is also deplored because of its association with male homosexuality, though most gay men in fact probably go in more for mutual masturbation. Others find it biologically unnatural as it cannot result in conception.

For one reason and another, then, the introduction of anal sex into the sex act is for many people a 'switch off'. But some may want to try it and if so their first experience should be carefully and gently handled if it is not going to result in bad association.

The penis must be introduced into the anus very gradually, and while the penis is pressing against the anus the woman should try to bear down as if she were defaecating; this will relax the anal sphincter and allow painless entry. A good lubricant (Margarine or KY Jelly) is essential.

The possibility of transferring infections from faecal material

65

should be borne in mind. Infection is not caused by the mere presence of bacteria any more than in the mouth; a breakdown of normal defences is required.

Many couples do not want full anal intercourse but enjoy a little anal stimulation with the aid of a well-lubricated finger. The French call it postillionage when the finger is inserted in the anus just before orgasm, thereby increasing the intensity of pleasure. It is in fact not necessary to penetrate the sphincter at all, for the whole area around the anus and between the buttocks is sensitive to erotic stimulation.

People must decide for themselves whether to use this area for sexual purposes; if they do so they are unlikely to come to much harm.

Fantasies

A fantasy is an imaginary scene, situation, or sequence. Like many films or novels it resembles reality but does not share all its constraints. It can be developed or 're-shot' at will, or like a dream it may seem to control itself and you may be carried away. Yet one is not alseep, and fantasies include the appropriate feelings. Sexual fantasies both grow out of and engender sexual feelings. They are also inventions – ideas for the future: new behaviour which can be added to the routine to vary and enrich the ordinary fare. As a 'fantasy person' one can do things which otherwise might be physically impossible or socially unwise; and although rationally one knows this to be the case, for a moment at least, suddenly one can fly. Like other mental abilities, fantasies can be practised and improved. The more one does it the better they become. It used to be believed that only men developed sexual fantasies. This is not so; both men and women have the ability to the same degree.

Most people use fantasy and sexual fantasy to some extent, but the richness of the fantasy life will vary from person to person. Where a person feels guilt about some sexual behaviour he or she may also feel guilt about fantasising and the fantasy life will be restricted. Patients with sexual problems often have a poorly-developed sexual fantasy life, and therapists will teach them afresh.

The ability to fantasise sexually is a good and useful ability. Couples who know one another to the point of boredom can use fantasy to enliven parts of the sexual act. These fantasies may be private or shared. If shared the fantasy potential may be doubled. Inventing sexual stories for a loved partner can be a pleasant way of doing very little and enjoying it.

People commonly use fantasy as rehearsal, and here the boundary between worry and fantasy is small. Worrying about something, concentrating repetitively and inconclusively on what may go wrong, is at best non-progressive and at worst may be harmful. A rehearsal fantasy should concentrate upon the desired result and the desired sequence so that snags are ironed out in advance and the sexual feelings confirm the projected behaviour.

There are many situations in life when, married or single, sexual arousal is considerable or even amounts to tension. Perhaps a sexual partner is not available, or the person wishes to be alone. Solitary sex can be both a necessity and a pleasure, and in either case fantasies can and should be readily conjured up as one's fancy dictates.

The content of sexual fantasy can be extraordinarily diverse. However, there are certain elements which, single or combined, frequently crop up. The first element is one of strangeness.

People like to imagine that they are having sexual relations with new, strange and beautiful people. The stranger may be some well-known figure in the entertainment world, a public figure or even royalty. The sexual fantasy contains elements of power, magnificence, wealth and success, which may be lacking for the individual.

Others may fantasise people known to them but believed to be sexually unavailable. Both men and women enjoy chance encounters in real life. Such encounters may end quite tamely but may implant the nucleus of a sexual fantasy which, once used in orgasm or foreplay, rounds off the encounter in a satisfactory way – possibly better than in reality. Housewives sometimes fantasise sexual relations with frequent callers at the house: the milkman, the postman or window cleaner.

Another common element is of group sexual activity: a sexual party or orgy. Meetings with friends can begin with games of strip poker or games with certain forfeits and end with openly sexual activity – a group intercourse in a tangle of couplings or group masturbation.

The elements of sado-masochism are also extremely common, rape fantasies being enjoyed by men and women equally. The violence may extend to whipping, torture and degradation. Men imagine they can force attractive women to do their bidding, with the free use of manacles and ropes. The idea of humiliating and defiling other human beings while obtaining sexual pleasures is not uncommon in sado-masochistic fantasies. Here the elements of strangeness and group situations are also brought in.

Masochistic attitudes are more common in women than in men but not confined to them. The idea of being overwhelmed, of being unable to resist, of being swept away, of being raped and of being seduced by attractive and powerful men provides common fantasy material. Some women imagine themselves going out into dangerous and sinister parts of the town where they surrender themselves to a brutal and insensitive sexual encounter. Men may imagine themselves overcome by a group of attractive women who may force him into sexual compliance or into cunnilingus under duress; alternatively they may stimulate him unendurably while helpless. Elements of violence and dominance with their opposites may occur as in 'gang bang' fantasies, which are imagined by both sexes.

The possibilities are endless and can be elaborated to the point of teetering improbability. But the ability to appreciate and generate the improbable may well be associated with the ability to enjoy abandonment. Anxious and obsessed people who are quite able to fantasise sexual events usually restrict themselves to the probable and possible. Despite this they can be encouraged to be more adventurous.

The position as observer is also much fantasised. Such fantasies are usually called voyeuristic, a *voyeur* being a person who habitually attempts to watch others during sexual activity. The idea of watching others who are unaware attracts nearly everyone to some degree. Children want to observe their parents in this way. Both sexes fantasise watching people undress from hidden and forbidden places, and the fantasy may go on to include secretly watched sexual activity between couples or groups. Men fantasise that they are watching their wives or partners in sexual relations with other men, sometimes with violence. Women imagine their husbands in sexual relations with both known and unknown partners. Again, the desire to watch other people in actual sexual activity is strong in most people – witness the appetite for films showing just this. Though whether jealous and possessive people are able to imagine their habitual partners in intercourse with others would be interesting to know. Voyeuristic fantasies extend also to all situations in which people undress in public; beach and sun-bathing situations are very common material for fantasy. Where the voyeuristic fantasies are mainly those of watching through windows and from a distance, without involving sexual activity and without known people involved, this may reflect a lonely or un-involved sexual attitude.

Occasionally elements of other sexual orientations are imagined. Normally heterosexual people imagine homosexual activity. Of course there are many people who would call themselves bisexual; they are interested in sex with either sex. Homosexuality has of course been terribly repressed in the past and many such fantasies may be guilty ones. There is no need for it to be so – sexual interest in the opposite sex is entirely normal and harmless. These remarks apply equally to both sexes. At the present time men are probably more afraid of homosexual fantasy and involvement than women; hence it is more frequent to learn of the fear of homosexual fantasy leading to overt homosexual behaviour in men than in women. Even so, rigid and upright women express similar fears.

An element of the forbidden often enters fantasy – breaking the rules of society; enjoying sexual behaviour in forbidden places, in public, in churches or on the beach; fantasies of sexual behaviour with children, girl guides, scouts and so on. Parents have incestuous fantasies more often than the prudish would like to admit. Similarly, children fantasise sex with their parents. It may be said that there is no prohibition which is not regularly broken in fantasy, and it would seem with very little harm. Human beings, being curious and adventurous, will ever be attracted to the forbidden merely because it is so. It is extremely unlikely that a well-adjusted person who has forbidden fantasies will act upon them; not only have they other outlets but have much to lose by defying the rules.

Women who imagine that they are prostitutes and are taking money for sexual favours are fantasising elements of power, in-difference, beauty, defilement and strangeness. The prostitute may be fantasised because she apparently pleases herself and is paid for it. She is not caught in a net of obligations nor is she constrained by good behaviour; she can be herself. Male fantasies of being employed as studs will probably increase, now that it is known that men are being used as surrogates by therapists working in California. Not that hustlers, gigolos and male prostitutes have not always existed.

The element of showing off and of being admired and watched comes into many a fantasy. People imagine themselves as if seen by others, transformed by clothes, by confidence and by youth. They imagine that they have more attractive features, more brilliant circumstances and more beautiful companions. They imagine themselves to be basking in a perpetual regard. Others imagine themselves more actively parading their sexuality. Women imagine themselves giving off sexual signals: subtly hip-swinging, thrusting forward the hips, crossing or uncrossing the legs in a revealing manner, giving lingering glances and movements of the tongue. Men stare boldly, they swagger, wear tight trousers to reveal their erections and so on. Such fantasies could be called exhibitionistic, though 'exhibitionism' is more commonly used in referring to men who expose their erect penises to women and girls. However, quite normal men, usually confined to clothes which conceal their figure and their sexual offerings, have the desire to show off their bodies and sexual parts to others: one only has to think of the scanty tight bathing costumes they wear to see this. So their exhibitionistic fantasising seems far from unnatural.

Women, after all, have been allowed to expose themselves far more freely than men in the last hundred and fifty years. Breasts, shoulders, arms and waists during the eighteenth, nineteenth and early twentieth century, and more recently legs, breasts and pretty well everything else, so perhaps they may have less need for fantasy, or guilt. Whereas society allows the power of men to show but not the sex. When men have freedom to flaunt and decorate themselves it will reflect a very profound change in the social order.

The female counterpart of male exhibitionism of course still exists both in fantasy and reality. Women fantasise exposing their breasts and genitals in a provocative and sexual manner, sometimes as part of a seduction scene in which they have the power and the allure to seduce an innocent to his or her ecstatic first experience. Women constantly fantasise themselves wearing both tight and revealing costumes which may in fantasy become loosened, torn or wet.

There are innumerable other varieties of fantasy and none should be rejected by a therapist. Fantasies have many uses – let us nurture and respect them.

3

Why do some people have sexual problems?

Sex – does one measure up?

As we have seen, society has reached a point where sexuality has become a subject of considerable attention and concern. Until this century sexual behaviour was a matter for the individual alone. Because of the conspiracy of silence people have been able to judge themselves sexually only by their ability to produce children. Those who were unable to produce children because of a failure of sexual performance had no access to ideas which would help them resolve their difficulties. They could only see themselves as unfortunate victims of chance and resign themselves to fate. For this reason, their difficulties must often have been lifelong. Certainly they would have been in danger of ridicule, a further barrier to any help.

Society today actively promotes the idea of sex as a pleasure, and a pleasure available to all. The limits of sexual pleasure are not well defined, but nevertheless people are able to get some idea of what constitutes normal behaviour, are able to some extent to compare themselves with others, and judge how their own behaviour rates.

It has never been difficult to judge whether someone is a success in terms of social position or wealth: the criteria are all readily available to us. This is not true of sexual behaviour. Neither sex therapists nor behavioural scientists have much idea how prevalent sex problems are, and the general public certainly has no way of telling. Some research has been done into sexual performance but this is limited in its scope and insufficiently known to the public at large. The Kinsey report, for example, provides a mass of interesting information, much of which has been discussed earlier.

However, the facts Kinsey presents are based on the experiences of a past generation, are often distorted in their re-presentation, and in any case reveal more about quantity than quality. They may tell us that, within a certain age group, orgasms are usually experienced, say, between two and six times per week, but they will give no information concerning the quality of the sexual perform- ance or the amount of pleasure derived from it. With the result that this kind of data does not really provide people with a fair gauge against which to measure their own performance and enjoy- ment.

The ideas an individual may form about his own performance and enjoyment are in fact gathered from a very limited number of sources. The sex films and erotic literature available in capital cities reach very few. Television stops very far short of detailed sexual information. The popular press contains much that is sexually lurid, but tends to lay more stress on the 'abnormal' than the normal.

So there is real difficulty in obtaining accurate information by which to judge oneself, and as a result, the problems encountered by an individual or a couple before they actually seek help are usually positively glaring.

It is on this kind of inadequate information that society at any time bases its vague definitions of what is normal and desirable. This will depend partly on such scientific information as is available, but it is impossible even to disentangle the contribution of currently accepted customs and morals from that of the new ideas generated by individual thinkers and scientists. Scientific theories are probably generated in response to changes within the structure of society itself, and the provision of new ideas creates in turn other changes.

The development of sexual behaviour

This chapter attempts to outline the ideas which enable people to understand sexual behaviour, and so determine to some extent why sexual difficulties arise at all and what can be done to correct them. An understanding of sexual behaviour is an understanding of a long process of development from the sexuality of early childhood through all the stages culminating in adult sexual behaviour. The adult patterns probably depend to a great extent on the manner in which the child and adolescent behaved and were encouraged to behave, but of course depend ultimately upon biological factors: upon the normal growth and change in the sexual organs; upon the adequate functioning of certain glands within the body, such as the pituitary and the sexual glands – the testes in the male and the ovaries in the female. Unless the hormones which these glands provide are produced, normal sexual behaviour will not emerge. However, this book will not give any account of these glandular and hormonal changes except to remark that they are part of a remarkably efficient system and that only rarely does a deficiency in this system lead to sexual inadequacy; when it does, it is obvious. The vast majority of sexual difficulties arise in people who are biologically normal.

Sex – learning to behave

Nature produces an individual who is capable of sexual behaviour. Society decides what sexual behaviour is desirable and instils this behaviour in innumerable ways: at home, at school, during play and work, and also through the medium of newspapers, books, films and television. The acquisition of sexual behaviour can be seen as a learning process like any other learning process. It is no different from learning how to swim, how to conduct a conversation or how to ride a bicycle. The manner in which learning takes place has been studied intensively in recent years and is explained by what is called learning theory. The terms 'learning theory' and 'behaviour theory' tend to be confused: in general, learning theory may be considered as one aspect of behaviour theory which comprehends the whole of animal and human behaviour. Behaviour therapy is derived from both. For simplification we shall in this book refer to the theory as learning theory and the therapy as behaviour therapy. And in order to understand the contribution of learning theory to the explanation of sexual behaviour and to the treatment of its problems, we shall examine its main ideas.

Learning theory – innate versus acquired

As we have seen, although sexual behaviour is to some extent biologically determined, a large part of it is learned. The implication is that although part of any piece of behaviour is innate or instinctive the remainder is learned or acquired during the experience of the individual. We do not need to learn how to pass water; the act of micturation is a reflex and can be described an innate or instinctive behaviour. But society demands more of a person than the ability to micturate. It requires that we pass water in suitable places and with a degree of privacy; it demands that we wait for a suitable opportunity before we micturate. Thus, learning is required. The infant has first to be taught these skills, but he will later build on this teaching and learn additional things about micturation and what is acceptable to society as experience expands his knowledge of the physical world and social structure. The final result is an individual with well defined behaviour in this particular area; part of the behaviour is instinctive and part learned.

However, the boundary between what is instinctive and what is learned is often less easy to determine, and this is certainly so for sexual behaviour.

Spontaneous erection and orgasm
A clear example of purely instinctive behaviour is the ability to form an erection and the ability to ejaculate. Erections appear in boyhood and it is also probable that even in the absence of any sexual stimulation the male would experience spontaneous ejaculations, perhaps in the form of wet dreams. However, it is learning which will instruct him in the manner in which to have intercourse and which will determine the pattern of his foreplay.

It is harder to point to any proven examples of purely instinctive behaviour in the sexuality of women, though it is probably true that spontaneous orgasms occur during middle childhood which are only accidentally released due to chance genital contact.

These examples of instinctive or innate behaviour are pitifully few because it is almost impossible to prove the absence of acquired influences in most sexual behaviour. And there is, indeed, fairly general agreement among scientists that a very large part of sexual activity is learned during childhood, adolescence and finally during early adult life.

Education and ignorance
This conclusion has certain consequences. It suggests that anyone's past history and experiences will determine the present state

74

of his sexual behaviour, and that an understanding of his present sexual behaviour can only be reached if every detail of every sexual encounter in the past can be known. Almost impossible to achieve, but therapists make a valiant attempt by taking the sexual history of each client in enormous detail before therapy begins.

Since learning plays such an important part in sexual perform-ance, we can easily see how sexual incompetence arises out of ignorance. A knowledge of how to stimulate the penis or the clitoris with the hand during masturbation is a matter of explora-tion. From the exploration and manipulation, the areas which pro-duce the greatest pleasure, or release the orgasm, are identified and used subsequently. In mutual love-making the male or female can only learn these facts indirectly, either from the signs of pleasure in their partner or from being told. This knowledge of how to give pleasure is often very incomplete, perhaps because of lack of imagination or because of shyness on the part of the other partner in discussing her needs or feelings, or for a number of other reasons.

Ignorance may exist in many areas. The anatomy of the genital organs is often only very vaguely understood. Many men do not understand that orgasm is just as essential a part of love-making for the woman as for the man. They are often ignorant of a woman's other erogenous zones. They often fail to understand the rate at which their partner wishes to be 'brought along' sexually, and the best way to go about it. Some couples know of no other position than the usual male superior position.

So it is not difficult to see that some sexual difficulties arise from ignorance alone. Where the man is ignorant of the sexual needs of his wife and the manner in which to give her pleasure, the wife frequently comes to see sex more as a duty than as a pleasure and eventually complains resentfully that she is unable to obtain an orgasm – in technical language, that she is anorgasmic.

Prejudice
Ignorance, that is a lack of knowledge, may also go hand in hand with harmful knowledge and prejudice. Many children have been taught to associate guilt with sexual behaviour: they have been discouraged from asking questions about sexual matters; they have been smacked for touching their genitals. Their parents have indicated that sex is not talked about openly. In later life people

find it difficult to discuss sexual feelings and needs with their spouse, when a simple discussion might make all the difference.

Prejudice may bar the way to new types of sexual behaviour. Prejudice may condemn oral sex or new positions for no better reason than that 'it is wrong' – with no further justification required. The repression can then extend even to that which is allowed and appear in the form of an inability to let go, an inability to abandon oneself completely to sexual pleasure. It is easy to understand how this kind of repression and constriction of the sexual life can lead to a loss of sexual pleasure and consequently to a loss of performance.

Fortunately, although ignorance and prejudice may bar the way to greater pleasure, the very fact that most sexual behaviour is learned and not innate means that sexual education even at a late date may remove such hindrances. Sex therapists who are dealing with problems of sexual performance and enjoyment believe that education, re-education and learning are the means of solving these distressing problems.

Bad habits

Sexual behaviour once learned becomes established in the form of a habit – a sequence of events which is, in a way, almost automatic. In the sexual act appropriate foreplay leads to sexual excitement which leads to intercourse which leads to orgasm. The step from excitement to orgasm may depend on a series of acts which, however often repeated, still produce the same results. A useful habit has been learned. When a woman either does not want to respond or is not given the necessary pleasure to respond, a sequence of acts during intercourse may lead to no orgasm – may cause the learning of a bad habit. Here the bad habit consists in not responding with orgasm. Some men have the bad habit of premature ejaculation which, if established, causes much unhappiness.

Learning theory believes that one habit, whether good or bad, may be replaced by another. (Learning theory of course is not concerned here with morality.) So bad habits may be unlearned and new habits learned in their place. A man may replace the 'bad' habitual response of impotence with the 'good' habit of potency by learning to relax or to maximise his pleasure in the sexual act.

So the therapist can also be seen as an educator and teacher.

The therapist removes ignorance and replaces it with new information and ideas. The greater the illumination produced, the greater becomes the possibility that the light will continue to shine.

Rewards and punishments
The second main idea of learning theory concerns the way in which things are learned. This hinges, learning theory maintains, on a system of rewards and punishments. Those activities which are rewarded will be adopted; those activities which are punished will be discarded. The range, frequency and success of sexual behaviour will have been determined by the rewards and punishments which have been associated with it during the experience of the individual. (The words 'reward' and 'punishment' are used in learning theory in a general sense. A reward in the sexual context is anything which brings pleasure; it may be a caress, a smile, a payment, a present, a kind word, a sexual feeling or perhaps a pleasant taste.)

If someone performs an act, any act, and soon after receives a reward, he or she will probably repeat the act. If the act is usually found to be rewarded, that act will become incorporated into that individual's repertoire of behaviour – it will be learned. This sequence of events will not necessarily of course be as simple or as immediate. When the first association is made between an act and an apparently associated reward, this information is stored. Whether the act is repeated or not will depend on various factors. Clearly, the physical opportunity has to arise; one cannot pick grapes in Greenland. Even if the opportunity arises there may be other possible actions which may reap an even greater reward. The opportunity might arise in a different social setting already associated with punishments for other acts. Will this act be classified with the acts which have been punished in the past? If the individual considers this to be likely the act may be inhibited or deferred.

The performance of a given act also depends on the internal physiological state or drive at the time the opportunity arises. Whether one steals a sandwich will depend partly on how hungry one is when tempted.

However, in general an act which has a history of reward, not punishment, or in which the balance is clearly tilted towards reward, is more likely to be repeated than an act which is not so endowed. (It should be added that sexual behaviour can also be influenced by purely intellectual or moral messages such as 'It is quite all right to masturbate' or 'If you masturbate you will get pleasure'.) And from this human beings will postulate new ways of behaving and hypothesise the reward or punishment that will follow. Indeed, the reward, punishment and behaviour itself may take place solely in the imagination – in fantasy, for instance, or in the imaginative rehearsal of some new sexual behaviour.

When two people come together sexually for the first time neither one knows just which piece of behaviour turns their partner 'on' most. For sensitive and intelligent lovers the first encounter will tell them a great deal. Each partner will behave in a general way – embracing, kissing, stroking, etc. – and each will be observing which action seems to give the most pleasure to the other. They will be judging this from various signs. It may be heavy or rapid breathing or perhaps groans of pleasure. These responses give pleasure in themselves; they act as rewards and encourage the repetition of the behaviour which produced them. This example is taken from sexual behaviour itself but it must be apparent that the system of rewards will have been operating earlier in life in many subtle ways. The sexual interests and questions of the child produce responses in the mother. If the mother responds with encouragement and smiles, the child will have been rewarded and will find open discussion of sexuality easier on a subsequent occasion. If the child receives encouragement in any form it will soon perceive that sexuality is permissible and good.

Punishment
'Punishment', too, has a similarly general meaning. The child which is brought up in a family which is sexually repressive will have been punished innumerable times before adolescence has been reached. Each time he has touched his genital organs he may have been smacked or frowned upon. If he has made a sexual comment or asked a sexual question, the parent may have turned away, snapped, or worse, hit the child. Sexual responding is thus always associated with displeasure. It is not surprising that such a child grows up haunted by guilt and inhibited in its sexual behaviour.

Single unpleasant events can also damage the sexual behaviour. Children of either sex may be assaulted or frightened in childhood, though it is commoner for such experiences to be reported to therapists by women. Violent sexual assaults on young girls may well provide a basis for later difficulties; the girl who has been raped under distressing circumstances has been given a punishment which may cause damage to her sexual responses for some time. Either she may become tense and anxious during sexual advances or she may refuse sex altogether.

The system of rewards and punishments is the means by which society moulds the individuals who are growing up. But it is usually far less clear-cut than the examples we have given. Reward and punishment are – for the child, often confusingly – mixed. The parents will selectively reward some responses while punishing others. And while most parents would have a clear idea about the young adult that they wished to produce and would be able to outline a definite policy which guided them in their dispensation of reward and punishment, some are rather inconsistent, which makes it difficult for the child to learn efficiently. This inconsistency is usually produced by guilty, prudish and over-emotional attitudes, which are thereby passed on to the child, who because he cannot altogether predict the parental responses, becomes anxious and uncertain. Sexual anxiety can be produced in this way.

Fear and anxiety

The mood states produced by rewards and punishments are also of considerable importance both to the learning theorist and to the therapist. Pleasure has been associated by definition with rewards. Punishment on the other hand is associated with degrees of fear. A slight to moderate degree of fear is called anxiety; there is no difference between fear and anxiety, except of degree. Fear and anxiety are felt in the body in various ways. The anxious person is often described as tense, since anxiety tends to make the muscles contract for no good reason; sweating is common; trembling may occur in considerable anxiety; palpitations and choking sensations may be felt; tension in the head may be felt as headaches or tight bands about the head. Some people suffer with anxiety for long stretches of time and are called anxious personalities. But for many patients with sexual problems the level of anxiety is not great except in connection with a particular situation. This may be a situation which was originally associated with some punishing event and which, repeated, has become associated with anxiety. For example, a young man's first experience of sexual intercourse may have been fraught with anxiety. Perhaps he was nervous; perhaps there was a chance that discovery was likely or possible; perhaps the noise of intercourse may have been obvious and felt as embarrassing; perhaps he was ridiculed or told to 'get on with it'; perhaps he was having to perform in front of his 'gang'. Any of these situations could produce anxiety, with resulting loss of erection. It is not possible to maintain an erection if one is either fearful or distracted. Unpleasant experiences become unpleasant memories, and on the next occasion there will be a degree of anxiety. Depending on how severe this is and upon how propitious the occasion may be, the man may or may not lose the erection again. Though the very fear of losing his erection again will have added to the anxiety, and hence to the chances of losing it. A lot of people probably shrug off a few failures, but some people do not; impotence is not always the result of these situations but it may be.

Furthermore, the anxiety experienced at the moment of impotence may also be recollected every time the man thinks back on the occasion and will appear every time the possibility of intercourse arises. Since both women and men avoid anxiety whenever possible, especially when it is severe, this anticipatory anxiety can lead to the avoidance of sexual situations, and the problem is never really faced.

The therapist is able to replace this sequence of punishments and anxiety with new sequences in which these feelings are dispelled by the alternative experience of pleasure and relaxation. For example, since fear of failure associated with impotence often leads to a situation in which the failure is very frequent, the usual recommendation is to stop all attempts at sexual intercourse and indulge only in some pleasanter sexual activity in which no performance, no erection is demanded. Some kind of slow and relaxed mutual massage is often prescribed. The calm, restful and undemanding experience of sexual behaviour in this new situation soon produces the state of mind in which erections naturally appear. From then on the therapist will recommend a graded series of new situations, all of which avoid anxiety and maximise pleasure and lead eventually to a relearning of 'good' sexual behaviour and successful intercourse.

Sex drive

The remaining important idea behind learning theory is that of drive. Every person has needs. Hunger and sex are two needs which are very obvious. When the body is hungry or sexually aroused a complex state is being experienced which reflects activity in the central nervous system (the brain and spinal cord) and within the body. By definition this internal state is called a need state or drive and is accompanied by a state of bodily preparedness. The stomach changes to receive food. The blood flow in the genital parts is increased.

This internal need state or drive can only be deduced in animals, but humans can say 'I feel sexy' or 'I feel hungry'. Humans can also estimate the strength of the drive concerned: 'I don't feel very sexy today' or 'I feel moderately sexy now'. They can also describe the amount of sexual drive they have felt over a longer period: 'I have felt very sexy this last week'. Drives vary in intensity over both short and long periods, and the level depends partly on the length of deprivation. For example, after two to three hours of food deprivation a hunger drive will lead the person to search for food. Similarly, sexual drive will increase more or less according to the length of time the individual has gone without sex, and this sexual drive will lead to behaviour which will, in turn, lead to opportunities for sexual behaviour. Within limits the longer the need remains unsatisfied the greater the sexual or other drive. One can talk then about a person being in different states of drive.

Further than this, different people and different groups show varying amounts of sex drive. Young people have more sex drive than old people, but in any group of people of the same age, the sexual drive will vary. Some individuals are labelled as very sexy and probably have more sexual drive than those who are described as sexless. To some extent such differences in drive are innate but it is also true that the state of sexual drive may be made to vary. Where there are many sexual opportunities drive will increase; where few opportunities present themselves the drive will be reduced. In crowded communities sex drive is probably increased; in isolated situations sexual drive may subside to some extent. Sexual drive depends far more on external events than does hunger, for example, though people will still eat more when food is abundant.

The therapist can take advantage of this situation to increase the sexual drive. This may be done by providing new stimulation in the form of new ideas for behaviour, or by removing obstacles in the way of sexual behaviour. By improving the sexual techniques of the person, the range of sexual opportunities will be increased. The intelligent use of literary and visual pornography may also serve to increase the sexual drive by making the person more aware of the possibilities of sexual behaviour. The removal of guilt and inhibition by permissive attitudes can also free the fantasy life so that fantasies themselves may act as internal stimuli, serving to increase the sexual drive.

As is argued elsewhere in this book, therapists believe that the dangers of pornography have been overrated. They see it rather as useful, informative and enjoyable, both in therapy and outside it; nor have they experienced any deviant impulses which could notionally arise from pornography. This is perhaps not surprising since most pornography deals with sexual behaviour which is quite acceptable to the majority: heterosexual intercourse in a variety of positions; foreplay; male and female masturbation; oral sex. The much less common pornography which concerns behaviour which is not approved by society is not used in therapy, though here again there is no real evidence that this fringe material is harmful. People probably soon loose interest in behaviour which does not conform to their own inclinations.

Sex and upbringing – how behaviour is formed

Why do some people have sex problems? During the consideration of learning theory we have given some examples of the way in which things may go wrong. The time has now come for a more systematic account which will trace the development of sexuality from the infant to the adult, with particular emphasis on the genesis of sexual disorders. For not all young men who have unfortunate initial experiences will develop impotence, and not all young women who are raped under distressing circumstances will end up with permanent sexual problems. Many other factors come into it, of which character, personality and upbringing are all important.

In attempting to understand why one person develops a sex problem where another does not, one must first recognise the impossibility of generalisation. Broadly speaking, any individual is the outcome of on the one hand what they were born with, that is, their genetic endowment, and on the other hand the experiences that they undergo during the long period of their development.

Genes

It is obvious that the experiences of any one child are extremely complex and subject to a great deal of chance. The genetic endowment received from the parents is no less complex. The genes may be thought of as a blueprint which lays down a set of possibilities which may or may not be realised. Two individuals with the same genes (identical twins) but brought up apart will be very similar but by no means identical. The differences will depend on their upbringing. Brothers and sisters who are genetically different but brought up in the same family may have similarities because of their shared environment but will yet present obvious differences as a result of their different genes. And even the environment does not remain constant, as family circumstances alter at different stages in each child's development. So you may have two quite different brothers or sisters within that family: one happy and confident, the other timid and nervous; one may resemble the mother, perhaps, the other the father. But the reasons will never be simple or easy to discern; it will always involve a complex interaction of genes and experiences.

In considering what follows, then, one must not forget this interaction, even though it is convenient to describe these factors separately.

Child and parents

The character and personality of the mother and father will largely determine the family atmosphere and, in particular, the attitude towards sex which pervades the home. Parents with an inhibited and guilty attitude towards sex will react quite differently towards the child from parents who are unashamed and free. Children begin to show rudimentary sexual behaviour from a very early age. Erections are common in the infant and all children get pleasure from touching and exploring their genitals. Repressive parents may discourage or even punish this behaviour and may gradually instil into the child the idea that the genital area is in some way forbidden territory. It is unlikely that even the most restrictive parents will succeed in preventing a child from playing with its genitals, but from being public, the behaviour may be made private; and from being an unalloyed pleasure it may become guilty and anxious.

The interactions between the child and its parents do not of course stop there. The child is watching how the parents behave towards each other, how loving and affectionate they are. Even though perhaps few parents become sexually excited in the presence of their children, in innumerable small ways they will give messages which make their sexual reaction to each other clear enough: how they kiss, how they sit together, how they smile and how they embrace. The child sees too how the parents respond to other people in social situations, and the child of parents who are easily embarrassed and lacking in confidence may come to feel that this is the normal way to behave. Children 'model' themselves upon their parents, who constantly offer them examples of their own behaviour, without always realising they are doing so.

Gender roles
One particular message which children receive is that of the sex roles. Men are expected to behave in one way, women in another. Of particular importance to a sex therapist is the question of sexual equality. In the past women have not been allowed 'equal say' in many areas; they have been expected to defer to masculine advantage too often. Girls who have seen their mothers dominated and exploited may find it difficult to assert themselves in the sexual situation in later life. Boys, on the contrary, may develop selfish attitudes towards sex, believing for example, that their orgasm is the only important consideration. Sex therapists are constantly finding couples in whom sexual inequality is distorting the relationship. The commonest situation is the one in which the husband is both demanding and unskilful. The wife feels that she is being used and in consequence does not 'join in' wholeheartedly and may complain that she never enjoys sex and never obtains an orgasm.

Sex education
In homes with a repressive sexual atmosphere the child's natural curiosity may be stifled. Simple questions about birth and sexual activity may be avoided or turned aside with inevitable harm. Such a child may enter adolescence quite unprepared and ignorant. Parents of course are not the only influence. Many children receive

most of their sex education from gossip and remarks gleaned from their peers. The sex education given in schools varies enormously. At one extreme, sex education may be given as a regular separate lesson in the curriculum and the subject dealt with thoroughly and well. At the other extreme the subject may be dealt with in such a cursory way as to leave the mystified child quite unaware of the connection between what he has been told and his own sexual behaviour. Very few schools spend enough time on sex education and much of the information is limited to the strictly biological. Simple questions such as 'What do Mummy and Daddy do when they make love?' 'Where does Daddy put his penis and why?' are fudged, and even where such explanations are given the question of giving sexual excitement is often avoided or glossed over, and information about contraception deliberately withheld on the grounds that if sex is made to sound both safe and attractive children will behave irresponsibly. The truth is that they will be far more likely to do so if they are not well informed.

Fortunately many such attitudes are changing and it is likely that future generations will be much better informed. Sex therapists believe firmly that well-informed people will have fewer sex problems than those who are ignorant.

Personality
It is probably true that some types of personality are more likely to develop problems than others. The type of person who is confident, cheerful and outgoing is probably less prone to encounter real problems, and will usually have more frequent sex experience and sex with more partners than his more withdrawn counterpart. Whereas people who are naturally timid and anxious may brood on a bad experience and be less ready to try again or to try with a different partner. Their inhibitions may also make it difficult for them to find sexual partners and make them fearful of loosing any they may get, with the result that they may become possessive or jealous. Those who encounter these difficulties may unhappily turn towards lonely sex as their main outlet, or even develop deviant sexual behaviour such as exhibitionism or fetishism.

Society's sexual programme
Long before adolescence the child will have formed a good idea of its relationship with other people: will have discovered how easy

it is to get others to cooperate, whether other children seem to like them, seem to want to play with them or to bully them, how easy it is to make friends and keep them, and so on. The child approaches adolescence with these ideas and those attitudes and ideas instilled by the parents. The actual details of adult sexual behaviour may still be something of a mystery.

Gradually society presses harder. The half-understood and furtive gossip of childhood begins to assume meaning. The messages of the media begin to spell out the expectations of the masculine and feminine roles (ignoring the individual and assuming that we are all made in the same mould): the young adult shall dress in a certain way, shall adopt certain ways of behaving, shall be as rich, beautiful and successful as possible, and shall achieve happiness through multiple seductions on golden beaches. Pop songs cover a wide range of 'what every child needs to know', many dealing with romantic love and its problems – frustrated love, enforced separation, the beginning and end of affairs, and so on. Many refer to sex in quite an open way.

Nowadays the child will appreciate that many forms of relationship are available, and that sexual relations are a possibility quite early in life. The very fact that schools are being encouraged to give information about contraception during sex education is in itself a message that society expects young people to have sex quite freely. The idea that marriage is the likely outcome is losing some ground, though most adolescents probably still see their future in marriage, particularly where children are envisaged.

However, the demands of this essentially fantasy world promulgated by the media, by advertising, by songs, put a tremendous strain on those adolescents who do not feel sufficiently confident to go their own way.

Whereas in reality
The realities of sex and relationships are somewhat different. People are not invariably beautiful, they differ in the amount of love they are able to feel, they differ in the amount of sex that they want. However, since they do not realise that it is quite normal to differ, they build up expectations and ideals which they may find difficult to achieve.

Confusion and dissatisfaction often arise as a result of this gap between people as real people and the fantasy people of fiction and film. Heroines of the screen do not have to cope with menstrual periods or with the fluctuation of sexual feelings; they do not become tired, bored, irritable or listless. They never fail to enjoy themselves enough, or at all, or fail to excite and satisfy their men to a point of ecstasy. Male heroes are always ready and able to make love through a whole night, with a number of orgasms best described as fabled. Since the average man does not know how many orgasms he might expect, even in the most ecstatic circumstances, he may in the face of reality believe he is less than adequate. Many men feel quite reassured when they see a 'live' sex show; they are able to compare their performance with the performance of a real person and not with the imagined image of some film or television producer who has been more concerned to show excitement than truth.

When adolescents begin sexual activity in earnest they still have little to guide them. So many of society's messages which should be instructive and helpful are in fact only partial, often mystifying and far too often misleading. The very mystery, of course, may be in itself an extremely exciting element, but the maintenance of this mystery amounts almost to a social conspiracy, and it is a mystery which produces its casualties. Young girls may be frightened or repelled by the contrast between the rough and heavy-handed boy encountered behind the local disco, and the romantic, gentle, tender lover of her imagination. The young boy, fumbling and uncertain of what to do with his erection and how to handle his girl can, only too easily, feel he has failed, or experience either impotence or premature ejaculation. Either way, he will be very unlikely to give a second thought to the orgasm of his girl friend or to her need for pleasure. Most people overcome these difficulties and establish their own pattern of sexuality, but the minority do not, and the number of people who manage to realise their complete potential is probably quite small.

Once again, full and sympathetically presented information beforehand could prevent many a casualty of a first encounter, and could help to build a good behaviour-pattern from the start.

As sexual information becomes increasingly accurate and available, people should be able to enjoy their sexuality more, and there should be fewer people with sexual problems.

However, while one may inveigh against the distortions and romance of much of the information available today, we must not

87

forget that in some areas even this is not available, and that in the very recent past people depended almost entirely on extremely inaccurate gossip – or the observation of animals. Thus many people with sex problems today are victims of an earlier, much more repressive society. The atmosphere of today calls not only the young but also the middle-aged to the sexual feast. A feast at which many of the dishes are unknown and for which the appetite is uncertain.

It is entirely possible, of course, that new manners will create new problems. If group sex becomes more popular, for instance, there will undoubtedly be individuals who do not feel competent and comfortable in that situation, and who end up feeling inadequate. A further possible consequence is a decline in romanticism. For romanticism depends to some extent on mystery and mystery upon ignorance, and feelings are certainly more intense where barriers exist to impede their open indulgence.

Fumbling towards a settled state
At some time between the ages of twenty and thirty most people try a permanent or semi-permanent relationship with another person. With the gradual disappearance of much prudery and ignorance most people are probably being much cannier before they enter any 'long-term' relationship. Despite this, the drive to settle down is strong, and many are still entering marriage after an inadequate look at their intended partner. This can be the cause of many a sexual problem.

The old long-standing prohibitions still make it difficult for young people to obtain adequate sexual experience before marriage and they are often not in any position to assess the potential mate as a husband or wife, or as a lover. Any difficulties which they encounter will probably have to be solved by themselves, as advice is hard to find, treatment more so, and although there are now a few excellent books available, written at a really simple level, comparatively few people come across them.

Some of the hazards of courtship have already been mentioned. For people of an anxious disposition or who have been raised in a sexually unsympathetic environment, this may be a crucial period. They will have to learn how to make love, whether this means sexual intercourse or, as it did a few years ago and still does in predominantly religious societies, mutual petting, often to climax.

Love-making which is learnt under difficult or disapproving circumstances may be badly learned. The natural anxieties of doing anything for the first time will be intensified. Over-excitement and urgency may spoil an otherwise beautiful event. Premature ejaculation is said to be caused by learning intercourse or at least sexual behaviour under hurried circumstances. And for young women who have been given no foreplay at all to expect to come to orgasm under these rushed circumstances is to expect a lot. Both partners are going to be left unsatisfied, and neither will have discovered that in giving skilled pleasure to the other, they will also gain more satisfaction for themselves.

Many women, brought up to believe that sex is dangerous and disgusting, marry with the idea that sex is primarily a duty, with the bearing of children the only good outcome. Others, less inhibited, have an intimation that sex could be pleasurable if only something were different. That 'something' was, and still is for some women, an unknown. Either way, the role into which many women have been educated demands that they are passive – that they neither command nor initiate events. This passivity deprives the relationship of something valuable, for where there is no decision there is no commitment, and where there is no commitment there is no responsibility. And such women contribute their share to the sexual problems of today.

Many women still argue that it is the responsibility of the man to 'bring her on', but the liberated woman of today must take equal responsibility for the success of the sexual event. She too will have to learn techniques of love-making; she too will initiate the act in order both to proclaim her commitment and her liberation.

Harmony achieved – problems past?

However difficult the original circumstances of love-making, there eventually comes a time when these pressures are relieved. The relationship may change from one of courtship to one of marriage, or a couple may decide to settle down and not to marry though having every intention of staying together and having children. The opportunities for love-making will now become extended. Sexual intercourse can be enjoyed without serious difficulties of time and place – except perhaps for a couple living in very crowded conditions. This easing of circumstances means that the techniques which were employed before settling down may either be abandoned or require change.

Earlier generations had to change from mutual petting to sexual intercourse. The so-called 'first night' was often a nerve-racking business, particularly if both partners were virginal: a complicated exchange of bodies and feelings by two people neither well-informed nor expert. The majority of people overcome these initial difficulties, though often at some cost, but both women and men have to learn to overcome a variety of problems in order to achieve some degree of synchrony. Where these problems are not solved the sexual life of the couple is vulnerable and larger problems may occur.

The body
The most obvious problem area concerns the body; love-making is partly a matter of how bodies are managed. Most people start with the male superior position and if things go smoothly it is usually only a passing difficulty for the penis to find the entrance to the vagina. The simple act of repetitive thrusting is easily learned and leads to male orgasm without difficulty, except again where the male is anxious and 'watching' himself too closely.

Where a satisfactory position is achieved, this for many couples will constitute the habitual position, with perhaps rare excursions into one or two other possibilities. This limitation is due usually to ignorance, but prudery too may curtail the imagination and prevent the couple from trying new ideas. Oral sex is a frequent casualty here. But both partners also have to learn the other's 'erogenous zones' (those areas of the body which, when stimulated, produce sexual excitement) and how to stimulate them. One woman will like to be tickled and stroked, another kneaded and pinched. For a really satisfactory sexual scene these have to be learned.

Timing for two
The next problem concerns timing. As far as women are concerned this is of the utmost importance.

Women vary over the course of the monthly cycle in the degree to which they feel sexually interested. This varies from woman to woman, but it means that on days where the woman is not feeling particularly sexual but is nevertheless willing to have sex, it is the man's duty to ensure she becomes adequately excited by spending sufficient time on foreplay and activities which excite her. Thus the man must learn how much time his woman requires and what activities please her.

Men also have timing problems but they are less obvious. Some men do not require much penile stimulation before they 'come', but the woman will soon learn the timing of this. A second act of sexual intercourse after the first is often possible, but for the man not usually immediately. After a variable time lapse the woman may begin to fondle and work upon her man to achieve another erection. The way in which to do this is fairly crucial and can only be discovered from the man himself. Usually some kind of fairly patient gentle manipulation of the penis will produce the desired result. A woman who proceeds heavily and hastily may well obtain a disappointing rebuff.

After a man has had his orgasm he may not always be aware of the situation of his partner. To remove the penis immediately is unkind, for the woman may still be in a state of excitement and love – to have the penis rudely removed from her inside appears abruptly selfish. If the man does not know whether his partner has had an orgasm and wants one, he should ask and some other means of bringing her to climax will have to be found. Where the desire is urgent the male can usually bring her to climax by rubbing the clitoris in the way she wants.

The pacing of the sexual encounter obviously has other problems but the general idea should be clear. In essence it concerns the idea that the sexual act between two people contains a large area of unselfishness. There must be concern for the partner but also abandonment to pleasure for oneself. To get this balance right, the balance between giving and taking, is a matter of sympathetic and intelligent experiment.

Controlling anxiety and excitement
In the early stages of love-making some couples or some individuals feel a great deal of anxiety. The control of this anxiety is one of the problems of successful sexuality. Anxiety has several sources. The more obvious is clearly derived from society's repressive attitude towards sex which engenders an unrelaxed attitude towards sexual behaviour. Here, mutual enjoyment may give way to anxiety over 'performance'; the sexual act is anticipated as an encounter which

may produce a good result or a poor one. Men are the worst offenders here.

How can anxiety be controlled? In the same way that it is controlled in everyday life, in other situations. Perhaps it is easiest to think of children's fears. A child who is afraid of the water can be taken slowly into the shallow end and encouraged to go a little deeper on each visit. In early sexual encounters the young adult is no different from the child; the unknown is always dangerous, and seen as more dangerous to some than to others. So the problem of anxiety can be dealt with by adopting a gradual and slow approach, combined with an effort of will. If one relaxes, does not allow oneself to rush or fumble, 'keeps one's cool', the anxiety will not spoil the act.

Anxiety may also arise from rigidity of thought. If one begins the sexual act with a definite plan of action in mind, not only will it limit the possibilities, but any change of plan may throw one off balance. For example, either partner may be 'put off' by a new suggestion made in the middle of the act. So after establishing initial confidence it is important to take a creative and flexible attitude towards each encounter in order to avoid such shocks.

An anxiety which used to spoil the sexuality of many women was fear of pregnancy. But since the advent of more reliable methods of contraception this fear is found less often, at least among married people. Because of the variety of contraception methods available, there is not usually much difficulty in overcoming such a fear, long before a sex therapist is required.

It may seem odd to say so, but it is also important to control excitement. The most obvious case of over-excitement causing a sexual problem is premature ejaculation. However, the woman may wish to achieve her climax near to the climax of her man, and here it is possible to learn to postpone the climax to some extent by an act of will. Likewise, if a man senses that his partner is nowhere near climax and clearly wishes to continue for longer, he can thrust more slowly or less deeply, or change to a position in which prolonging intercourse is made easier. Where one has the knowledge to make such decisions, sexual problems may well appear trifling.

Fantasy
One area where anxiety, prudery and rigidity may combine to

stifle sexuality is in fantasy. By fantasy is meant the 'calling up' of images of a sexual nature – not necessarily fantastic or bizarre in themselves. As we have seen earlier, fantasies may well be beneficial: some are rehearsals for events which are yet to come; if they are anticipated with pleasure, these rehearsals simply provide additional and often stimulating pleasure. If the events are anticipated with anxiety then their function may be that of 'problem solving' in advance. Difficulties can be foreseen, analysed, and overcome with benefit. Fantasy may also help one to envisage some new sexual activity, which may in turn lead to further fantasising, for it is in the nature of fantasy to develop and expand beyond the original thought.

However, on the adverse side, some people get 'hung up' on their fantasies. They may believe that their fantasies would be unacceptable to their spouse, perhaps because they fantasise activities which are unusual or deviant; perhaps because the fantasies concern other people, known or unknown, who seem sexually very desirable. To reveal such thoughts might either seem to be a criticism of one's partner, or be taken as evidence of a kind of mental adultery. Insecure people may feel that such fantasies indicate they do not really 'love' their partner, or that if their partner has such fantasies, he or she does not really 'love' them. There may of course be elements of truth in these fears, but if so it is better to bring them out into the open, especially in therapy, where they can be intelligently and calmly discussed.

To remain in a private fantasy world is to create unnecessary difficulties for oneself, since private, unshared fantasies can only too easily become guilty fantasies, and guilty secrets create real problems. Another problem can arise if one partner spends the whole of the sexual act fantasising to such a degree that the other partner is forgotten.

Fantasies should be brought into the open, to be encouraged, used and shared in the service of a more open love and of an increased flexibility. In this way the shared fantasies will become part of the sexual relationship between two really honest people, who are more concerned with giving pleasure than with any thought of censure.

Communication and constraint

If people felt able to talk openly about sex there would be far fewer sexual difficulties. Where difficulties are not discussed they are frequently not solved. Difficulties that are not solved may cause resentments which in turn may make communication even more difficult. Of course it is not only sex and sexual feelings which are difficult to talk about but feelings themselves: feelings of anger, of distress, of suspicion and of love are all sometimes difficult to discuss openly.

Adults find it especially difficult to admit anxiety about a situation which they feel they are expected to face easily. Men, for example, hate to admit anxiety about speaking in public, or about approaching a woman. Women do not like to admit to anxieties concerning their dress or sexual attractiveness. Society lays down standards of competence and adults know what is expected of them in most given circumstances; where they have doubts they often keep quiet out of shame.

In general the rules of sexual conduct are well known; the places where sexual intercourse may take place, for example, are well defined. There are, however, some aspects of sexual behaviour about which many people feel doubtful and therefore anxious, and about which they find it difficult to speak. Oral sex is felt to be wrong or disgusting by some people. Many would feel anal intercourse to be definitely wrong or undesirable. Between any couple there are areas where behaviour is not quite certain, and what may seem acceptable to one may be repugnant to the other. These areas need above all to be discussed openly, but unfortunately there still exists a taboo on talking both about feelings and about sex.

Reality and romance

The difficulty in talking about feelings extends also to bodies and bodily functions. The Victorians did not like to think of themselves as animals and in order to affirm their superiority over the animal kingdom demanded that the animal nature of man be suppressed. Thus it became taboo to expose the body freely, taboo to talk about bodily odours (polite people spent much time washing and perfuming themselves); farting and belching were both extremely bad form, and even the yawn had to be covered.

Many of these taboos are being relaxed today: far more of the body may be revealed and there is much more freedom in talking about bodily functions. However, it still remains hard for many people to talk about sex either in public or in private. And it is in private that problems arise, and they usually arise where real discussion has not taken place.

Past generations saw sexual behaviour as animal behaviour, and since there was no way of avoiding it, they merely suppressed all public and private reference to it and surrounded it with as much romance as possible. Relations between courting couples were supposed to be spiritual and platonic, and the appropriate language of this love was poetry, and certainly not descriptive prose. To be open, frank and unsentimental threatened the romantic illusion: the illusion that all love had little to do with sexuality.

Learning to talk about sex
Romantic attitudes still persist, and the problem of sexual disorders is partly a matter of language. The average person is just not equipped with the technical vocabulary to talk freely about the parts of the body concerned, or their activities. Learning the vocabulary and learning to overcome the prudery and anxiety go hand in hand. In part the sex therapist begins the treatment by saying, in effect, 'Let us learn to talk about sex together.' The therapist who says, 'Do you have oral sex?' is saying firstly that 'oral sex' is a convenient way of referring to oral-genital contact. The act of referring to oral sex represents an encouragement from the therapist to the couple to begin to refer to it in this way.

Gradually, the therapist will proceed to be more specific, and will probably introduce the whole technical vocabulary and demonstrate its use, using various synonyms at the same time. People find it useful to have alternative, more informal expressions for orgasm and sexual intercourse at times. The adoption of a casual vocabulary reflected in such expressions as 'to come' and 'to have it', or in the use of basic words such as 'fuck' and 'cunt', probably represents a more relaxed and realistic attitude.

Talking about sex in an open way without using formal or vague words inevitably leads to a similar need for frankness in talking about feelings. Both men and women have difficulty in describing their feelings. People often say they don't 'like' doing something, but what exactly do they mean by this? Do they mean that they feel this something to be wrong, or disgusting, or frightening? It is valuable to be able to describe feelings accurately, and to describe them is also, of course, to identify them. In addition, the therapist can also make sure that words describing positive feelings – love, warmth, excitement, etc. – are brought into the talk in a reassuring and approving way. In this way the course of therapy should leave the couple equipped to communicate with ease and facility when talking to one another about emotions and sex.

Regrettably, by the time most people reach adult years the habit of secrecy and reticence over sex is well ingrained. People will often say, 'It just doesn't seem right to talk about it', meaning that they have been thoroughly conditioned not to do so. Unfortunately such an announcement often signifies not only that the subject is closed but the mind too, which means that the problem-solving intellect is denied a chance to change what may be a bad situation. One may also have the problem of one partner being prepared to enter into discussion of sexual matters while the other is not. A woman, for example, has come across some of the newer magazines dealing with sexuality, and wants to start talking about a subject which has not been discussed for years. Her man may immediately feel that he is being criticised in some way, and may react with anger. Or the man, for example, may attempt to open discussion on his wife's 'lack of responsiveness', and she instantly believes that he no longer loves her. If they are unable to get beyond this kind of over-sensitive reaction, a serious barrier to further communication is built up.

Where a therapist becomes involved, time would be spent on reassuring each partner that the expression of suggestions and ideas should not be taken as criticism but as a means of increasing the pleasure each is able to give and receive.

Equal partners? Marital difficulties

Earlier in this chapter it was pointed out that the inculcation of exaggerated male (chauvinistic) or female (subservient/passive) roles, took place at an early stage. Such attitudes lead to various inequalities and difficulties. In theory, nearly all couples would agree that the maintenance of the relationship should be a shared and equal responsibility. In practice it is common for one partner to be more dominant than the other, and this dominant partner may like to take all the decisions and assume the main responsibilities. One partner may also always take the sexual initiative – will always be the one to suggest sex.

The exact balance within a relationship is a matter for each couple to work out but it is not a good thing for the balance to be permanently and irrevocably tilted in one direction, especially where sexual activity is concerned. The partner who always initiates sex will also be made to take the responsibility for the act. The passive partner may simply 'opt out' of the responsibility of participation, of giving as well as receiving. Even worse, perhaps, the dominant partner may be insisting on his or her right to dominance. In either case the problem of shared responsibility should be recognised and discussed.

The mention of dominance problems within relationships raises the whole question of the relationships themselves. Making a relationship is a very complex affair and a lot can go wrong. Many wives nurse resentments against their husbands. Common complaints are that the husband makes no contribution to the domestic duties of the household; that he stays out late, leaving his wife alone; that he does not take his share in the upbringing of the children; that he does not consult his wife on money matters; and that the wife never gets a chance to go out alone. Husbands complain that their wives are always busy; they never have time from domestic chores just to sit down and be pleasant; that they care more about the children than their husband; that the wife does not bother with her personal appearance; that the house is untidy or too tidy; that he can't abide her relatives, and so on. Husbands and wives both complain that the other 'lets them down' in front of other people, damaging their self-esteem. Relatives or other people in the house often add to the difficulties. Either partner may begin to feel trapped by circumstances from which they see no way out. These and other problems often lead to quarrelling, especially when one partner 'takes it out' of the other partner, or of the children, because of general dissatisfaction with their lives or achievements. Quarrelling in turn leads to ill-feeling and resentment, and quite frequently one partner will withdraw sexual favours from the other, either partially or completely.

On the other hand, if a couple have a sexual problem this itself may lead to resentment and quarrelling. For this reason it is

97

important to distinguish between a difficulty which is basically sexual and one which is basically marital. Sex therapists try to confine themselves to problems which are basically sexual but since sexual difficulties and relationship difficulties are often mixed together, they involve themselves to some degree in the marital relationship as well. This book does not examine purely marital or relationship problems but for any couple it is wise to be aware of the need to maintain each area of relationship in good repair. This activity of renewal can only take place where a habit of communication is established and the problems of talking together openly have been solved.

Sex as a casualty
Ideally, most of the problem areas that have been examined should have been solved in the first few years of a relationship. Even where they are not dealt with openly or consciously a couple may make what appears to be a fairly good adjustment. Their sex life may have been somewhat infrequent and rather routine but at the same time it did not seem to be a problem. Often such couples reach middle-age before there is any hint of real trouble. When trouble does appear it may have various causes, and the causes may have been operating for some time before the couple are aware of anything being wrong.

Take the problem of tiredness due to overwork, which affects both men and women. For the man who is hoping to 'get on' in his career, or who works overtime, the immediate result is a reduction in the amount of time he spends with the family, and a reduction in energy level. Rather than make love he may prefer to be mesmerised by the T.V. or flop into bed. Initially the frequency of intercourse is reduced, but eventually enthusiasm is reduced also.

This tiredness is often mixed with boredom. The excitement of the early relationship naturally wanes. Only too often it wanes to a point where sex is very infrequent and minimal in its enthusiasm. The act may be reduced to its mere essentials.

As one gets older
Difficulties occurring in middle-age may be compounded with feelings of depression because of lost youth, feelings that neither oneself nor one's spouse are any longer attractive. The loss of youthful energy and attractiveness in one partner may cause the

sexuality of the other to be focused upon younger people. It may be difficult not to be jealous of the sexuality of one's children and their friends. Men, more frequently than women, begin to feel that their hope of achieving anything significant has been decided by middle-age, and where youthful ambitions have not been realised it is only too easy to allow an element of depressive inertia to creep into one's life. And this will inevitably affect the sex life too.

There are other factors which may also cause trouble: heavy drinking, often a symptom of maladjustment, will affect any relationship and may also cause potency problems; excessive smoking only produces an effect after many years but in the long run the general health of the smoker will be reduced and this may be detrimental to sexuality; declining health, for whatever reason, will undoubtedly reduce sexual desire and performance. It is beyond the scope of this book to describe a solution to all these problems, but help can usually be found from marital, medical or psychological counsellors.

Either or both partners of a couple who have lived together for many years may become emotionally and sexually involved with other people. When such a relationship is concealed things may go either way: sometimes there is an increase in the sexual activity between the original couple; sometimes the sexual activity falls off disastrously. Occasionally, a chance sexual encounter or affair may cause some psychological upset, and guilt may affect the performance of the erring partner. This guilt can probably best be dealt with by open discussion between the couple and possibly with a sex therapist or marriage counsellor.

These various factors which may cause problems after many years are often present in combination. For instance, some measure of physical decline is apparent by the forties. Neither partner is as active and tireless as before. Overworked and tired people may begin to smoke or drink more than is advisable. People who have neglected their relationship or who have been unable to resolve psychological conflicts over many years may have reached a state of constant quarrelling or a state of boredom. It must also be faced that not all people who may appear suitable mates during the early years of marriage will remain so. It is common to find one member of a partnership flourishing while the other declines. This may happen for many reasons, some psychological, some due to ill health. There are other couples who only stay together for the sake of their children, or because it is difficult to part.

Tired and overworked people often lose interest and hope in the future, and stick apathetically to the known routine. They may show a lack of creative interest in their sexuality as well as in their lives, and begin to neglect their bodies. Overeating and too little exercise will make them less fit for sexual exercise, and they may even find themselves severely out of breath because of the physical strain alone. Unfitness of a severe degree will probably eventually impair the erection and the ability to achieve orgasm. The effect may not be so apparent in women; however, no woman who hopes to maintain her relationship in a happy condition can allow herself to become seriously overweight or neglect her fitness or her attractiveness.

Sex for the old as well
In the last decade sexual activity in old people has been more discussed. Adjustment is required in old age as much as during middle-age. Sexual expectations may be too high. If a couple expects to be able to achieve orgasm just as easily and frequently as when they were young they will be disappointed and frustrated. People tend to believe that each sexual act should end in orgasm, but there is no absolute need for this. An elderly couple may decide not to aim for orgasm in either or both partners. They may decide to have more rest pauses during intercourse, which can be allowed to take longer. Where there is some reduction in energy and physical capacity, a new position for sexual intercourse may be adopted. For instance, a position in which neither partner is supporting their own weight: a side-to-side position might be the answer. Alternatively, mutual masturbation may be found less stressful. If there is a deficiency of natural lubricants, some lubricating oil may be applied. The need to continue to talk occasionally both about the relationship and about their sexuality should not be neglected. A couple who have managed to avoid the difficulties facing middle-aged people should not neglect the new difficulties of old age. Where old couples continue to be flexible and creative, their sexual lives will continue longer, probably very much to their benefit and happiness.

4

Who needs sex therapy?

Most people experience mild sexual dysfunction at some time during their lives, either from fatigue, drugs, reduced drive, ill-feelings, or various other causes. Indeed, variations in sexual performance and pleasure are part of the normal scene. It would be surprising if it were not so, since every other human capacity has similar variations. A slight variation – an orgasm of low intensity; a delayed orgasm; a transient mild failure of the erection, and so on – are only matters of slight disappointment. It is only where such variations become more obvious – and this is a matter of degree – that the word dysfunction should be used. Again, to suffer a dysfunction is not in itself abnormal. It is when such a dysfunction is persistent and distressing that the question of sex therapy should be considered. Of course the threshold for distress is lowered where the person has high rigid expectations of their performance, any departure from which is seen as threatening or disastrous. Here it is the expectations which are at fault, not necessarily the sexual potential.

One problem can arise between couples today as a result of woman's sexual expectations being considerably increased and better defined. The emphasis is shifting away from male performance and pleasure, and males now are seen to have a duty to ensure an adequate sexual experience for their partners, who will otherwise feel deprived. Women today expect men to develop a degree of skill during foreplay and to become aware of the female's state of sexual arousal in order to achieve a tempo which will lead to a good orgasm for both parties. These demands, and they should be no less, may threaten the male ego and cause temporary sexual problems. However, if the male is able to recognise the justice of this new current, he should also recognise the potential for greater pleasure which it offers. Once the sexuality of women is really accepted as a fact of life such problems will disappear.

1 Low sex drive

Problems of varying degree of severity arise where there is a considerable disparity in the sex drive between the couple. One partner may want sex twice a day while the other is quite satisfied by sexual relations once a week. On the surface this difficulty appears more extreme where the male has the low drive, for in the opposite case the female can at least lay herself out even if she does not want to participate. However, it becomes a problem where she does not want it and is expected to respond.

These problems of disparity of sex drive should always be looked at very carefully; they often turn out to be due to problems of communication and of sexual technique. The partner who is of low drive may require more time or more skilful attention in order to respond more frequently. The so-called high drive partner may be prepared to abstain either in the interests of greater cooperation or of enhanced intensity of experience. Disparities may also conceal psychological problems; the high drive partner may feel uncertain of the affection of the spouse and require constant reassurance, or may long to be invited into sexual activity in a situation where the low drive partner is refusing or baulking at the initiation of sexual activity. In any case careful analysis of each couple's particular problems can often lead to an acceptable solution.

There is of course no problem if both partners have a low sex drive and are not making sexual demands on each other. If that couple wish to have a family and have fertility problems they might need sex therapy to enable them to increase their sex drive. Usually, however, couples come for sex therapy when there is a marked disparity between their sex drives.

Low sex drive may be chronic and apparently part of the personality. This would go with a chronic indifference to sexual acts, fantasies and thoughts. This type of person almost never gets 'turned on'. This chronic state of low drive can also be caused by addiction to alcohol, sedatives, barbiturates, or heroin. It may also be caused by permanent fatigue, depression, medical disability, epilepsy, diabetes, hormonal deficiencies and some prescribed drugs, but these causes are usually obvious.

The occurrence of a state of low sex drive of fairly sudden onset in the course of a life of normal drive is usually symptomatic of some temporary disorder. Common causes of such temporary reduction are depression, anxiety, stress, fatigue, personal life upheaval, illness, pregnancy, and marital disharmony. Chronic reductions in sexual activity occur in unhappy marriages. These, however, are not so much reductions in sex drive, as a failure to cooperate in sexual activity. Masturbation or other outlets may have taken the place of mutual sex.

The level of sexual activity which is present for any given person at any given time is of course determined by many factors. Circumstances may have led to a situation in which the person is not using their sexual capacity to the full. It may be that they have very little contact with sexually active people; they may be isolated; they may believe that their sexual life should really be over; they may have experienced a sexually repressive upbringing that in later life leads them to ignore or suppress sexual arousal. Women particularly have often been programmed to behave with a low sexual profile: to present a demure and chaste front. Or they may have united themselves to a sexually inactive partner, or live in a repressive clique. People in such situations may be quite content, and to offer sex therapy would be quite intrusive. There is after all no reason why a person should not carry a spare capacity. Most of us do in any case – having more talents than we can use. However, if help is sought, therapy can always introduce such a person into a more active sex life by means of an erotic education.

2 Painful sexual intercourse

Sex therapy may need to be given to people who complain of pain associated with sexual contact.

Problems associated with pain are common to both sexes. Dyspareunia is the name given to this; it means painful sexual intercourse. Once it was thought that this was an exclusively female problem, but this is not so. It is, however, less frequent in men. Some men complain of pain during intercourse, and this can be caused by the abnormal sensitivity of the glans associated with poor hygiene and infection. One condition called phimosis (when the opening of the foreskin is too small to be pulled back over the head of the penis), can also cause pain.

Women sometimes experience pain in the vagina due to poor lubrication. This is most commonly caused by inadequate excitement or insufficient foreplay, and if the vagina is poorly lubricated pain may also be experienced by the penis, which does not slide along with its expected freedom. When natural lubrication is insufficient there are a variety of commercial lubricants available, some a pleasure in themselves. Mild pain in the vagina may also be seen as a protest associated with: low sex drive and excitement; partner dissatisfaction; fear of pregnancy, or with the anxieties attached to repressive rearing or unfortunate experiences.

Infections of the vagina, the commonest being trichomonas (a small organism) or thrush (a type of fungal yeast), may inflame the mucous membrane lining and alter the acidity of the secretions, making intercourse painful. Sometimes when a patient is cured of this type of infection she still associates sexual intercourse with pain.

Mrs W. was referred for treatment because she had suffered from a bad attack of thrush six months previously. She had been treated for this and there was no sign of any further infection, but she still complained of pain during intercourse. She was twenty-three and her husband was twenty-nine. They had been married for two years and were keen to have children. During the initial interview she revealed that her husband did not particularly excite her and had never given her clitoral stimulation. She had felt embarrassed about this but unwilling to communicate her desire for clitoral stimulation. She said that she had always enjoyed masturbating on her own. Her parents were not very strict and were regular Church of England supporters. She had been confirmed but had abandoned religion at the age of fourteen. She had enjoyed relations with boys and had tried sexual intercourse at the age of seventeen, but had been in a rather anxiety-provoking situation and had not allowed herelf fully to enjoy insertion, and had not climaxed. She met her husband at the local discotheque. She was not particularly attracted to him physically but liked his personality and his attentions. A year later they got engaged and enjoyed sex twice a week in the man above position. After the wedding they became more experimental over positions but she was not keen on any of them, whereas he liked them all. He rapidly turned over and went to sleep after intercourse, while she lay awake feeling frustrated.

Following a chest infection, for which penicillin was prescribed, she developed thrush and suffered a great deal of vaginal pain.

Treatment left her cured, but she still found it painful to make love and only permitted intercourse on a monthly basis. She said she only felt the pain when his penis went inside her and he started thrusting. They had used a lubricant jelly, but this did not help.

Since there was no physical explanation for this pain, perhaps it was being sustained by psychological conflicts? Sex therapy was given a trial with considerable success.

Cases have been recorded where anal intercourse followed by vaginal intercourse has caused infection of the vagina. If vaginal intercourse is to follow anal insertion during the same session, the penis should be washed carefully between the two encounters.

Pain from locally applied substances is also to be considered. Deodorant sprays and applications have been implicated as, also, have certain contraceptive substances now largely superseded. The symptom from such local applications is often burning sensations and irritation.

Post-menopausal women may also complain of pain – it is thought that this pain is caused by thinning of the vaginal walls, due to the changes of the menopause. This problem may be solved either by extra lubrication or by hormone replacement therapy.

Deep pain in the pelvis can also be caused by psychological factors, but a physical cause must be decisively excluded before a conclusion is reached. Pains of this kind may have a deep, sickening quality, depending on the structures involved. The symptoms may arise from injuries and infections sustained during childbirth, or during unskilful abortion procedures. Infections and other conditions of the cervix, tubes, uterus, ovaries and other pelvic structures will also have to be considered. Where these symptoms persist a gynaecological opinion should be obtained.

Mrs G., a housewife and mother, had complained about pain since the birth of her baby. After this birth she had stitches and overheard the nurse saying, 'It looks a bit frayed', and the doctor saying 'It's all right'. Aged twenty-two, she was a pretty-looking, rather flashily dressed girl. She said that she wanted sex and could get excited and lubricated but could not bear having intercourse as it hurt her, although the gynaecologist had checked that the stitches were all right. Just at the moment of penetration she became tense, her legs went rigid, and when her husband entered she felt pain.

She had tried the 'woman above' position but this did not help. She talked about masturbation and how she enjoyed this activity with her husband who had shown her where her clitoris was. She had enjoyed orgasms before the birth of the baby and since had masturbated when on her own, but wanted to have an orgasm with her husband, and definitely wanted more children. It was felt that Mrs G. was reacting to the unpleasant events of the recent birth, in particular the wound and stitches, and that her symptoms could be treated with sex therapy.

3 Vaginismus

Vaginismus is a spasm of the muscles surrounding the vaginal introitus, the purpose of which is to prevent entry into the vagina of any intrusion. The condition may be present to varying degrees. However, in a severe form penetration is almost impossible without considerable force. Vaginismus is a dramatic and compelling reason for sex therapy. The condition is usually obvious from the description. The spasm is not confined only to the vaginal inlet but may affect the whole body – in an extreme degree the knees are firmly held together, not even allowing a vaginal approach. The couple have usually abandoned all attempts at intercourse, and usually all sexual contact involving the female genitalia. Vaginismus is a frequent cause of marital non-consummation. The history is usually sufficient to clinch the diagnosis but a physical examination is always necessary. The attempt to insert a finger or fingers into the vagina in the usual manner will be almost impossible and certainly inadvisable. The woman may back away and take any avoiding action as the finger approaches. When the condition is less severe a finger may be allowed entrance, but encounters an increased resistance. While the examination is pending, signs of fear may be evident.

The majority of cases of vaginismus are produced by unfortunate experiences during attempts at intercourse, or during rape episodes. The vaginismus is then seen as a conditioned fear response which persists in the face of any further repetitions of similar behaviour. Vaginismus may be either primary, that is, there has been no period of normal penetration beforehand, or secondary, in which case it develops in a woman who up to that time was able to allow normal penetrations. In cases of primary vaginismus, a repressive sexual upbringing is frequent. Secondary cases may also be the result of unpleasant experiences or psychic trauma.

In addition to these cases which could be called psychosomatic, there are cases of secondary vaginismus which follow upon painful intercourse caused by injuries or diseases of the locality. The cure of such cases is of course first the cure of the physical disorder. Careful history taking will elicit dyspareunia anteceding the vaginismus.

In a marriage in which the woman has vaginismus it is not uncommon for the male to develop a degree of impotence.

Mr and Mrs R. attended for treatment. Mrs R. was an attractive woman who could be described as 'too heavily made up'. Her vivid orange coat clashed with her auburn hair and certainly made her look conspicuous. Mr R. was a soberly dressed, quiet, bespectacled man with a somewhat timid manner. Mrs R. had been told the facts of life by her mother, but prior to this her mother had caught her masturbating, and in Mrs R.'s words: 'She clouted me and I felt bad.' She ceased to masturbate and felt guilty about the activity she had enjoyed previously. She had several boy friends at school, and when she left she became a shorthand typist and enjoyed going to parties and dances. She met her accountant husband at work when she was twenty-four and he was twenty-six. She was attracted to him but thought he was rather fussy about accounts being neat and tidy. Mr R. had led a sheltered life and Mrs R. was his first 'date'. He knew exactly what to do, because he had read books about sex, and gave her some very arousing clitoral stimulation, but thought they should wait until marriage before they had sex. He insisted on a long engagement, although she was quite ready for marriage. They had a big white wedding and went to Bournemouth for a disastrous honeymoon. She talked about 'closing up' when he put his finger near her vagina, and being very anxious.

A year later, at the age of twenty-seven, she was 'stretched' at the local hospital as her hymen was rather thick, but this still made no difference to ease of penetration. When physically examined at the clinic when she arrived for assessment, it was impossible for the examining doctor to insert her little finger, even with reassurance that it would not be painful. She said she hated the whole procedure, had perfectly satisfactory sex by means of clitoral stimulation and that, in any case, her husband did not get erections.

He admitted that this was true, that since the honeymoon he had found it difficult to get an erection; when he tried to penetrate her he lost his erection. Mr R.'s impotence probably resulted from his wife's vaginismus.

Masters and Johnson cite two cases in which women preferred lesbian partners, and this appeared to influence the development of vaginismus.

Vaginismus, though dramatic, is fortunately not difficult to treat, many women being returned to full penetration within quite a short time.

4 Orgasmic dysfunction

Many women request sex therapy because they find it difficult, or impossible, to obtain orgasm during sexual intercourse without some manual stimulation. Implicit in this request is usually the feeling that a woman should be able to obtain an orgasm by intercourse alone. In order to decide whether this difficulty is to be regarded as abnormal we need to know what percentage of women have suffered and, of these, the proportion who have had a liberated upbringing, and also what is considered ideal. As the incidence of the difficulty is unknown we can only attempt the last question. Most women would probably like to achieve orgasm by intercourse alone, at least part of the time. According to a *Forum* magazine questionnaire only one fifth of women in the survey found they could obtain an orgasm without manual clitoral stimulation, while three fifths needed vaginal plus manual stimulation.

For the therapist it is not really a difficult decision. If the woman or man wants to attempt to change the behavioural pattern, why not? All varieties of adjustment are found. The saddest situation is the one in which the man has intercourse to orgasm, then disengages, ignoring the state of his partner. At worst these men will not allow any manual self-manipulation or provide any themselves. But in a knowledgeable and cooperative partnership, a position can often be found that will allow manual stimulation to take place by either partner.

One could say of the woman who is only able to obtain an orgasm by manual stimulation during intercourse that she has a mild degree of orgasmic dysfunction. A greater degree of orgasmic dysfunction is represented by the woman who has frequent or severe difficulty in coming to climax by any method during sexual inter-course, and perhaps also during self-stimulation, if this has been attempted. This difficulty used to be called 'frigidity' but the word was also used for almost any female disorder. Masters and Johnson stigmatised it, both because of its vagueness and its emotional over-tones.

Orgasmic dysfunction does not imply low sex drive or low sexual response. The woman often responds sexually with normal responses as far as the plateau phase. Her difficulty may be solely the inability to succeed with orgasm, despite every effort, during which she is both excited and lubricated. After much effort she may become sore, embarrassed or fed-up, and desist. This leaves her to face a lengthy 'resolution phase' in a state of unrelieved sexual tension.

This failure to achieve orgasm can be primary, that is, it has always been difficult or impossible to climax, either in intercourse or in masturbation; it can be secondary, in which case the difficulty only supervenes after a preliminary period of normal orgasm. Occasionally a woman will find herself unable to climax with one man, but able to quite normally with another. Other women only suffer from this dysfunction during parts of their cycle, or for no apparent reason.

Most therapists believe the commonest cause to be psychological, although occasionally the dysfunction may be related to serious illness or the action of drugs – particularly those used for depres-sion and anxiety. Some women ascribe their difficulty to the contraceptive pill which may well alter sexual responses. There is also a current belief that slack pubococcygeal muscles may make orgasm more difficult. A better formulation here would be to say that PC muscle-training may institute orgastic potency.

Psychological causes are probably numerous, ranging from in-adequate stimulation to a poor relationship. Masters and Johnson investigated the causes of both primary and secondary cases. Com-mon to many of the primary cases was a religious upbringing in which sex was equated with sin and punishment. They felt some of their women patients were emotionally immature and that others had partners whose potency was insecure.

Mrs K. is a good example of a woman suffering from primary orgasmic dysfunction, who had been brought up with a strict religious Roman Catholic background in England. Her parents had avoided telling her about the facts of life. She had been unpleasantly surprised by her periods, but had managed to bring herself to discuss this with some of the convent girls at school. She had never discussed masturbation and did not know what it was when she was initially interviewed. She had led a hard life. At the age of sixteen, while still at school, she had been seduced by her uncle – it had been a painful and frightening experience, though afterwards he had given her affection. The result of the experience was a pregnancy; she had never dared to reveal her uncle as father of the child and her parents were disgusted and punitive when they discovered that she was pregnant. They made her leave school to go to a home for unmarried mothers, where she had the baby. All the girls in the home lived in dread of the time that they would have to 'hand over their babies' for adoption, never to see them again. Mrs K. felt broken-hearted when this happened and decided not to go home, but to get a training as a children's nurse.

She arrived at the clinic having weathered the years well for she looked younger than her thirty-eight years; she had a fresh complexion and a fashionable upswept curly hairstyle. She filled in the years between sixteen and thirty-eight and described her marriage to a rather dull paediatrician whom she had met during the course of her training. She said that she had not been able to tell him about her illegitimate baby until just before the birth of their first child. He had been calm and reassuring, but she had felt ashamed and upset. He was a solid dependable chap who never switched her on sufficiently. She felt initially excited but could not 'take herself over the edge' and achieve an orgasm. She found him too quiet and well-mannered, and found herself behaving in a restrained manner, never daring to let herself go fully. She remarked that she had become obsessed with having a climax, desperately wanted it, and felt disappointed that she could not attain it.

The causes of secondary orgasmic dysfunction are less clear cut, according to Masters and Johnson. Some cases were attributed to low sex drive and others to lesbian preference. Other theorists believe that the inability to completely 'let go', to abandon oneself, is the basis of the problem. Theoretically this inability might be caused by anxiety or guilt; on the other hand the woman may be holding back from this abandonment out of an incomplete love or trust in her partner. For her, the moment of orgasm represents a loss of control, a state of potential vulnerability where she reveals herself as she really is. Other therapists associated secondary anorgasmia with a disturbed marital relationship.

Where the woman's chief concern is to satisfy and please her partner she will be watching his performance with anxiety and not concerning herself with her own pleasure. If her own orgasm approaches she may believe she might disturb or interrupt her partner by allowing it to happen. She may, by experience or intuition, know that if she has an orgasm her partner will feel that the chief goal in the event – the male orgasm – has been upstaged. A woman who wishes to connive in the maintenance of such an inequality may learn to delay orgasm. Unfortunately, to persist with such a practice leads to loss of sexual interest – the inhibition has gone too far – orgasms become elusive. While such formulations may help to explain anorgasmia, it is also useful to remember that more obvious causes such as ignorance and poor technique are often present.

Miss T., a nineteen-year-old, baby blonde, plump secretary, was very ignorant of the facts of life and her own anatomy. She was not originally referred for a sexual problem but for a 'plane phobia. She and her boy friend wanted to go on a trip to Majorca, but she was afraid to go on a 'plane. She also complained about her sex life during the routine interview, reporting that she did not get good sex with her boy friend, and asked if she could have help with this problem too. She described a form of masturbation in the bath, induced by pouring water on herself with a sponge. She had never told anyone about this and thought it was a nice thing to do, having discovered the pleasure when she was sixteen. She had discussed periods with her girl friends, and her mother had told her about menstruation but had omitted any mention of the facts of life. She did not know of the clitoris.

She had led quite a sheltered life until the age of eighteen, when she came to London to work and made up for lost time. In London she met boys, one of whom was older than most of the others, and he sexually initiated her. She enjoyed the experience and reached her climax. However, he sounded rather a cad for he abandoned her shortly afterwards. Within a year she knew what she wanted and had found a nice reliable and steady boy friend. The only snag was that he did not sound a very experienced lover. His foreplay was too short and from what Miss T. said, he did not even touch her in the right places, but she did not know what to do about this. She liked the feeling he gave her, but felt disappointed that she did not climax. She did not want to change her boy friend as they had by then decided to live together, and she felt genuinely fond of him.

Many people with phobias also have sex problems. Miss T. and her boy friend were quite ignorant in sexual matters and sex therapy seemed an obvious choice of treatment, which in fact was very successful.

5 Impotence

The word impotence is derived from the Latin *impotentia* which means a lack of power. Impotence is the persistent inability to obtain and/or maintain an erection sufficient to penetrate the vagina and conclude sexual intercourse to the satisfaction of the male. Masters and Johnson considered that a failure of erection in twenty-five per cent of attempts at sexual intercourse was a 'persistent' inability. Usually the man who is impotent is unable to get erect before sexual intercourse, but some impotent men lose the erection during or shortly after penetration. Impotence can be diagnosed despite ejaculations since the mechanism for each is independent.

There are of course degrees of impotence. Some men only obtain a full erection immediately before the ejaculation. Some men may be able to maintain an erection quite satisfactorily during masturbation but not during intercourse. Such a person would by definition be considered impotent.

A diagnosis of primary impotence is made when a man has never been able to achieve normal intercourse because of his erectile failure even though during masturbation he can get an erection. Primary impotence is rare and Masters and Johnson found only thirty-two such men over an eleven-year period. Much more common is the man who has been potent for some time then for some reason becomes impotent. Such a state is called 'secondary impotence'.

It is difficult to assess how common impotence is in the general population. It is twenty years since Kinsey found that it affected one male per thousand at the age of twenty, rising to twenty-six per thousand at forty-five. In a recent *Forum* magazine an advertisement for impotent volunteers to test a new serum for impotency brought in 3,457 replies when only one hundred subjects were needed.

Possibly the incidence of impotence has increased since the 1950s. There are both physical and psychological causes of impotence. Occasionally the two operate together. The psychological causes are a complex of personal and socio-cultural effects. Most authorities suggest that physical causes account for five to ten per cent of all cases of impotence. Perhaps nowadays this figure should be slightly increased to take account of the increased incidence of drug-induced impotence.

The possibility of organic disease should always be considered before the condition is diagnosed as psychological. An important question will help to make the distinction. Can the patient obtain a good erection during masturbation, during dreams, when awakening, or with another partner? If the answer is 'Yes he can', then physical and organic causes can be excluded. Where doubt remains a physical examination will have to be performed in order to exclude local causes such as phimosis or deformities of the penis. A careful neurological examination will be able to exclude general brain damage and diseases of the spinal cord. There is a strong presumption of a physical cause where there is a co-existing disorder of the act of micturition. Diabetic effects should always be looked for. Glandular disorders, including diseases of the thyroid, will usually be sufficiently obvious at an early stage as to cause little confusion.

Various drugs may cause impotence. A definite relationship between a given drug and impotence is often noticed by the patient. This is especially true of drugs used to control high blood pressure (anti-hypertensive drugs) which affect the mechanism of erection directly. Alcohol, sedatives and opiates taken in quantities sufficient to produce drowsiness, low sexual drive or debilitation can cause various degrees of impotence though the relationship is often not clear. Difficulties also arise when such drugs have been prescribed for psychiatric conditions which themselves may affect potency. In such cases a detailed enquiry will usually allow a decision to be reached. Anti-depressants, mainly of the Tricyclic series such as Imipramine, have been blamed for impotence in addition to their well-established effect of inhibition of ejaculation. Again, since such drugs are usually prescribed for depression, it is not always easy to decide whether it is the depression or the drug which is producing the effect. The same remarks apply equally to the Pheno-thiazines which have similar pharmacological effects.

One of the commonest psychological causes of impotence is

negative conditioning. Sexual behaviour or the sexual act has become associated with some unpleasant anxiety-producing event or events and this association has been learned and incorporated into the mind of the person concerned. Thus, when the need for erection arises, instead of feeling the pleasure of sexual arousal the person feels worried or anxious. Unpleasant emotions inhibit the erection. Anxieties of this kind may be related to multiple unpleasant events which have taken place or are anticipated: a sexually repressive childhood, hostility towards the partner, a fear of pregnancy, of disease, of discovery or rejection, anxiety that sexual performance may be insufficient to satisfy either internal ideals or the imagined demands of the partner, fear that impotence will recur, stress, overwork, a fear of past physical illness recurring (such as heart attack), and also a fear of premature ejaculation. The association of such fears with erectile failure is an example of negative conditioning.

The case of impotence arising from premature ejaculation is a special case, since here the primary abnormality is the premature ejaculation. The impotence which develops in association with this condition usually comes on after a long experience with the ejaculatory difficulty. Repeated frustration over an inability to delay the ejaculation eventually leads to a sense of helplessness and often to marital discord. This is the setting in which erectile failure may appear. In a proportion of cases the erectile failure does not prevent premature ejaculation occurring despite a flaccid penis. In the remainder, the erectile impotence may stifle all response.

The negative conditioning produced by a repressive upbringing is probably one of the commonest, most pervasive causes. Typically the boy has had a dominant mother or father who strongly disapproved of sexual behaviour. Early masturbatory experiences are guilty and spoiled by a fear of parental discovery. Over-religious attitudes are often found in such families and the concept of sin is freely attached to proscribed behaviour. The idea that sex is sinful and dirty is the result.

Mr F., a rather ruddy-complexioned, paunchy prep. school teacher of fifty-two was referred for his secondary impotence. He had always been guilty about masturbation and remembered his father telling him that if he ever caught him at it he would be flogged. Mr F. was a normally sexed young lad and could not resist masturbating, which he did in fear and trepidation that his father would find out. His public school environment was hardly more sympathetic and relaxing and he recalls worrying that one of his masters would discover him. He associated masturbation and sex with the dirty and forbidden. The other boys were constantly discussing sex and he felt reassured by their activities but was rather shocked when one of the boys described how he had had sex with his older female cousin during the Easter holidays. Mr F. wondered what it would be like to lie with a girl, but had no opportunity during his schooldays or when he left because he joined the army and there was a shortage of girls in both these male dominated communities. Eventually his luck changed when he met his future wife at one of the military tattoos. She was a pretty, slimly-built debutante, dressed in frilly silk with a straw hat. He loved her 'Dresden-like beauty' as soon as he saw her. He invited her to the pictures the next day and she became his first and only girl friend. Physically things when well and he had good erections but they both wanted to wait until they married before they had intercourse. When they married things went smoothly, he had good erections and penetration was good. Two wanted children were born and they were both delighted.

One day Mr F. was slightly tipsy and he lost his erection when he tried to penetrate. He immediately felt that he was being punished for his past masturbation and became very anxious indeed. They avoided sex for a week and he worried more and more about the next opportunity, but when he tried again the same thing happened. This pattern continued until he found that he could not even raise an erection. He accepted this unfortunate occurrence as a due punishment for his past sins and said 'I knew things would catch up with me eventually'.

Sexual guilt may be produced in other ways, as for instance in the man who has an extra-marital affair or who visits a prostitute, perhaps for the first time. Impotence may be caused by marital difficulties and the therapist must have the answer to certain questions. How much marital disharmony is there? Is the interaction between the couple in some way destructive or over-competitive? Did the disharmony antedate the impotence or has the impotence always existed? Careful analysis is always necessary since resentment and hostility may exist on both sides. Where it is the male who feels resentful, hostile or unloving, impotence may result. The man may unconsciously 'punish' his wife by witholding sexual favours, whereas the woman may express her aggression in criticisms of his performance. The couple who are bored with one another but stay together from habit or convenience may fail to excite each other sufficiently for adequate sexual arousal to take place. Many such couples have long since failed to introduce any novelty into their relationship and may be helped with new approaches and new ideas – the interaction with a sex therapist is in itself exciting and interesting – as would be the interaction with any third party.

A rather neglected form of impotence but one which seems to be occurring more frequently, at least in Britain, is that of low sex drive. The man with a low sex drive is today especially vulnerable to a high drive partner who makes excessive demands of him. Men used to have a monopoly of overt sexual persuasion but liberation is changing that. The modern woman can ask for what she wants – the initiative is hers to grasp.

It is probable, though not certain, that impotence is more frequent in men of neurotic personality (anxious, tense, insecure; liable to phobias, insomnia and mild depression; lacking in confidence, obsessional, hypochondriacal and so on). This type of personality is partly inherited.

Some males are impotent with women because they are homosexually orientated. Presumably in this case the presence of women is insufficiently exciting for sexual excitement to become sufficient.

Mr J., a twenty-three-year-old Spanish waiter, presented with primary impotence. He had never been potent with a woman although he had excellent erections with other men. He was exquisitely dressed and groomed. He had been born a bastard and his mother had pretended that his father had died. She became penniless and between the ages of seven and thirteen he was sent to an orphanage. The priests were sadistic but the boys were affectionate and warm. He enjoyed mutual masturbation with the other boys but felt guilty after these pleasurable experiences. At the age of thirteen he was adopted by older parents (his foster father was sixty-three and foster mother fifty-nine). They showed affection but never discussed the facts of life; these he had learned from the other boys at the orphanage. He continued to enjoy other boys.

His first contact with a girl was with a Parisian prostitute; he found this a most sordid experience. He failed to get an erection and felt dirty as she would not even let him kiss her. He later met an English girl in Majorca where he got a job as a waiter. She gave him a sheath to wear when he had a good erection but he had never seen one before and promptly lost his erection.

He had arrived in London and had been lonely so had started an affair with another man in the same lodgings. This had been a failure because his friend had been jealous and possessive to an almost paranoid degree. He then met a waitress at the restaurant in which he worked. She was Spanish and they both had a lot in common; they were sensitive and both appreciated the writings of Garcia Lorca. They had kissed and he had felt very excited initially but had become more anxious when he failed to 'keep a hard on'.

Mr J. had been sufficiently excited to get an initial erection, but probably his positive conditioning was more related to boys than to girls.

Impotence can also be associated with disgust, usually conditioned by a faulty sex education, ignorance, and an inadequate explanation of the facts of life. Some boys find a wet dream a traumatic experience if they are ignorant of such matters, and then associate sperm with something dirty and disgusting, especially if they have been made to scrub the sheets afterwards. Some men have associations of disgust with vaginal odours and the female genitalia.

The occurrence of transient impotence is the experience of the majority of men. The experience may be quite unnerving for some men who have high sexual expectations, or for others who are prone to worry. The first experience of impotence may cause so much anxiety that impotence may follow on a subsequent occasion. Fortunately such cases only require a patient and sympathetic woman for the situation to be reversed. Reassurance alone may be sufficient.

The crucial personality difference between the men who become impotent and those who do not may determine the speed and thoroughness with which negative conditioning becomes established. One unpleasant experience may be sufficient to make some men very anxious and subsequently impotent, whereas other men would not even remember it. People of neurotic or unstable character tend to condition more readily than stable types.

Psychoanalysts have offered their own explanations. Here it is unconscious castration anxiety which produces the effect. The Oedipus complex demands that the boy has incestuous and possessive wishes towards his mother – he is competing with his father for her favours and he wishes to kill him; the punishment may be castration and thus by generalisation the sex act is perceived as dangerous. From a historical point of view the importance of many psychoanalytical ideas cannot be overstated and even now they permeate much modern thinking. However, ideas and concepts have to be viewed as aids to thinking, explaining and predicting, and in this role psychoanalytical ideas are not as effective as more modern concepts. Many are too vaguely stated to be scientifically examined and are now best discarded or more accurately reformulated. There is no danger that their most important insights will be lost.

6 Premature ejaculation

Premature ejaculation can be described as that condition wherein orgasm and ejaculation persistently occur before or immediately after penetration of the female during coitus; this is a definition that is widely used. Masters and Johnson consider a man to be a premature ejaculator if he cannot control his ejaculatory process for a sufficient length of time during intra-vaginal containment to satisfy his partner in at least fifty per cent of their coital connections. They do add that if the female partner is persistently non-orgasmic for reasons other than the rapidity of the male's ejaculation, there is no validity to the definition, but at least it moves away from the stop-watch concept which has been proposed. For example, the definition has been suggested that a man suffers from premature ejaculation if he 'comes' within thirty to sixty seconds or less after entry. The trouble with any definition is that in practice it tends to rigidify thinking about a phenomenon which has a wide range of expression. In practice therapists might prefer to talk of degrees of PE; for example, 'He has a mild degree of premature ejaculation.' The central idea is clear: the man comes too soon, that is, either before entry or shortly after; he is not deficient in arousal or erection, indeed it may be he is over-aroused.

Kinsey questioned the abnormality of such a condition. He stated that in the U.S. it is usual for males of lower educational levels to try to achieve an orgasm as soon as possible once they have entered their female partner. Upper class males more often attempt to delay orgasm. Kinsey went on to say that for perhaps three-quarters of all males, orgasm is reached within two minutes after the penis has been inserted, and that many males reach a climax within less than a minute or even within ten or twenty seconds after coital entrance. He continued to examine other mammals in which the male ejaculates almost instantly upon intromission, and remarked that this is true of man's closest relatives among the primates. Chimpanzees only take ten to twenty seconds to effect ejaculation.

One cannot of course argue that what is true of one species is necessarily true of another; however, new ideas and attitudes may follow from such knowledge. In this case it is valuable to bear in mind that not all human behaviour labelled as dysfunction is a biological dysfunction; it may be alternatively a failure to live up to some ideal.

Whatever the cause, premature ejaculation is associated with much misery and breakdown of marriage, because the partners in such a situation seem unable to manage it themselves. The condition may be commoner in the States, but the number of cases referred in Britain is increasing. Fortunately it is not difficult to cure.

Physical causes are probably very rare but should be considered in a man who became a PE after years of normality. The American author Helen Kaplan cites cases caused by inflammation of the male urethra or of the prostate. Again, where there is a loss of urinary or defaecatory control of neurological origin, the same may bring about ejaculatory incontinence. This may be found in disseminated sclerosis and other diseases causing degeneration in the central nervous system.

Those who have studied the background of many cases of premature ejaculation believe that most cases are referred at the female partner's instigation – it is usually her dissatisfaction which brings the matter to a therapist.

It is usually found that the condition has been present during the whole sexual life of the sufferer. Even during adolescent masturbation the ejaculatory response is reported to have been very rapid. Some of these men appear to have an excessive sexual drive and to have married sexually inhibited women; but perhaps that is mere chance.

Who needs sex therapy?

There is a further group of men who tend to have anxious, insecure and neurotic personalities. These men usually had a poor relationship with their parents during early childhood, but whether one should blame the parents or the child is a moot point – probably both.

In a series of cases collected by John Johnson there were three out of eighteen in whom the premature ejaculation came on after a lengthy period of normality. In two cases the man married again; one to a 'frigid' and one to a 'passionate' woman. The third man's wife began to lose sexual interest after a child was born. Two of these men had a very high sexual drive.

Masters and Johnson believe that it is mainly among the educated that the condition leads to a sex therapist, perhaps because poorly educated males feel less responsibility for the sexuality of their partners. Middle class and educated women are also more likely to encourage or demand that their husbands seek help. Some psychiatrists in America consider that the sexual freedom enjoyed by women could now be a cause of increasing male problems. Obviously there is considerable frustration for the woman when she becomes aroused during foreplay, excited by penetration and then let down as her man comes prematurely and loses his interest and his erection. For the man who has a tendency to prematurity of ejaculation, an increasingly demanding wife may further shorten the response. This effect may be produced either by her excitement or by the anxiety she may induce in her spouse. Unfortunately, when sexual difficulties occur the interval between sexual encounters may lengthen. This naturally produces a state of greater excitement which in turn may hasten the ejaculation.

There is also a suggestion from some laboratory work in London that the refractory period of men with premature ejaculation may be quite short. That is, they will be able to obtain a satisfactory erection and orgasm soon after the first failure. As this second orgasm does not usually arrive with the speed of the first, this immediately suggests a method of cure; this is discussed in the chapter on treatment.

It is thought by many therapists that the experiences of first intercourse may influence the development of the subsequent 'time to ejaculation'. Among American males over forty, Masters and Johnson estimated that initial experience with a prostitute was common. They felt that the impatient demands of prostitutes with one eye on their purse might have conditioned a rapid response. Subsequent generations may also have been hustled into premature ejaculation by initial sexual experiences taking place at speed in the back of the parental car, in the lounge when the parents retire, in various public places such as cinemas and on public transport, and, in rural districts, in gardens and fields. Here discovery is imminent and prematurity an advantage.

It is also believed by Clifford Allen that the practice of coitus interruptus can establish a pattern of premature ejaculation. Coitus interruptus is the 'withdrawal' technique : when orgasm is imminent the male withdraws as quickly as possible. Such a method requires considerable control – it requires a close monitoring of the state of excitement – it is associated with anxiety over pregnancy and, for some at least, it may encourage haste. When a pattern of rapid performance is established it may be difficult to break. Since the method is a contraceptive technique perhaps it will be less used, except for those for whom contraception is forbidden. Masters and Johnson believe the method to be harmful on account of the unrelaxed state of mind it engenders. For the female, the rapid mounting followed by a few frantic thrusts before abrupt withdrawal and male orgasm, can be a very unsatisfactory business. However, if coitus interruptus is unavoidable, the whole process can be slowed down and the female brought to orgasm either by good foreplay or, alternatively, by post-coital pleasuring.

Alan Cooper found many of his patients with premature ejaculation reported bodily manifestations of anxiety during the sexual act. These bodily manifestations of anxiety include dry mouth or eyes, palpitations, rapid or irregular breathing, tremulousness, tense muscles, and various other less common and idiosyncratic effects. There may also be psychic anxiety mixed up with the sexual excitement. People of neurotic character are more liable to show anxiety in more situations than are normal people. When Alan Cooper compared men with premature ejaculation against men with impotence, he found the former to be more neurotic.

One fairly common sign of anxiety is a desire to pass water. Nervous people often want to pass water more frequently than those who are calm. At an extreme degree of anxiety, when, for instance, the anxiety is of sudden onset or simply amounts to fear, there may be an involuntary passage of urine. Clifford Allen has compared the loss of control over urine, urinary incontinence due

121

to fear, to the loss of control of semen. The hypothesis may be stated: urinary continence is learned but may be broken by fear – ejaculatory control may be learned but may be breached where strong fear is present. The source of this fear is thought to lie in adolescence or childhood, as, for instance, with the boy who had been brought up to believe masturbation was harmful, perhaps believing that his youthful masturbation had produced an incurable and hopeless disease. He views the next intercourse with a mixture of hope and dread. This fear itself is enough to produce a further attack and so a vicious circle is set up.

Mr Y. was referred because of premature ejaculation which had resulted in occasional impotence. He was a neatly dressed, slim, grey-haired man of forty-five. His father had been a leading barrister and a disciplinarian. He had wanted his son to follow in his footsteps and had been delighted when Mr Y. was accepted by an Oxford college to read law, but infuriated when he learned that Mr Y. rejected the idea of being a barrister and chose to be a solicitor. Mr Y. chose this because he was such a timid, non-assertive man. In his own words 'the idea of spending the rest of my days debating frightened me so I went against my father's wishes for the first time'.

Mr Y.'s parents never told him about sex, which he had discussed in any case with boys at his public school, but they did give him a book to read on the subject. He described himself as very highly sexed as he masturbated daily and managed to pet furtively with his sister's friend during school holidays, despite feeling anxious about being caught. Sometimes when he was petting he was able to ejaculate by rubbing himself on the girl's leg. He mentioned how excited he had been when he had his initial experience with a girl after they had been swimming in the nude and she had directly stimulated his penis with her hand, but he had come before he had been able to enter her. Later he had his first sexual intercourse with the same girl when they were both nineteen, at a Commemoration Ball. This had been successful but rather hasty, although she had been satisfied quickly (it was her first experience; her hymen had been torn while fox-hunting).

He had been very much in love with this girl and was hurt when she married a friend of his. He met her cousin at the wedding and was immediately attracted to her. Both girls had the same ginger hair, blue eyes and small firm breasts and it was hardly surprising when he married her a year later.

Mrs Y. was very different from her pleasure-loving cousin. She refused to have sex before marriage and was only willing to indulge in light petting, insisting on waiting until the honeymoon (spent in Barbados). It was hardly surprising that he ejaculated almost immediately he entered her. She 'got nothing out of it' and remained a virgin for a week before he managed to penetrate fully. She admitted that she was not very well lubricated in those days and rather badly informed about sex. Later things improved somewhat but Mr Y. failed to maintain an erection long enough to excite his wife much. By the time their first child was born (fifteen months after the marriage) she had never been near an orgasm. She decided to remain faithful to him and bore two more children and then had a hysterectomy because she wanted no more children. Mr Y. was having sex three nights a week with his wife and getting very turned on by her in spite of her lack of response and frustration. Eventually she decided to have an affair and met a man she described as 'her social inferior' but with a good technique which gave her the climax she had missed during her marriage. She cruelly informed her husband she had made an arrangement for a 'stud' to come on a fortnightly basis, and also taunted him for his lack of virility compared with the lover, which caused him to become even more anxious and resulted in partial impotence for he lost his erection while entering once he heard of his wife's arrangement.

The hypothesis that it is anxiety which produces premature ejaculation requires more research. It may not be easy to make a laboratory distinction between anxiety and sexual arousal because, although the experiences are different, many of the somatic effects are similar.

Kinsey found that men suffering from premature ejaculation had a lower sex drive than similar members of the normal population. This was judged by orgasm frequency. This result is quite contrary to the hypersexuality of some of John Johnson's cases and illustrates the complexity of the issue. Much may depend on the stage of the disorder. After many years of premature ejaculation the hopelessness of the disorder may itself begin to inhibit sexual performance. Masters and Johnson indeed found that persistent premature ejaculation led to secondary erectile impotence. They found that some couples tried to avoid the difficulty by setting up a 'no touch' system designed to cope with the 'hair trigger' response. Probably the mere fact of behaving in this way draws attention to the disorder – it may increase the anxiety and thus promote the condition or the development of erectile failure.

Psychoanalysts of the Freudian school believe men with this condition have intense but unconscious sadistic feelings towards women. The early ejaculation is a punishment. What is certain is that analytic treatment does not offer, even with years of treatment, the cure which behavioural methods can produce quite quickly.

7 Delayed ejaculation

This is the persistent inability to ejaculate in the vagina during sexual intercourse, but the same problem can occur when masturbating with or without a partner being present. It is the opposite of premature ejaculation and is a much less common disorder. Masters and Johnson had only seventeen cases of what they call 'ejaculatory incompetence'.

Cases can be primary, when the man has never been able to ejaculate, or secondary, when he has lost the ability. Sex therapy is moderately successful in this condition. The female equivalent of this is anorgasmia or the failure to obtain an orgasm.

Few cases of delayed ejaculation have a physical cause but sometimes hypertensive drugs and Phenothiazines prescribed for psychotic illnesses can affect the ejaculation and produce retardation. Other physical causes are diabetes, prostatic diseases and scarring of the posterior urethra by gonorrhea, but these are rare.

Clinical experience with cases of delayed ejaculation suggests that some cases are due to low sex drive, and some to sexual boredom or lack of imagination. But the condition also occurs in men who appear adequately sexed. One can only hypothesise that such men are either insufficiently excited or, on the other hand, are unable to relax sufficiently to permit the orgasm. The inability to surrender oneself to the sexual excitement – to abandon that part of the mind which is calculating, watching and worrying – may help one to understand the difficulty. It is tempting to treat such cases by inducing abandonment in other spheres – by singing, shouting, dancing or writhing.

As with many other sexual difficulties a sexually repressive upbringing with much guilt and many prohibitions often appears in the history. Single traumatic experiences may possibly also cause some cases; for example, being caught or interrupted during the sexual act by disapproving authority figures. Masters and Johnson quote a case in which the condition was established in a man who caught his wife in adulterous intercourse. The same authors cite four cases out of a total of twelve in which an episode of a burst condom figured in the antecedents. Such an episode would be more likely, one supposes, in a man who had some degree of ejaculatory delay – the condom being subjected to more trauma. There is a suspicion in some cases that a fear of pregnancy may produce delayed ejaculation: there was a case where the man claimed to his wife that he wanted pregnancy, but admitted some doubts to the therapist.

Mr R., a thirty-year-old bus driver, was referred to the clinic because of delayed ejaculation and the fact that he and his wife had been married for eight years but had remained childless. He was of medium height, muscular, casually dressed and relaxed. She looked rather frail and unhealthy but had a good work record at the local toy factory.

Mrs R. had attended the gynaecology clinic in order to have her 'infertility' problem investigated, and it was soon discovered that delayed ejaculation was the reason for this. Mrs R. seemed desperate to have children but her husband seemed more interested in motor cycle racing. He even incorporated motor cycles into his fantasy life and commented that he was switched on by Marianne Faithful revving up in 'Girl on a Motorcycle'. He said that even these fantasies wore off after 'fucking for two hours'. He just kept going by moving in and out and still had a good erection, although Mrs R. said it made her sore. He had not lacked imagination over sexual positions. They had tried and enjoyed oral sex but had never had mutual masturbation. They had not made love completely before marriage. He remarked that maybe he would be really turned on if Mrs R. wore tight-fitting black leather gear and rode a motor cycle herself. He had once asked her to do so but she had refused even to drive the family banger because she felt unsafe. She was even more scared of a motor cycle and had not enjoyed being a pillion passenger.

Marital problems appear to cause 'a condition' in some couples. The commonest problem is the husband who feels the wife is dominant and controlling; he resents her for this and his response is a lack of sexual enthusiasm or a failure to trust his sexual partner. Such feelings act as a barrier to the final sexual response which becomes delayed. Some commentators are prepared to call this an act of rebellion.

Some retardation of ejaculation is normally present after a great deal of sexual activity over a short period, or during intercourse which takes place during the refractory period (the normal period after one ejaculation – lasting for a variable interval – during which a further ejaculation is impossible, though an erection can be obtained). The condition may occur more frequently in old age, when ejaculation may not be attained or even desired on every occasion.

The act of coitus reservatus is an act in which the semen is retained. It is an unusual practice which can probably only be acquired with much practice and determination. The revelance of delayed ejaculation is more apparent than real.

8 Marital causes of sexual dysfunction

Marital problems are often the cause of sexual dysfunctions. However, some couples may have a poor marital relationship and yet have a good sex life in spite of their quarrelling and nagging. Marital difficulties can both cause and reflect sexual disharmony.

Probably one of the commonest causes of poor sex for a couple is the failure to communicate what they want. This can result in a lack of harmony which is fatal for successful sex. Many couples who fail to communicate their wishes never even get to the 'excitement' or 'plateau' phases of sexual response. They do not tell each other how or where they want to be stroked or, if there is anger, they punish one another by failing to provide the right foreplay. Some couples, having failed to communicate what turns them on and off, still expect immediate sexual responses. One partner may know that the other enjoys certain sexual behaviour, such as oral sex, but chooses to ignore such wishes, causing much frustration.

The communication between Mr and Mrs P. was exceptionally poor and there were frequent quarrels. Mr P. was particularly insensitive and chauvinistic and refused to help in the house, although they both worked as dentists. Mrs P. was no angel and frequently lost her temper and smashed crockery during quarrels. Originally they were referred for help by the Marriage Guidance Council as they were making no progress in their marital therapy. Mrs P. had been examined by her gynaecologist because of pain during intercourse, which was assessed as psychological rather than physical.

Mrs P. was a rather hippy-looking twenty-seven-year-old woman with large owl-like spectacles. Mr P. was twenty-eight and rather a striking, tall man with vivid blue eyes. They had met at one of the London dental hospitals and had both fallen in love at first sight, but Mrs P.'s parents had insisted that she should finish her dental training before marriage. They had both enjoyed good sexual relations with other people before they met, and when engaged continued to feel excited by one another but did not have much opportunity for prolonged love-making. When they finally married the sexual side rapidly deteriorated. Mr P. acted as though he had a right to his wife's sexual cooperation, never seemed to notice when Mrs P. wanted to make love, and tended to start kissing her when she did not want to be touched. Her protests often led to bitter rows and he felt unwanted. Even when they proceeded to sexual intercourse there was only one speed for him – the satisfaction of his desires the only aim. She said, 'I might be a rubber doll for all he seems to care.' Yet, he definitely seemed to be fond of her and wanted to make the relationship succeed.

Difficulties can also arise when partners fail to coordinate their timing. Perhaps one partner feels sexy and suggests making love, but the other partner takes an hour to get ready and then not surprisingly finds the initiator irritated or turned off. Advances which are made at clearly unsuitable times will also cause trouble. It is unwise to make sexual advances when the partner is tired, anxious, or intoxicated beyond performance.

Probably the most successful way of preventing sexual arousal and desire is to make a partner angry or hostile. This interferes with sex drive and switches a person off, with the result that there is no relaxation and no pleasure. Some couples pick quarrels, insult and criticise each other just before making love. Another way of killing desire is deliberately to pressurise a partner to perform sexually, perhaps mentioning that last time he was not 'hard enough' or she was not well enough lubricated.

Some couples do not confine themselves to quarrelling just before love-making, but nag and criticise each other most of the time, and quarrelling of this kind can develop into a pastime. Though the process may appear painful it is quite possible that one or both the partners are obtaining a certain excitement otherwise lacking in their relationship. The emotional arousal and anger, often followed by the release of tears and forgiveness, may be a substitute for sexual interaction which has neither stimulation nor release. There is often a two-way emotional system operating, combining a fear of being rejected or abandoned by the partner with actual anger and hostility towards that partner, often resulting in hatred.

Arguments and quarrelling can represent a continuous power struggle in a relationship. Both partners wish to dominate and control each other. The man might respond to this power struggle by failing to get erect or to ejaculate – fully realising that this thwarts his wife. The woman might refuse to have sex or orgasms for similar reasons. It is an important finding by Lobitz and LoPiccolo that women who have secondary anorgasmia tend to fail to respond to sex therapy if they have a poor relationship in which there is conflict with the partner.

Another source of marital discord and conflict is that of role playing. Some partners fail to take the male or female role that the other demands. Often, if a man refuses to assert himself in everyday activities his partner will not give him the opportunity to assert himself in bed; she will refuse to cooperate during foreplay. The difficulty only arises, of course, where one partner wants the other to adopt a certain role and that partner finds such a role uncongenial.

Again, there is the partner who is really looking for a re-enactment of a child/parent relationship, the partner who wishes to be dependant – a demand which may not satisfy the other, and gives rise to conflict. Some men like their women to be more passive and coy than they want to be. This is even more likely to cause conflict today when women have become more liberated and demand equal sexual rights.

Another way of expressing hostility towards the partner is deliberately to set out to be unattractive: unshaven; unwashed; smelling of garlic or alcohol when the partner dislikes this; being too fat or too thin; smoking; taking a wig off to make love, and so on.

The areas of conflict between some couples are multiple; for example, in the upbringing of children, the management of the household budget, the quality or timing of the food, the housework, the shopping, and the washing-up. There may be problems with the parents, in-laws, or other relatives, especially if they live in the house. The housing circumstances themselves may be inadequate. In other families both the adults may go out to work, making both tired and irritable. Couples who have numerous burdens find sex is often sacrificed in one way or another.

Couples who spend their time quarrelling over such day-to-day problems may in reality be using such issues as an excuse to join combat. The real cause of irritability may be in the relationship, in the poor sexual encounter, or in some factor outside the relationship altogether. Therapists must be prepared to look beneath the surface.

The last delicate area is that of trust. Many partners feel insecure and worry about fidelity. This leads to jealous anxiety and a failure to respond sexually, on the one hand, or on the other to an increase in sexual demands that the other partner may find impossible to meet.

9 Neurotic and psychosomatic symptoms
Having a sex problem is often the last thing a patient will admit. This may be because he has been brought up in a sexually restrictive family and does not talk or think about sex with any freedom, or it may be because he is ashamed of this possibility. A sexual failure may threaten the patient's whole self-respect. Again, to believe that a sexual problem exists entails the possibility of therapy, embarrassment, and maybe worst of all, renewed sexual contact.

For many reasons, then, it becomes more convenient and less threatening to present the unhappiness or dissatisfaction in some other way – with an explanation or symptom which is related to but does not bear directly on the problem. A typical complaint might be backache or perhaps itching of the vulva (pruritus vulvae) or anus (pruritus ani). On a closer questioning the patient may also reveal a degree of unhappiness and depression with life itself.

There is also the situation of people who are totally unaware of the cause of their difficulties; they come with a complaint and

129

believe with unshakeable conviction that no further enquiry need be made as to causes. Suppose here the complaint is likewise backache or pruritus; to suggest that sexual difficulties underlie the complaint may be met with indignation.

Complaints or illness arising in this manner are called psychosomatic. The difficulty lies in the mind (the psyche), for example, fear of intercourse. Instead of being felt as a psychological disorder it is changed into a bodily (or somatic) presentation.

This shift of attention from a psychic to a somatic symptom is not the only type of diversionary presentation. The patient may equally complain of tension headaches, depression or anxiety, all of which may be quite genuine, but nevertheless secondary.

Long continued unhappiness and stress may produce other kinds of psychosomatic disorders, which can also be thought of as stress diseases; for example, peptic ulcer or colitis. While such people may also have sexual problems, it is usual to find that other maladjustments are more prominent, or that the situation is of great complexity and long duration.

Where the therapist has come to believe a problem is psychosomatic, great care is required in case some physical illness is being ignored. The patient may need to be seen by a specialist surgeon or physician, and even then certainty cannot always be achieved. However, the surgeon or physician can usually eliminate the possibility of physical conditions requiring treatment and if the symptoms indicate possible underlying sexual causes, some sex therapy may be attempted as a hypothesis. If the symptoms are caused by sexual difficulties and these difficulties are successfully treated the symptoms should disappear.

A failure of the sex life, instead of producing bodily symptoms, may on the other hand cause purely psychic symptoms which the person may or may not relate to sexual frustration. At its simplest, sexual frustration may be felt as anxiety or an inability to relax, a symptom not far removed from ordinary frustration. More serious degrees of unhappiness, felt as chronic depression of varying degree, usually result from a mixture of dissatisfactions with life in general or the relationship in particular, of which sexual frustration is part.

Other psychic symptoms may also be in part caused by sexual failure. Secondary orgasm dysfunction occurs rather frequently in agoraphobic women (agoraphobia being a fear of leaving certain secure places such as the house).

Mrs D. could be described as a very beautiful but highly neurotic woman. She wanted treatment for her agoraphobia, and had to be accompanied to the clinic by her husband. They made a bizarre pair. She would have been a suitable model girl if she had not decided to become a full-time mother and housewife. She was well-groomed and pale, with dark chestnut hair framing her rather thin and sensitive face. Each time she came for treatment she wore a strikingly different outfit, and obviously enjoyed spending Mr D.'s money and looking young for her thirty-six years. Their age gap was not great but Mr D. looked more like fifty-four than forty-four, as he was excessively over-weight. They looked rather like Beauty and the Beast; he in the form of a huge, fat, blond, red-faced creature.

She had been agoraphobic for eleven years and it appeared that nothing in particular had triggered this off. She did not know why she had become shaky, nervous and panicky. She remarked that tranquillisers made her feel worse, and she certainly could not enjoy her three small children. She found that she could do many of the things her husband wanted her to without going out, as this mainly involved entertaining his business friends and providing large dinner parties.

It turned out that she had 'hang-ups' when questioned about sex. She said so emphatically that her sex life was all right and had nothing to do with her agoraphobia that it was necessary to find out tactfully about it. Eventually it turned out that she had disliked sex since the marriage eleven years earlier. She had liked masturbating before the marriage, and had felt excited by Mr D. when they were engaged, although he did not bring her to orgasm. When they married she had her first child and gradually grew to dislike sexual contact with her husband, who was increasingly gaining weight. She found him heavy on top of her and as he did not want any other position she tolerated his advances reluctantly because she wanted more children. It turned out that they had not had sex for four years, since the birth of her last child. She masturbated to fantasies of slim men, excluding her husband from her fantasy life. She remarked, 'I like a man with a trim figure, although some women might like a Teddy Bear husband.' Mr D. said that

131

initially in the marriage he had felt so contented that he could not help gaining weight. He realised this had affected her, and that he was less physically attractive. This made him anxious and created a vicious circle for he then ate more, while Mrs D. had been expressing her sexual frustration through her agoraphobia.

Similarly, certain neurotic symptoms such as claustrophobia (a fear of confined places: lifts, crowded places, small rooms and so on) are frequently found in men with erectile impotence. Sexual problems in general also probably occur more frequently in people of an anxious disposition. Such neurotic symptoms are probably not usually the cause of the sexual difficulties, but tend to co-exist in any particular character.

Certain psychosomatic symptoms seem to exist in order to make sex impossible or difficult. Some women who complain of backache report that intercourse makes it worse, and this may lead gradually to a complete avoidance of sex. Other symptoms of anxiety may occur during sexual advances and foreplay, and completely inhibit the development of the normal state of excitement – the erection may not appear or may not be sustained, or vaginal lubrication will not take place. The person may complain of tension, difficulty in breathing, nausea or sweating, among a variety of other complaints.

Vaginismus is the most dramatic psychosomatic presentation, the object of which is sexual avoidance. Some cases of impotence may also be understood in this way.

5

Evaluation of individual problems

1 The initial assessment interview

Treatment of sexual disorders is in the nature of a contract between the patients and the therapist. Before such a contract can be agreed upon, the patients must know what is offered and the therapist must feel that he or she has a clear idea of the problem and its cause – which may be complex. Neither therapy nor reassurance will be efficacious unless the individuals are known both as people and as histories.

The complete account of the problem; its development; the sexual history; the story of the relationships which have been made; the current relationship; the couple's attitudes and personalities; their life style; the way in which leisure is spent; how they use their imaginations; and the nature of their work. These are all important elements and together constitute the patients' history.

There are really two partly overlapping histories to consider: the personal history of each partner and the history of the relationship, be it marriage or otherwise.

The therapist will first and most importantly want to know the nature of the problem. Patients may wrongly 'label' themselves as abnormal, perhaps claiming they are impotent or frigid when, for example, they are able to enjoy an orgasm when making love but cannot obtain another until twelve hours later. It is essential to find out exactly what the patient means when he or she initially presents a 'labelled disorder'.

The source from which the referral has been made may be useful here: if the patient has been seen by a psychiatrist or gynaecologist a detailed history may have been taken. However, many patients have been seen by physicians and others who have not taken a full history, or perhaps even made a valid diagnosis. In such cases the history will have to be taken in considerable detail.

Clinics specialising in sexual disorders always take a full history, and this is regarded both as an opportunity to get the facts and as an opportunity to begin to get to know and evaluate the patients as people. Clinics vary in the amount of time they can give to each patient and to each area of the history, and some ask the patients first to fill in various forms giving background information not directly concerned with the sexual history or problem: age, occupation, family, previous health and illnesses, birth control methods, and so on. After this, the initial interview can begin.

Some clinics in the U.S.A. use the full routine of Masters and Johnson, devoting a whole day to the history. In their method, therapists of opposite sexes work together as a unit and each therapist begins by taking the history from the same-sex patient. When this is complete the patients change over to the therapist of the opposite sex, giving a female/male situation. The benefits of this arrangement appear obvious. Both patients may find it easier to discuss embarrassing matters with someone of their own sex. Women may initially prefer to talk about masturbation and orgasm with another woman who has shared such intimate problems, and similarly, men may find wet dreams and masturbation methods easier to describe when talking to another man who has faced similar problems himself. When the 'changeover' takes place, the potentially embarrassing material, the difficult admissions, have already hopefully been made and the material is available for the second encounter. Learning to talk about one's sexuality is, in itself, a beginning. In the second, opposite-sex encounter, each therapist discusses the couple's relationship and attitudes towards each other.

It is not yet clear whether the co-therapist partnership of Masters and Johnson offers substantial advantages, and there are in any event many sex therapists who work alone, either from desire or necessity. In addition, while Masters and Johnson may devote a whole day to the clients' history, this is not usually practicable in busier clinics. It is not really possible, however, to take the history of an individual in much less than an hour, and for a clinic or therapist to show haste is to approach a point of diminishing return. Patients do not respond to haste, any more than does sex itself.

If the therapist is working alone there are various ways of taking the history. One system is to see the patient presenting the problem first, another system is to take the same-sexed partner first, and although there may be some difficulty in approaching sensitive or 'taboo' areas with the patient of opposite sex this can usually be overcome with tact and experience.

All therapists should be familiar with the sexual vocabulary in current use and that of previous generations. It goes without saying that therapists should not show embarrassment when hearing or using common colloquialisms such as 'screw' or 'fuck'; nor should they show surprise if some words are not understood. If the patient looks blank, the term should be explained or a synonym used; for example, masturbation may be better understood as self-stimulation, self-relief, wanking, tossing- or jerking-off, or the religious pejorative 'self-abuse'.

During the initial interview the therapist is able to deduce a great deal more than is conveyed by the patient's verbal answers. The patient's general demeanour is revealing whether he or she is confident and assertive or uncertain and timid. The way in which he or she looks at the therapist will also indicate not only social skills and attitudes but also the areas where there is some embarrassment. Many people are embarrassed by discussing their masturbations, their erections, their clitoris or their orgasms, and they will show this in many ways: their glance may drop; their voice falter; they may become restless; the hands may fidget or be constantly touching their face, nose or lips.

The way people sit is probably significant too: some sit bolt upright, suggesting alert preparedness; others lounge with apparent ease; some cross their legs which may suggest a defensive attitude; others seem unaware of their sexual parts, behaving as though they did not exist; some seem to flaunt their bodies in a manner of challenge. The interview is the time to study and be studied – a two-way communication is taking place. The clothes and other details carry signals which are usually quickly and even unconsciously evaluated: hairstyle; decorations; the quality and cut of the clothing; the general colour scheme; the amount of make-up and the way it is applied; the amount of exposure, either direct or indirect, given to neck, arms, legs, breasts and genital area. The patient walks in as a self-advertisement, an advertisement which may proclaim, at a single glance, what might take hours to discover over a telephone. Those who are uncertain, hesitant or depressed will be advertised in one way, those happy, confident and keen in another; the sexually repressed will present themselves in one way, the liberated another. The game of reading people is slightly complicated by those who wear uniforms or very formal dress; but even bankers and businessmen manage to find ways of advertising themselves as individuals.

There are also the signs of nervousness: sweating may be observed on the forehead or felt during the handshake. Nervous people may tremble in the hands or in the voice and may show frequent blinking. Occasionally the therapist may even see a pulse beating in a patient's neck. Blushing and red mottling of the skin are common signs of embarrassment and tension, as are dry mouths and lips. The breathing is another 'give away' which the nervous or highly aroused person cannot easily conceal.

Anger or suspicion may also produce similar reactions, and here the facial expression will often give the clue. Frowning, flushing, engorgement, sweating, lip-licking and an intimidatory gaze may warn of anger. When the teeth are shown this may express fear as well. The person who is continually smiling may be signalling that they wish to placate, allure or charm the therapist, whom they fear. Therapists have to face the fact that most patients will respond to them as sexual beings and that while they are reading the patients, the patients are reading them. It is a narrow path the therapist and patients must tread. The encounter concerns sex, sexual arousal will occur, sexual signals will be exchanged. Present manners dictate that a barrier should exist – sexual behaviour between the patients and the therapists is taboo. However, the therapist must be warm and easy – to put down the patients' sexuality is no part of the scheme.

To call the first interview the evaluation and history-taking session is only to name its most obvious function. At many points the therapist is already giving therapy by giving reassurance, by opening up difficult areas, by demonstrating that certain subjects are not the danger they were supposed to be, by being relaxed about things that cause the patient tension, and so on. The therapist may take the role of an arbiter of what is normal: informing the patient, for example, that to masturbate after marriage is quite normal and healthy or that oral sex is perfectly permissible, even desirable.

History-taking is a skill that has to be learned. It is possible to forget to ask even the most obvious things in the mass of detail, especially when the 'going' is difficult. The safest and easiest way to make sure that all the important things have been covered is to follow the same sequence each time and begin with a structure that can be referred to.

A golden rule of sex therapy is that the therapist should never impose his or her value judgements upon the patient. The therapist may attempt to introduce new ideas, but the couple is not constrained to accept them, and the therapist is principally there to help the patient attain his own goals. The patient's behaviour should never be judged as good, bad or wrong except in relation to the effect such behaviour may have on reaching the desired goal. And this goal should be spelt out and agreed on between the couple and the therapist. Where there seem to be differences in the goals of each partner then a compromise will have to be reached. Where the goals are seen to be unattainable, or where no agreement can be reached by the couple, or where the goals may damage others, the treatment should not begin.

Sexual development
This part of the history is naturally taken in a lot of detail. It should be established first how the patient learned the facts of life: were they picked up piecemeal from other children or were they given some sex education either by the school or by their parents? If their parents did not discuss the matter, why not? Were the early sexual associations good or bad; associated with pleasure or guilt?

A woman should be asked about the onset of menstruation: how old was she? Was she prepared? Did she understand what was happening? Who told her? Was she frightened? Details should be taken of her early periods: were they painful, frequent or irregular? How did she feel emotionally about her periods – happy that she was a woman and could have children, or just inconvenienced or embarrassed by them?

A man may be asked to describe his early experiences of erection. Did he have wet dreams? How did he feel about it and did he understand at all? Was he punished or made to feel guilt in

137

association with these early experiences?

Both boys and girls have early orgasms, sometimes during dreams and sometimes occurring during the day. Ask about these – they occur before puberty as well as after.

The changes of puberty can now be enquired about: was the patient upset by the growth of hair? breast development? the size of the penis? the occurrence of acne? blushing? Did he or she believe himself or herself to be deficient in any sexual way? Unattractive perhaps? How did parents and family treat the new self? How did he or she 'make out' with the opposite sex? Did they have opposite-sexed friends or mainly same-sexed? All patients should be asked if they were pleased to be the sex they were and also if their parents were pleased. Masculine and feminine attitudes depend to some extent on parental attitudes. Ask what roles they liked in children's games and whether such roles were consonant with their sex. Did they spend much time dressing up in opposite-sexed clothes or in their parents' underwear?

When talking of this early period ask if any adult made sexual advances to them or seduced them into sexual activity. Did they ever witness adults in sexual activity by chance or by intention? How did they feel? Has rape ever happened?

Enquire about the family atmosphere and the attitude of the parents: were they easily embarrassed by sex, by sexual questions, by sexual events on the television? Were they loving towards one another when around the children? Ask if the parents ever punished the patient for any sexual act or any act involving sexual organs. Did the patient play any sexual games with or without dolls, for example, games relating to babies or love – games involving fantasies of doctors or nurses – sexual games with pets and so on? Were they ever punished for doing this?

Here it is a good idea to fill in some important details about the family unit in which the patient was reared. Find out how old the parents were when the patient was born. Are they still alive? What kind of relationship did they have (loving, distant, formal, quarrelsome, warm, and so forth)? Estimate their social circumstances and attitude towards leisure, money and friends. Was the family 'outward-looking' or closed against strangers? Did the patient have brothers and sisters? If so, how did they relate together? Did sex ever come into it? Did the patient believe that his parents had a good sex life? For some people it is difficult to imagine their parents in sexual activity of any kind, which is probably due to the blanket of silence which they have thrown over the subject. Ask whether the patient feels he or she is repeating any of their faults or shortcomings? What kind of work did the father or mother do? Did they spend much time at home? Ask what the relationship with each parent was like – was it loving and affectionate? If the parents have separated ask why and how it affected your patient. Who brought the patient up? Did the parents remarry? Ask whether religion was important in the family, and get an idea of the moral values prevailing.

Try and find out how the patient learned to masturbate and what techniques he used. Although such questions may prove embarrassing, the answers will nevertheless reveal how adventurous and imaginative the patient used to be and could still be. Many people use some kind of fantasy during masturbation – ask what kind of fantasies were used most frequently and did such fantasies develop over the years? Many people deny the use of fantasy at all. Ask also how long it took to come to orgasm and whether any mechanical aids were used. Was it necessary to dress up or masturbate in any particular place? Where was it usually done?

During this kind of discussion the answers the patient gives may reveal ignorance or mistaken beliefs – be on the look-out for these and if there is not time to discuss them make a note to deal with them later. Do not be afraid to say, 'We can deal with that during the next session.'

The sexual development of the individual during adolescence can then be explored. Enquire about the amount of contact with the opposite sex. Did they make early sexual contact such as dating, kissing and petting? How far did they go? Was their contact with the opposite sex easy, frequent and pleasurable, or full of anxiety and embarrassment? Were they attractive or unpopular, dominant or submissive? Sexy or demure? Find out the age and circumstances of the first genital contact and their feelings about mutual masturbation, deep kissing, stimulation of other erogenous zones. Was the attitude towards sex primarily romantic or purely sexual? Was the first genital contact against their will? Rough or clumsy? How did they feel?

Where sexual intercourse was established as a routine ask for some description of the course of events: was the foreplay adequate in manner and duration? Did they talk to their partner about sex during the act? Did their sexual behaviour depart from the entirely conventional? What positions were employed? Was the light usually left on? Did they ever have sex in the open? Usually dressed or undressed? Ask either sex how many orgasms were aimed at and obtained. Ask women whether they came to orgasm during penetration alone or was some clitoral stimulation necessary? Did the partner do this, or did she do it herself? Did she consider it permissible?

Either partner may have had several sexual partners. Discuss how sex differed in each relationship. Ask what qualities seemed to attract the patient and ask if such qualities still retain their power? Find out if the patient had any difficulty in finding partners for sexual or social activity. Were they ever engaged to be married to another person, or were they married previously? Describe these relationships. Are there children from a previous marriage?

Did the first sexual or genital contact with the same sex involve an older or younger person? Homosexual and other unconventional experiences should be approached with tact but also treated in a matter-of-fact way – such contacts are, after all, very common. Enquire about homosexuality in practice and in fantasy. Many people are bisexual; some among them give expression to this entirely natural tendency. Others find unusual sexual outlets such as transvestism, exhibitionism and voyeurism. Some sexual activities bring people in contact with the law. All these should be asked about.

The partner
In this part of the enquiry the nature of the relationship and the qualities of the partner can be examined. Why was the patient first attracted to this particular person? The appearance? The personality? Did love develop? Love at first sight or mainly sexual desire? How much attraction was there to the qualities of mind showed by the partner, or to qualities of personality? Were they qualities which the patient possessed or did the patient like his partner because of the differences? Did they have many similar interests or activities? In what way did their personalities differ? Was one of them more dominant? More assertive? More confident? To what degree was either of them anxious, neurotic or insecure? Was there any quality which they really disliked in the partner even from the first?

Find out the way in which the relationship has changed. Was the transition from passion and infatuation to a more companionable existence difficult? Did the partners really get to know each other before settling down together? In what way have the partners changed during the relationship? Have they remained physically healthy and attractive or not? Have they developed bad habits such as smoking, drinking or gambling?

The nature of the contract between the couple should be enquired into, and whether the partners believe this contract is being observed by them both. Does the contract need to be renegotiated in any sense? Are they free to alter the agreement if they wish? Contracts vary of course, but whether within marriage or without, there usually exists a complex of understandings which regulate the behaviour of each partner but which may be broken or disregarded unless regularly redefined. Do they sometimes discuss the nature of the contract between them?

The sexual relationship should be covered at this point. If the details of early sexual behaviour have not already been elicited they should now be obtained. At the present state of their relationship what is the pattern of their sexual behaviour? Who usually takes the initiative – is it always the same partner? Do they always make love at the same time or expect to do so? Or does sexual behaviour arise spontaneously, at any time? Are they usually too busy for love? Where do they usually make love – in bed? Do they ever make love in the lounge or elsewhere? Do the couple use a particular position for intercourse and do they ever depart from this? Do they experiment with unusual positions? Do they both like the same activities and positions? The therapist will need to have details of the foreplay: how it is done, what the sequence is, whether the way in which the partners handle each other is satisfactory, or, if it could be improved, have they asked one another?

Many couples are too inhibited to ask their partners for special favours, too shy to indicate the best manner of stimulation, and this should be investigated as well as whether they talk to one another during sexual play. Does genital manipulation play a large part in foreplay? If so, how is it done – mutually or sequentially? Does mutual masturbation ever replace intercourse and does it satisfy? Each partner should be asked if they have oral sex and if they do, whether it is enjoyable: does the man like cunnilingus or the woman fellatio? Are they skilled at it? Do they know how and where to use the tongue and teeth? How does the woman deal with the ejaculate: swallow it, some of it, none of it? Would she like to? Would he like to ejaculate in her mouth? These questions may seem too intimate during the history taking, and the therapist may judge it better to leave them until oral sex is discussed during therapy.

Discover also the manner of intercourse and the length of time necessary for insertion before orgasm. Do both partners come to orgasm during intercourse: sometimes? Always? Never? Do they attempt to regulate their orgasms so that both partners may come together or does one come before the other? Some women feel they must delay their pleasure until the man has arrived. The man should be asked whether he would like his partner to come first and if not, why? How many orgasms are attempted and achieved by each partner can then be discussed. So often orgasm activity is primarily male-beneficial – the female may not even be aware that she may be able to have several orgasms with little or no refractory period. Is this capacity present or unexploited?

After the orgasm has been achieved does the person feel satisfied and relaxed? What do they do next: make sure the partner has completed their immediate sexual needs? Or lose interest, go to sleep, want to talk, to smoke? Does the male assist the female manually to her orgasm if it is necessary? Ask if the couple usually go on to a second act of intercourse and examine its pattern. How long after the first? How long may sexual activity continue? Does either partner ever wake the other for sexual purposes and how does the awakened one respond?

In long-standing relationships people have usually established a characteristic sexual or orgastic frequency; find out what it is. Also, is there any disparity between the needs of each partner? Does it cause conflict? Orgasm frequency may of course include orgasm induced by masturbation.

Careful enquiries should be made as to the sexual taste of either partner. One partner may have asked for some activity – perhaps dressing-up or role-playing – and have been rebuffed. Or again he may have been afraid to ask – for example, a desire for anal manipulation or penetration is often concealed. The question here might be phrased: 'Is there any sexual activity you have wanted or fantasised, for which you have not dared to ask or which you have been denied?'

Has the couple or the person ever had group sex, been to an orgy, or had sexual relations with another couple? Has the patient ever been unfaithful? Tried bondage?

At some point in the discussion of sexuality the nature and occurrence of fantasy should be examined. What is the subject of fantasy? When is the fantasy used? People use fantasy idly – during masturbation and during intercourse. Fantasies which are used during intercourse are sometimes used throughout the act all the way to orgasm. They may be attended to so closely that the partner is forgotten – is this so? Inhibited people rarely tell their partners of their fantasy. Does this particular person do so? Again, some people have no fantasies at all. Does the patient have sexual dreams?

The relationship must also be seen in its non-sexual, personal and social setting. Ask about the social life of the couple. Do they share it with mutual friends? Do they have some social activity which they do alone? Does either insist on always being together every day and every evening of the year? Ask the person whether they are possessive or jealous to any degree. At a party or social event do they keep together? Would they mind if their spouse was flirting with another person or dancing intimately with that person? Do they believe in one standard for men and another for women in social or sexual behaviour?

As a functioning unit who makes the decisions? How are the household tasks apportioned? Does the husband help with the housework, the washing-up and with the children? Are the finances discussed and agreed? Does either partner feel any major injustice exists? How many children are there? Were they planned? Did they agree? If there are none, why? Is the couple trying to have children at present? The therapist should ask carefully about each child and its relationship with each parent. There may be disagreements over the upbringing practices. Parents sometimes use the children as pawns in their own conflicts.

At this point the financial background to the relationship should be discussed: is it fairly secure? The type and amount of work each has to do should be enquired into. Is either partner worn out by excessive work or worried about their social status? Does work dominate the patients' lives? Has their work suffered because of their sexual problem?

Contraceptive practices may already have been discussed, especially if these have caused problems. In any case they should be asked about since a fear of pregnancy or a failure of fertility may underlie some problems, as may some contraceptive techniques.

It may be quite apparent by this stage how the sexual problem has affected the relationship. Has it driven the couple further apart or had little apparent effect upon their mutual fondness? At worst the couple may wish to part. Has this been discussed? Does either partner feel trapped – that they have no options at all? The position at this stage may look black but if some pleasure can be obtained love can be revived.

The senses

The last part of the interview is an attempt to assess the sensuality of the couple and how ready they are to respond to sensation in whatever form it may present. To find out what sensations they commonly seek out. To find out if they go through life as though programmed to some single inflexible goal – as if the instructions would allow no deviation into the unexpected and novel. To find out how responsive they are, how flexible – to estimate their ability to change.

Many people are not fully aware of the effect of the senses on sexual arousal. Indeed, many people are unaware of the wide range of sexual stimuli with which their senses can provide them. Many people are conditioned to respond sexually to certain types of stimuli. The process starts at home and continues throughout a person's life. It is probably at its most powerful when the individual is sexually developing and makes the initial association between sexual excitement and whatever event or stimulus happened to be around at the critical moment. This may explain why people respond sexually to such a wide range of stimuli, ranging from rubber aprons to the colour purple. These stimuli may vary in their power to evoke a sexual feeling; they may be very slight or have all the power of a fetish.

Every person has different switches; the stimulus which turns one person on leaves another indifferent. What is it that arouses this person sexually? Is it touching, caressing, kissing, looking or listening? While some people seem to respond mainly to visual cues, others respond mainly to voices and sounds, others still to warmth, touch and closeness.

The partners should be asked what they find visually exciting: particular parts of the body? Clothed? Unclothed? In transition from one to the other? Or the clothes themselves? Colours or texture? Furry or shiny? Black materials with a sheen are very popular. Many people like pictures of the opposite sex – pictures of sexual arousal or sexual activity. Such people would probably prefer the stimuli to be either alive or at least moving in films, but erotic films are not easy to find and are often of rather sleazy quality. The beauty of human sexuality is not often filmed with understanding. Do the partners like watching or looking at other people who are displayed in this manner? Would they like to see a live sex show? To watch others engaged in sexual activity can be erotic and sometimes instructive – such films can be a valuable part of sex therapy.

Both men and women occasionally reveal anxiety that they become sexually aroused by the sight of a person of the same sex; for example, a man sees another man in a film with a rising erection, becomes aroused himself and may say, 'How terrible, I am a homosexual.' They can rest easy; it is quite normal to have a degree of homosexual interest – in fact the more things there are that turn a person on the luckier they are.

Do the partners watch each other during sexual arousal? Do they like to do so? What excites them most of all? Does one partner like the other to dress in any special way? On special social occasions or during intercourse or foreplay?

The partners are next questioned about the sounds of sex. Do they like to utter or hear verbal caresses? Do they like to discuss sex as it goes along? Are they switched on by sexual sounds – breathing, sighing, giggling, groaning or screaming? Do the partners allow themselves to be noisy during orgasms? Does this excite them in itself? What kind of voice do they like? What kind of music? Do they find any kind of music sexually exciting? Do they ever use it during sex itself? What? Pop? Reggae? Madrigals or ragas? Some strong rhythms can have a sexually arousing effect – people have reported being carried away by making love to Ravel's 'Bolero', and Indian evening ragas and Reggae music can be stimulating. The beat of a primitive drum can lead to frenzied sexual activity among tribes who practise ritualistic sexual orgies.

Other people find the spoken word very exciting and can get sexually aroused by listening to excerpts from erotic literature. Other people prefer to listen to erotic tapes of people making love.

Many people are stimulated by stories in which there are detailed descriptions of sexual behaviour. They may prefer this to films because they can use their imagination in a much freer way; or perhaps they have a literary and not a visual imagination. Perhaps people of this kind would like to have erotic stories read to them? Have they ever tried it or would they?

The sense of touch is much more alive in some than in others, but is often neglected. Women are probably conditioned into being more sensitive to touch than men. Children are less self-conscious than adults and will approach a piece of sculpture in an art gallery and immediately explore it by touching it. The need to be stroked, tickled, held, caressed or massaged during sexual contact is very strong in some people. The partners should be asked how they like to be touched, and how they like to touch in return. Are there any special surfaces which switch them on, that they find particularly sensual: silk, nylon, skin, rubber, hair, velvet, fur, tweed, or whatever? Have they ever thought of touching surfaces with a new attention – learning to feel anew? Would they like to have a session with their partner in which they massage or touch their partner in as sensual a manner as possible – first one partner then the other – the sole object being to give and receive pleasure? Do they do this already? Have they ever used a cream for massaging each other? Do they like it or would they like to try it? Masters and Johnson have emphasised the importance of using a smooth slippery cream for touching during treatment. They reported that patients who disliked such cream or lotion sometimes did badly in treatment, so a patient's initial reaction to this discussion could provide clues about how careful the therapist will need to be in reassuring patients when touching exercises are prescribed.

The sense of smell comes last, though a partner with no smell is unthinkable. The sense of smell can be just as exciting as the other senses. People vary considerably in this respect, and conditioning has often been a powerful influence. A man might, for example, associate a certain scent with a particular woman he

146

was jilted by, and this might make him dislike another woman who wore the same perfume. During sexual excitement sweat glands produce considerable odour which both sexes may find arousing. What do the partners like? Do they prefer each other to wear scent or only the natural bodily odours? Does the smell of sweat excite them as it does many people? The specifically sexual smells of the genitalia – how does the patient respond to them? Some people like them at any time; others not at all; some only when sexually aroused. Do sexual smells disgust the patient?

At the end of this enquiry on sensation the therapist will know how sensual the partners are; whether the patients need to be taught the pleasures of the senses anew; whether they want to learn.

2 The physical examination

The physical examination may take place during the initial attendance, depending on how things go. It is usual to have a 'round table' discussion after the two individual assessments, and some discussion of the treatment programme, and if there is time, then the physical examination may also be undertaken.

The procedure is based on some American formulae which require both therapists and both partners to be present. Assuming that one of the therapists is medically qualified, then it is that therapist who does the examination. If neither therapist is medically trained, a medical colleague can be called in to help. If the clinic treats single patients at any stage of the treatment, then the patient will have to be examined alone.

The physical examination has several aims – to exclude the presence of physical disease and to educate each partner in the sexual anatomy of the other. Many people have never examined the genitalia of the opposite sex in real detail. Male patients are particularly ignorant here. The physical examination will ensure that the therapists and the patients are all talking about the same 'named' parts. The manner and thoroughness of the examination are intended to reassure the couple and to convey to them the idea that genitalia are not to be hidden or concealed out of shame. The examination must be done in complete privacy.

Initially the examination is done by the medical therapist wearing surgical gloves. Then the patient is examined by his or her partner, who should not wear gloves. The other therapist should remain in the room looking on and appearing relaxed and friendly.

The examination is done for both partners in turn. The general anatomy of the sexual parts is carefully indicated both in technical and colloquial language – which should help to make the examination less formal. The patients can be examined in any order, and the one to be examined first is asked to strip from the waist downwards and to lie on a couch – a sheet or blanket can be provided if required.

The examination by the therapist should be leisurely, calm and complete. This examination then constitutes a 'model' for the partner who then repeats it. To some extent the conduct of the examination is intended as a desensitisation for those who may be afraid of touching their partners or even their own genitals.

While each partner is examining the genitals of the other, they should be carefully observed. How do they approach the task? Delicately, roughly or with about the appropriate touch? Are they nervous or embarrassed? Watch also to see if the patient flinches or draws away – as do women with vaginismus.

The female examination
The therapist begins by examining the vagina. A rubber glove is usually worn and a lubricant applied which makes for more comfortable entry. The therapist first inserts the index finger then the index and middle. The range of response to vaginal examination is very wide, and the manner in which the woman responds is important to note. The woman with any degree of vaginismus will tense herself in various parts depending on the severity of her condition. Women who are severely affected draw away and close their legs; in lesser degrees it is the vaginal entrance which is constricted, and in very mild cases the therapist may only note a slight tightness or withdrawal. Where there is no problem of fear and where the woman is used to such examinations, the entrance and examination reveal complete relaxation. Women who have training in deep relaxation also respond very easily. The majority of quite normal women come between the extremes of complete relaxation and severe vaginismus. A woman who shows a slight tenseness is not necessarily abnormal, for she is after all being examined rather publicly by a stranger.

Where it is possible for the medical therapist to conduct a deep digital penetration he should examine for any local pathology: for example, fibroids, prolapse, tenderness, discharge, painful scars, ovarian cysts and so on.

The woman is then asked to contract the pubococcygeal muscle. If she is not familiar with this she should be told to pretend she is attempting to stop the flow of urine, which is similar to, but not quite the same as, preventing defaecation. She should be familiar with both muscular skills, which are well understood. This facility with the pubococcygeal muscle plays a part in the training of orgasm response and is a pleasuring activity for the male, which may be used during intercourse.

Her partner is then asked to try inserting his index finger, using again a suitable lubricant, and then if possible the index and middle fingers. When in position the woman is asked to squeeze these fingers, using her pubococcygeus muscle as before. She should then be asked to demonstrate her anatomical parts with the help of a mirror. The clitoris, the clitoral hood, the labia minora, the labia majora, the urethral outlet and the vaginal entrance. At all points both the colloquial and formal terms should be repeated. If she has never done this before, the act of seeing her genitalia from a new angle may add to the information which she already has. The woman is then asked to show her partner which of her parts are most sexually sensitive. She may be very shy over this; it is a matter of judgement whether she should be pressed. If she does not indicate the sensitive areas the female therapist should do it for her. During such an examination it is quite usual for a small amount of sexual excitement to be manifest – it is probably a good sign.

Occasionally the examination may reveal some abnormality which requires further examination on another occasion by a gynaecologist, or the use of a vaginal speculum (a device which allows the physician to look up the vagina directly and to examine, among other things, the cervix). If a woman wants to see her own cervix, show her with the help of a mirror.

The male examination
This examination is again undertaken first by the medical therapist and then by the partner. The man's scrotum, testicles and associated parts are examined. The penis is palpated and inspected and the

foreskin, where present, is drawn back and the glans examined. The physician must also examine the local lymph glands in the groin. The presence of any urethral discharge is noted, any sores, infections, hernia and so forth. When the medical therapist is satisfied that all parts are normal, the female partner should examine them herself. The details of the anatomy of the testicles are not very important but may be explained briefly. The penis should be examined in detail. The foreskin (if present), the glans, the circumcoronal sulcus, the frenum or frenulum, the shaft, and the course of the urethra on the underside – all should be shown, felt and named both formally and colloquially. The man is then asked to say which parts, when touched, give sexual pleasure. He may again be diffident, in which case the male therapist can join in, pointing out the areas he finds exciting himself and giving some indication of how exciting each may be.

Attitudes

It is vitally important to include both partners at the physical examination, not only in order to ensure that all important parts are known to them both, but also in order to understand their attitude towards the situation. Those who are fearful and hesitant will not be able to conceal it during the examination, either as a subject or as an object. The act of cooperating in this new and semi-public situation also indicates a more open attitude; the patient who refuses or objects may be unwilling to change. It is also a learning situation. Patients who are very nervous, for whatever reason, may in the unhurried atmosphere of the examination be able to change their attitude beneficially. The patient who is rough and insensitive will also be revealed and can be given some insight into his or her behaviour.

The acts of examination and exposure may also be seen as a kind of ceremony – a new social situation which forms a bond between the couple and the therapists and which promotes that degree of trust and intimacy in which therapy can flourish. There will doubtless come the day when full sexual activity in therapy is quite a natural part of the teaching programme but that time has not quite arrived.

3 The measurement of attitudes

In addition to history-taking, questionnaires can provide further useful information. These may be filled in by the patient alone and can supplement the history-taking in important ways. In a busy clinic a lot of information may be gathered while the therapist is engaged elsewhere, and this information may be used during the history-taking either to introduce certain subjects or to check on the impressions given during normal conversation, or to make sure no question is forgotten. The questionnaire asks a standard set of questions and these are framed in such a way that the strength of a given opinion is recorded. There are also research advantages: since the form is standard, people can be compared with one another, couples can be compared, men and women can be compared, the differences between the women and men among many couples can be examined, and all these findings can be adjudged in the light of the success of treatment, which becomes known later. It can also be used as a gauge to measure the effect of treatment and the changes in attitude in the couple under consideration, and also to compare them with other similar couples in the population.

The use of questionnaires is by no means essential and may make some patients feel that the clinic is impersonal; however, where the questionnaires are given out in a friendly manner, with the explanation that they are only a helpful preliminary, few therapists find patients are offended.

A very useful scale has been developed at the Netherlands Institute for Social Sexological Research. The questionnaire is called Sexuality Experience Scales (s.e.s.). There are two sets of questions, one for men and one for women. Partners fill in their forms separately and should not compare answers. The therapist wants their separate attitudes and there are some areas in which female and male sexuality differ, requiring different questions. The s.e.s. has eighty-four questions and may be completed in under twenty minutes.

The questionnaire covers many different areas such as sexual morals, the sexuality of children, premarital sex, the sex education of children, the manner in which people respond to different types of sexual stimulation, fantasy, preferences for different sexual activities, attitudes towards marriage and the actual marriage, affairs and sexual compatibility. To give some examples of the questions:

M19 How do you like trying out different positions in intercourse? *M14* Is it a good thing for children up to ten years old to see their parents in the nude? *M12* Is your husband sexually inhibited and prudish?

Under each question there is a set of standard answers expressing degrees of agreement and disagreement. The respondent has to tick the one which is nearest to his or her attitude. An example of a complete question is:

M5 I find seeing sexually exciting photos or pictures

( ) 1   very pleasant
( ) 2   fairly pleasant
( ) 3   a little unpleasant
( ) 4   very unpleasant

Whether or not an individual therapist or clinic uses such scales is up to them; in practice, many clinics find them useful.

There are other scales available, some very good. In addition there are scales designed to measure change from one point in time to another. Using such a scale could, for example, measure the change brought about by education or time alone.

6

Treatment

There are two considerations in treatment: theory and procedure. To some extent decisions about procedure are based on theory, but often they are influenced by questions of convenience or morality. We will deal first with the practical question of procedure and secondly with the fundamentals of the treatment. Neither the procedure nor the treatment is identical for any given patient, or patients, so the available options are also examined.

1 Procedure

The clinic
Patients usually visit the therapist at a clinic on an appointment basis. The therapist will try to ensure that the meetings take place in an attractive, informal environment, though this is often difficult to achieve in institutional surroundings. It is better if the therapist does not sit behind a desk except while taking the extensive notes necessary during the history-taking. It is important to do away with the stereotyped image many people have of clinics, therapists and doctors as formal, grave and authoritarian, and during treatment itself it is better for the therapist to adopt an informal attitude, wear normal clothes and no white coats, and provide comfortable chairs in a room with pleasant, moderate lighting. It is also better not to receive telephone calls during the treatment sessions, since they break the sequence of thought and may give the patients the impression that the therapist does not have time for them. The aim should be a calm and relaxed atmosphere and if it is also possible to be light-hearted and humorous, the treatment will go better all round.

The therapists

Some clinics are able to provide two therapists of opposite sex for each case, following the Masters and Johnson plan. Some therapists regard such an arrangement as essential and undoubtedly there are advantages.

Patient–therapist interaction may be easier as some people find it much easier to talk to, and relate with, a person of the same sex, especially where intimate and sexual matters have to be discussed. Two therapists also make it possible for either patient to request to talk to either therapist in private when he or she is unwilling to deliver up to open examination.

The treatment interaction will also more closely resemble a common social situation – one couple meeting another. There is a certain pleasure and challenge, both personal and sexual, when the opposite sex is present. Both men and women behave better and aggression is reduced.

A couple meeting a single therapist form a triangular relationship. In such a situation the couple may compete for the liking or attention of the therapist. Either patient may try to make an alliance with the therapist against the remaining partner. Therapists are human and have to be on their guard. The initial interviews with some couples can be quite stressful to any therapist, however well-adjusted. Often there is some anxiety present, and the patients may be aggressive and hostile towards one another and also towards the therapist. Two therapists can deal with this and other situations more readily. In any verbal exchange one therapist may be active, talking and making points, and the other passive. The passive therapist may notice things that the active one does not, and because he is not for the moment immediately involved, can be more thoughtful and detached.

The passive therapist may intervene to break up some argument or potential hostility; a female therapist may intervene to reassure either patient if they seem uncertain or anxious. Women can often say things to a hostile man which another man would hesitate to say. Male therapists, on the other hand, may be able to impress a female patient with an idea she would not accept from a female therapist. Either therapist may use charm to overcome difficult situations. Certainly, some of the strain on the therapist is lifted in a partnership.

154

After a therapeutic interview the two therapists may compare impressions and actively plan the ensuing treatment, and here two minds and two different points of view are often, though not invariably, better than one. For relatively inexperienced therapists it is an excellent training method to work for a time with a more experienced person on a number of cases.

However, there is no firm proof that two therapists have better results than one, and clinics will have to choose which method they adopt. The two-therapist system has some theoretical advantages: the law of chance makes it more likely for patients to meet one good therapist or one therapist that they like; two minds and two personalities are in most situations better than one; and the system is more comfortable and interesting for the therapist, and probably for the patients too.

However, therapists who, either through choice or necessity, work alone should not be discouraged. One therapist is nearly always better than none at all and sometimes better than two. And there is also the great shortage of sex therapists to consider.

Appointments

Most clinics will develop a routine session length; most clinics consider between three-quarters and one hour to be about right. Where there is a lot to be discussed the whole hour may be taken up; when the therapy is going well or is very stressful the time could be reduced. Towards the end of therapy, or after therapy is really finished, the couple may come up to the clinic for shorter periods just to report that all is well or to get advice on some additional problem.

Some clinics treat the patients by an intensive course; some by spaced interviews. In the intensive method the patients stay in a nearby hotel and visit the clinic daily, or several times per week, over a period of about two weeks, after which the therapy is often complete. During such an intensive course the patients may have received up to fourteen hours of therapy.

This arrangement demands that the therapists have sole use of the interview facilities, which is not always possible in an institution. It is also necessary for the patients to be able to find the necessary time away from work, children and other responsibilities. For many patients the financial strain would also be too great. Some clinics are run on a fee-paying private practice basis; this is almost universal in the United States. In Europe some free clinics exist as well.

The majority of clinics in Europe use the 'spaced interview' method. This is partly a matter of convenience, partly a matter of allegiance to the medical model, and partly a matter of belief. Most European therapists believe the spaced method to be as efficacious as the intensive method, which is more in vogue in the U.S.A. In the spaced method patients are given appointments of about one hour each, at intervals which can vary from weekly to monthly: in the early phases of treatment, usually weekly; later on, near the end of treatment, monthly. There is often a so-called 'follow-up' appointment after a variable period, say six months. If this is inconvenient, the 'follow-up' may be established by letter. The 'follow-up' is a matter of mutual benefit – for the patient for obvious reasons, and for the therapist to check up on the results of the method.

During the initial meetings the therapist has an opportunity to assess the likelihood of treatment success. Patients are usually taken on for treatment even if the chances of success may appear small. If a chance exists at all, treatment is worthwhile. If no progress is made after a few treatment sessions the therapy can be terminated, but sex therapists have a high rate of success, even though the success is sometimes only partial.

The contract for therapy
The decision to undertake treatment lies with the therapists and the clinic and the 'contract' will then be presented to the patients: they are offered therapy, the therapist explaining what it is like and how it proceeds, and they will have to decide whether to accept. The therapist will on his side make certain demands which have to be met, and the patients on their side will often require a lot of reassurance that they will not have to do anything against their will, that there will be no sex in front of other witnesses, and so on.

In the therapy recommended in this book the following ideas will figure and should be outlined to the patients. The therapist will explain that the treatment will consist of a series of meetings, of a certain average duration and frequency, at which there will be a free discussion of the sexual problems of the patients. At each meeting the therapist will set tasks or homework assignments which the patients must carry out as best they can. At first these tasks will be easy and undemanding, but will become more and more ambitious until full sexual behaviour is attained. They begin with touching, stroking, tickling and massage of non-genital areas – this is called sensate focusing. In the next stage – called genital sensate focusing – the genitals are stimulated. Orgasm is not demanded at this stage but may occur. Oral sex follows next. The techniques will be fully explained when the patient reaches the appropriate stage in therapy, and patients will be given every encouragement to include them in their regular behaviour. The patients may be told that oral sex is entirely optional but that it would be helpful if they felt able to try it eventually. The therapist might say, 'Let it depend on how the earlier stages go.' The last steps will concern sexual intercourse and some teaching of positions.

Where either partner has a lot of anxiety, the therapist will reassure them that techniques will be used to deal with this. The techniques include relaxation and graduation, and the anxieties will be fully discussed.

The therapist should explain that the patients will not only go through these stages of treatment but may also be expected to try and take a new attitude towards their whole sexual life. The therapist will explain that he or she will try to open their minds to new ideas to encourage a relaxed outlook on sex – to make sex fun. This will involve a willingness on the patients' part to read and look at matter perhaps previously ignored or rejected as pornographic, with the purpose of knowing more about sex in general and having pleasure as well.

The individual life style of the patients will also be discussed, as some people live a life inimical to sexual pleasure; the therapist will try to persuade them to rethink their lives and to use their imagination and creativity not only in new sexual behaviours but also in liberating their fantasies.

The more general reshaping of attitudes and the persuasion to lead a life more pleasure-oriented – encouragement to be sensual – is called 'reorientation'. Reorientation is a stage in treatment but not in the same sequential sense of the other stages, since re-orientation ideas are discussed at every session. Reorientation is dealt with fully in section 3 of this chapter but the general idea should be clear.

In this initial briefing the therapist will emphasise that if a couple is being treated, then they must take the attitude that they are being treated as a couple. Should either partner refuse to regard themselves as involved in the success of the treatment, it is likely it will fail. Should either partner be continuing an affair it will have to be given up in order to maximise the chances of sexual unity and pleasure between the original pair.

Patients may ask if their marital problems can be discussed, to which the answer is 'yes', provided the sex therapy usually occupies the major part of the interview time. The therapist may point out that when the couple start to get sexual pleasure from one another some of the so-called marital problems may disappear. Some problems may best be redefined rather than met 'head-on'.

Many patients are curious about the reasons for a given recommendation or task and some will be better motivated if the rationale is explained. So the therapist will reassure the patients that no step is taken without a good reason, and that this reason will be explained to them if they wish.

Having discussed all these matters, the patients decide whether they would like treatment. If so, arrangements are made and treatment can start. The decision, though complex, can usually be made in the session following the history-taking session or sessions.

2 Fundamentals

We will now pass on to the fundamentals of treatment and the options which the therapist has for overcoming individual difficulties in a flexible manner.

Anxiety relief

One of the main principles of the treatment described in this book is the relief of anxiety associated with sexual behaviour. Often patients have become extremely anxious about everything related to the sexual act and sexual behaviour. Some patients show anxiety when they just touch their partner or hold hands. This anxiety has usually built up during a series of painful failures. In the language of learning theory the anxiety has been generated by repeated punishments. For the therapist, then, an excellent starting-point is to remove any further fear of failure. Where the failures have occurred during sexual intercourse, the patients are told that to begin with no attempt must be made to have sexual intercourse. The only sexual behaviour to be allowed is touching, massaging and fondling each other. The relief of performance anxiety immediately releases the patients from inhibition, and pleasure becomes possible again. Punishment has been replaced by reward. The patients no longer need dwell upon the idea of failure.

Anxiety relief is embodied in the idea of the graded 'tasks'. Initially very little is expected of the couple, and since success is probable they gain in confidence. Couples often return after only a single task showing considerable pleasure and hope. The sexual confidence will grow with each successful step.

Where the anxiety is very severe and makes even the first easy steps difficult, anxiety relief may be attempted by means of relaxation followed by desensitisation. As physical relaxation is achieved it will also be found that the mind becomes relaxed. The patients become able to clear the mind of anxiety and exist for at least short stretches with a blank and calm mind.

This relaxation can be used in two ways. The patients can be told to begin to use it during sexual relations – perhaps during parts of the sexual act where anxiety is experienced. The second use is in desensitisation, as follows. Firstly, graded lists ('hierarchies') are made of the patients' anxieties. At the foot of the lists are minor anxieties such as simple touching of the partner's body. Above this are listed slightly greater anxieties, such as, say, touching the partner's genitalia. At the top of the list are serious anxieties: a serious anxiety might be the moment when the penis is about to penetrate the vagina.

The patients are told to relax, and when relaxed, are asked to imagine a minor fear. If this causes anxiety they are asked to relax again, clear the mind, and again conjure up the thought. Eventually this cycle of relaxation and fear-imagining will remove the anxiety from the thought: the fear has been associated with relaxation and calm and not with anxiety. The sequence is then repeated for the next fear up the list. In a full course of desensitisation the therapist could go from the bottom of the hierarchy to the very top; however, it is more usual to employ relaxation-desensitisation as an adjunct to the graded homework tasks of the main treatment. The similarity of the graded tasks of the main treatment to the graded fears of the desensitisation procedure will be obvious.

Sex education and learning

The idea of proceeding from one task, one behaviour, one response to another has two aims. The first is the relief of anxiety and the acquisition of confidence. The second is the formation of new behavioural patterns, of new behavioural responses. The patient is learning new ways. It is a process of education. This education and learning is the second main principle of treatment.

The therapist spends much time discussing sexual behaviour with the patients. During the discussions, areas of misconception and ignorance will be discovered and, if possible, changed. The therapist will attempt to introduce discussion on as many areas of sexuality as possible so that the patients may be given as many opportunities as possible to reveal their attitudes or fears, even if they wish to conceal them. Some of this exploration can be done during the history-taking and some during therapy when the patients usually mention their fears spontaneously.

The therapist is playing the role of educator throughout. He will be giving lessons in behaviour, and in technique.

On matters of technique the therapist can give verbal, written, illustrated and videotape instruction and the couple can then try the behaviour out at home. This technical instruction may be in masturbation techniques, in the techniques of oral sex and in the art of intercourse. The actual behaviour, together with its associated responses and feelings, the patients learn for themselves. The progression from the simple and easy behaviours such as touching and massage through mutual masturbation to oral sex and, later, intercourse may be looked upon as the building of a total sexual response. Each part of the total response is taught and established separately until the whole sexual response is eventually built up.

The idea of building forms the basis of another concept, that of 'shaping'. The therapist finds out what part of the sexual act is already established in the patient's repertoire. This can then form a basis for new ideas and activities. The patient can go from the known to the unknown in easy steps. A response can be fashioned from one skill to another. This is called 'shaping'. The therapist might start from the ability of an impotent man to masturbate himself. The response is the established skill upon which the next response can be built. In this case, perhaps, the female partner could then masturbate the male. This is a small but new step. From being masturbated the next new behaviour could be oral sex. The man would learn to obtain pleasure from the presence of his glans penis in the mouth of the partner, all the while maintaining the erection. The last step may be insertion and thrusting in the vagina. The behaviourist would say the response had been 'shaped'. The concept may be applied to other sexual behaviours in which one proceeds by the process of successive approximation until the behaviour is attained.

Stimulation therapy

Stimulation therapy is the last fundamental of the method. If the sex drive can be increased, the sexual performance and enjoyment can only benefit. The therapist mainly achieves this result in two ways: firstly by removing prohibitions which prevent enjoyable sexual activity and secondly by increasing the patients' range of sexual interests and behaviours. For many patients the whole range of sexual behaviours is not open to them because of anxiety, but for others this is because of prohibition or ignorance. The methods by which sexual drive may be increased will be described, under reorientation, in the section which follows.

Marital therapy

During therapy, and even before this is really started, it may become clear that some time will have to be devoted to talking about the marriage. The possibilities of bad interaction between two people are endless and range from minor irritations all the way up to violence or mental cruelty. Relationships can become very complex, partners may have taken up positions of no retreat, and it is only too easy to get hopelessly involved or confused.

In this method marital difficulties are approached in two ways. One says: improve your sexual interaction and the relationship will improve as a consequence – which is very often true. The other approach is to look carefully at the area of concern and see if some simple analysis may suggest a 'give to get' solution. At a very simple level, where both partners have, shall we say, a niggling complaint about the other, an exchange agreement can be negotiated. For example, 'If you will tell me the details of the family finances so I can play a part in them, I will be more willing to help entertain your friends'; or perhaps at a deeper level, 'If you spend some time talking with me, I will try to put some enthusiasm into my sex life'; or, 'I will come out with you more often if you will show more interest in the children.' Any couple may have numerous areas of disagreement which may be paired off in this way.

When this approach is made systematic it is called 'Contract Therapy'. The couple are remotivated to make certain sacrifices in the interests of greater harmony and increased sexual cooperation. But it must be presented positively so that the tasks are requested and not forbidden (not 'I won't sleep with you unless ...').

It may also be a valuable lesson to teach a couple how to talk to one another. Previous discussions may have failed because the couple could not keep up a dialogue without quarrelling. This may be because one partner, or both, begin to feel threatened in some way and retreat into sulking, hostility or pretended indifference. The therapist may suggest ways of overcoming this. One method is to set aside a time each week for marital discussion when it is a rule to keep calm. Another rule could be to break off the discussion at a given time – not to try to solve everything at once. Once a habit of communication is established both marital and sexual matters may be talked about.

Sex therapists do not as a rule spend much time on offering interpretations of reasons why a person behaves in a certain general way. They do, however, make rational behavioural suggestions why a person is behaving in a certain way if that behaviour is a threat to the marriage or to the sex therapy: 'You spend all your time watching T.V. sport as you wish to fantasise yourself as a success, perhaps to make up for your other failures'; 'Perhaps you don't take care over your appearance because you will not test yourself out as an attractive being – you refuse to run the risk of rejection or ridicule'. Many similar interpretations may suggest themselves during the periods of discussion, but in general, sex therapists draw their explanations from behavioural principles and try to appeal to the common sense of the client rather than to his deeper psyche. The explanations or interpretations should be simply expressed; if the patient does not understand them the therapist is probably either being too general or is unsure what he or she means – in either case it needs rethinking. Incidentally, it is perfectly reasonable for a therapist to say, 'I don't really know', or 'I can only speculate',

since many behaviours are difficult to explain. The patient who
expects the therapist to have all the answers will be disappointed,
but should be satisfied if he can be persuaded that treatment can
often work just because it has been found to do so.

There are numerous other approaches to marital therapy but it
is not the purpose of this book to describe them. The marital
aspects of therapy may occupy quite a large part of the treatment
but we recommend that it is kept at a behavioural, specific and
readily understandable level.

3 Reorientation

After the history has been taken, therapy as such can begin and
this section will describe the first stage. Of course, in reality, it is
impossible to take the history without at the same time responding
to the patient in a way that is both appropriate and therapeutic.
The tone of voice, the inflections of speech and the construction
of sentences will vary for each partner and some kind of relationship will gradually be established. In most cases the couple will
have gone away with a new sense of hope and with the idea that
their sexual relationship might be built anew. This at least should be
the aim.

People who have a problem are 'stuck' in a situation which they
have failed to solve for themselves. No one likes to fail, the more
so in an area so important for self-respect, and repeated attempts
at solution have only served to confirm the failure. New ideas are
needed; the soil has to be prepared afresh.

Equal involvement
The first stage of treatment is called reorientation – though, as we
have explained, this is not a 'sequential' stage of treatment since
reorientation ideas are discussed at every session. Reorientation
reflects the hope that both the man and the woman will, in a sense,
learn to work together with a common aim and attitude – two
people with the same orientation.

Often, before arriving at the clinic one of the couple will have
decided that he or she is the 'ill' partner and that the other is
normal, or at least more nearly so. This attitude is found in all
degrees. At worst, the 'ill' partner takes on himself or herself all the

guilt and blame, often associated with depression and a sense of failure – failure to live up to an ideal. Conversely, in extreme cases, the 'normal' partner may take a smug or detached attitude as if to say, 'I have only come to help my sick partner.'

During the interaction of the history-taking the attitude of the patients will have been observed by the therapist and will have given him or her some ideas. The partner who offers himself as 'ill' can easily be identified, and the distance separating the couple may begin to be clear almost immediately. Where one partner denies all blame, all involvement, the distance may be very great. The real attitudes of the couple may of course only reveal themselves in full as therapy proceeds, since one or both partners may be 'stuck' with an attitude towards the spouse which they believe to be a true one but which is in fact concealing the true one, and also the attitude towards the therapist may be designed to conceal feelings such as hostility which the patient believes to be disgraceful and therefore unacceptable to the therapist.

First, then, establish the right attitudes. As a statement of principle the couple should be introduced to the idea that neither may any longer consider themselves as being free from responsibility for the situation. If anything is to be 'officially' treated it is the sexual relationship *of the couple*. It may be the case that one partner shows more abnormalities than the other; nevertheless the aim of therapy is the creation of a new sexual climate between *this* woman and *this* man. (Naturally a blunt statement to the effect that both are to blame would risk evoking indignation or anger which might only serve to reinforce the difficulty. No one should enter therapy who cannot summon up and command a good deal of tact.)

If it is a problem to get one partner to accept the idea of responsibility, the therapist could point out that his or her own technique or approach may need improving and that love-making is a two-way situation. The difficulty may be only partially overcome and one partner may still insist on a degree of detachment, but provided some readiness to join in is expressed, treatment can start – the difficulty may gradually be outflanked.

The idea of equal involvement and equal responsibility naturally entails that the couple attend for therapy together. Only when one partner has some severe additional personality problems should they be seen alone to discuss matters which are not directly related to the marriage. In all other situations the couple should attend as partners for the treatment of a common problem: their relationship.

Reassurance and embarrassment

Unless exceptional circumstances prevent it, the couple should now be given some firm reassurance as to the successful outcome of the treatment. Until now the therapist has probably said, 'I will be able to assess the situation better when we have all the details we require', and although only an experienced therapist can give a really well-informed guess about the likely outcome and success of the treatment, optimism can be based on the results which have been obtained by others. Modern methods of sex therapy do have a good chance of success, and it is part of the treatment to approach the problem with optimism. The patients will have their own questions, of course, but some kind of positive reassurance can easily be worked into the conversation: 'Many people have been treated by these methods and with your degree of difficulty there is a good chance of success'; 'We employ a modified Masters and Johnson method in which we also aim to increase your sexual appetites'; 'You will need to attend about x times', and so on.

Where embarrassment is a problem it is part of treatment to overcome it. Many people find it very difficult to talk openly about sexual matters, but it should be explained that it is as essential a part of treatment as it should be of everyone's education. Patients can be reassured that they will simply be given the opportunity to learn about certain sexual facts which other patients might already have learned at school or from books. Therapists find that embarrassment is easily overcome by leading the discussion in an open and frank manner. When patients see that their therapist talks about taboo subjects such as masturbation simply and without evasion, they fairly quickly join in. It is often possible to recognise 'embarrassment' areas when the patients are initially interviewed. The therapist can see how patients react to certain questions. Taboo subjects, taboo fantasies, and many sexual topics associated with fallacies can cause concern and embarrassment, but if they are discussed in a relaxed and open manner this is in itself a relief and the embarrassment soon disappears. The therapist should always try to reassure the patients about 'taboo thoughts and fantasies' and treatment may consist of 'rewarding' the inhibited person for open and frank responses by means of smiles and verbal encouragement.

Behaviour therapy does not consider it necessary to understand the manner in which the symptoms have been produced in order to treat them. At the same time, where the patient is ready and able to understand such explanations it is likely that he or she will want to hear them and will find them helpful and in a sense re-assuring.

Some explanations are drawn from such experimentalists as Pavlov and Skinner, some are based on physiological facts and speculations, but there remain areas in which theory is not supported by experimental facts, and where one is guided solely by new ideals, by custom or by morality. For instance it is fundamental to the method that women should play an equally active, though naturally different, role in sexual behaviour to that of her partner. Again, neither physiology nor behavioural science is sufficiently advanced to specify the relationship between a good sexual adjustment and a state of happiness. There are inumerable other examples. But despite these areas of uncertainty no behaviour therapist need fear exposing the rationale of the method whose strength resides in its documented results, quite apart from the simplicity of the facts that help to support them.

Patients are also reassured that the treatment steps are carefully worked out and they will only be asked to attempt each stage when they are ready to do so. They will also be reassured that their physiological responses will develop naturally during the different stages of treatment, but that no sexual responses can be willed or forced. If they concentrate on the different touching tasks and try to let themselves go and enjoy the feelings they experience, rather than striving for an orgasm or an erection, then these rewards will follow. If the patients are always watching themselves (spectatoring) to see their reactions, they will become too self-conscious and sexual responses will not take place. If partners become involved with trying to please and pleasure each other they will get involved in the tasks and sexual responses and excitement will naturally take place.

Anxiety

Some anxiety is almost invariably associated with any problem and an experienced therapist will be aware of its manifestations –

as they have been described earlier in the book. As in normal social situations, such anxiety should gradually subside to levels which will not be experienced as distressing. If this does not happen the therapist must ask him or herself what is causing it and try to reduce it by further reassurance or relaxation techniques. The therapist must always remember that people conceal some areas and often distort the truth in both large and small ways. However, a reasonable degree of honesty should not be too difficult to obtain where it is clear that an atmosphere of good will and friendliness exists.

Patients who show a lot of anxiety may be deliberately concealing thoughts, feelings or fallacies. They may feel that to reveal these will show them up as inadequate or weak, or will force them to admit to themselves that they fall short of some ideal, for which reason they may be ridiculed or rejected. They may feel that their feelings are for some reason unacceptable. In some cases the patient may not really know why he is anxious, and it is this type of apparently causeless anxiety which many couples interpret as hostility towards each other. It is common to feel hostility where one is threatened either by other people or by external events, but one may feel equally threatened by one's own impulses such as anger or grief which, if expressed, may lead to rejection. Some patients fear to show affection and love because they have learned in the past that a display of such feelings has met with disapproval or rejection. Others, for a variety of reasons, may never have learned to express these feelings in a free and open way. Because of this, when such feelings arise anxiety appears and often under the guise of hostility. Sharing emotions is part of good communication between a couple and usually leads to a deeper understanding, a reduction of anxiety, and better sexual involvement.

Assertion

Some people who are anxious are also timid. They lack the ability to assert themselves and thereby to control important events in their daily lives. For example, unassertive people often talk in a rather quiet voice and may find it difficult to look directly into the eyes of the person to whom they are talking. They may also find it difficult to express their emotions openly. This applies equally to love and to anger. Unassertive people often, though not always, cannot get their own way and more assertive people are able to impose upon them.

In a marital partnership an inability to be assertive may have serious results. The unassertive partner may feel a helpless resentment which may easily amount to a passive hostility manifesting itself as a lack of warmth, a lack of enthusiasm, a lack of sexual cooperation and initiative, or perhaps a sulking or moodiness. The therapist will quickly discover such behaviour, even if one of the partners does not mention it. It will be apparent during the early sessions. The more assertive partner will talk more and is more emphatic. He or she will often adopt an aggressive stance, have a louder voice and a more impelling gaze. The more timid partner is more readily squashed.

Methods have been developed in the last few years to deal with this problem. They are generally referred to as assertion training or personal effectiveness therapy. These techniques may be given by a single therapist, but they are usually taught in a group situation (that is with therapists and a group of patients). Where assertion training is required in sex therapy it is given by both the therapist and co-therapist if there is one.

Assertion training, briefly, is based on advice and practice. The therapist will give direct advice on how to behave and then demonstrate what he had been suggesting. He might, for example, say to the patient: 'When you are talking with your wife you should adopt a patient but firm attitude; you must try to look her straight in the eye from time to time. Watch while I show you how to do this, then you have a try.'

This demonstration of behaviour is called modelling. If the wife is complaining of her husband's overbearing manner, the female therapist could take the role of the wife and maintain a more assertive attitude in a mock argument with the real husband. When the 'model' of assertion has been given, the wife may try it herself in the presence of the therapists. Similarly, if the husband complains that he finds it difficult to show affection, the male therapist can give a demonstration by putting his arm around the female therapist in an appropriately warm manner, together with other suitable expressions. Then this 'model' may be enacted by the man with his partner. Suggestions and discussion can always follow.

The accent is always kept on encouragement and reward and not upon criticism. Even where a patient clearly fails in some way, the therapist should only remark, 'I am sure you will do it better next time', or perhaps draw attention to some way in which the patient did succeed, however small.

Like other aspects of reorientation, assertive training can take place throughout the therapy and of course since it is sex therapy there will be most emphasis upon sexual assertiveness. If the therapist believes that the failure of assertion is serious, then the assertion training could take place at a different centre. The techniques of this type of training are excellently described in some of the books listed in the appendix.

A new life style
Because of their background many people with sexual problems have only developed a small part of their sexual potential. Sexual activity need not be thought of as an activity of the bedroom; it is an activity or a potential activity of almost any situation. Sexual activity is in part just one side of a total attitude towards sensuality. Many people today shut themselves off from the sensual pleasures of life, being too abstracted, preoccupied and worried to find time for the smell of flowers, the beauties of nature, the enjoyment of rest, of activity, of food, of their babies and numerous other pleasures. The therapist teaches people to enjoy their sensations to the full, not to be ashamed of feeling sexual attraction towards people in the street or colleagues at work, not to inhibit oneself from thinking about sexual fantasies. Therapy is attempting the liberation of all the senses.

The therapist may suggest relaxed ways of enjoying leisure time more: the couple might dine out together more often, go for walks with friends, seek out and visit erotic films or read erotic or pornographic books for pleasure. Pornography can also of course be used to enhance sexual excitement, and couples who have sexual problems sometimes do not spend long enough on sexual activity. They may have the idea that the whole sexual encounter should be over in under half an hour. Ultimately, this may be the best style for them, but there is no reason why they should not try a more leisurely approach. Instead of embarking on sexual activity straight after the washing-up, the therapist should advise a period of relaxation with music or some other distraction. Perhaps the couple should occasionally spend the whole day in bed; or have sex in a different room or out-of-doors. Patients may have been too shy to ask their partner for some fantasised variation of sexual activity. When such inhibitions are revealed the therapist could suggest the realisation of the fantasy. Many men would like their women to leave

169

on their stockings, their brassières, or other exciting underwear during the sexual act. Women might like a more or less vigorous intercourse, more foreplay, and often more sexual stimulation after the first orgasm. Patients should be encouraged to build a more extensive repertoire of sexual activity and to continue to do so.

But above all, they should be encouraged to achieve a new sensual awareness of all aspects of their life.

Fantasy

A vital part of reorientation is the encouragement and development of fantasy. The use of imagination can accomplish so much in other activities that it is unthinkable that fantasy should not be allowed to enhance the sexual life and creativity of everyone. For patients who have had their sexuality repressed during childhood it is common for the fantasy life to be repressed also. Sexual fantasies have become guilty or dirty thoughts. This attitude has to be relieved. The fantasy life of the patients will already have been explored but now the therapist can attempt to mould or shape its direction and content, making a direct suggestion that fantasies are useful and enjoyable. Patients who find it impossible to imagine arousing fantasies can be helped by the therapist with a list of possible fantasy material. Some patients will be asked to invent and write down sexual fantasies which can be discussed and improved by the partner and the therapist, or made into a game perhaps. For other patients, pornographic novels or pictures can be suggested from which they can draw ideas of their own. Books of actual fantasies have been published and are listed in the appendix. Fantasies from the early adolescent years may be revived. Erotic or 'blue' films may allow the patients to visualise fantasies more clearly. Like other activities, the ability to fantasise can improve with practice.

Some people do allow themselves a limited fantasy life but feel it is wrong while engaged in sexual behaviour with their partner. This can be discussed. Most therapists would say that to have sexual fantasies during the early part of foreplay and love-making was quite normal and desirable, and recommend the use of fantasies during the parts of treatment known as self-focusing and sensate and genital sensate focusing. The therapist might suggest that as sexual excitement mounts the person should surrender himself to sensation rather than to thought. However, there are no rules, and the partners should discuss this with the therapist.

4 Relaxation and muscle training

Relaxation training

Relaxation is a useful first technique for the patients to learn. It can be applied whenever the patients feel tense, before or during the homework tasks, and can also aid the patients in learning a new life style, helping them to take things at a leisurely pace and to calm down at work or during other non-sexual activities.

The patients should sit in a comfortable chair, remove their shoes and loosen any tight clothing. They are instructed to close their eyes and to try to become aware of their bodies. They should notice how they are breathing, and where the muscular tensions are in their bodies.

Deep breathing is the first part of relaxation to be learned. The patients are asked to breathe slowly and deeply, expanding the abdomen as they breathe in, then raising the rib cage to let more air in until the lungs are completely filled. While inhaling, a hand can be lightly placed on the lower abdomen and pushed upwards during inhalation. The patients are then instructed to hold their breath for a couple of seconds and then to breathe out slowly through the mouth, letting the abdomen fall and allowing the rib cage and stomach to relax, pushing the air out of the lungs further than usual. Breathing out can be accompanied by an audible sigh. They are asked to do this five times, without strain – being reassured that with practice it will become easier. This method of deep rhythmic breathing is recommended throughout the relaxation session.

After the breathing pattern is established the next sequence teaches patients the difference between muscular tension and relaxation. Various tension tasks are demonstrated by the therapist, who then goes through the exercises with the patients, checking that the instructions are being followed correctly. The patients are asked to do each tension task in turn during an inhalation, to hold the tension for ten seconds, then to relax as they exhale. The tension tasks in order of practice are: curling the toes hard and pressing the feet down; pressing the heels down and bending the feet up; tensing the thigh muscles, straightening the knees and making the legs stiff; tightening the buttocks; tensing the stomach as if to receive a punch; bending the elbows and tensing the muscles of the arms; clenching the jaws, frowning and screwing up the eyes really tight; tensing all the muscles together.

Once the tasks are completed, the patients are told to remain sitting with their eyes closed and to take a few slow, deep breaths, and to become aware of their physical well-being – a state of heaviness spreading through the body for about three minutes. Next they are instructed to imagine a white rose on a black background as clearly as possible, concentrating attention on it for one minute, breathing deeply throughout. Next the therapist might ask the patients to visualise other scenes, e.g. sitting at home relaxing. To end the session the therapist tells the patients to open their eyes after a count of three, and suggests that when their eyes are open they will feel relaxed but alert.

Patients are given a relaxation instruction sheet to remind them of the sequence of tasks and are asked to repeat their exercises daily; after a meal is a good time.

Sensate focusing instructions follow next; if patients seem anxious about them they can imagine them during a relaxation session.

The pubococcygeus (PC) muscle

The Kegel exercises are designed to help patients to strengthen and to obtain greater voluntary control over the PC muscle. This muscle is the support muscle for the genitals in both males and females. There is a correlation between good tone in the PC muscle and orgasmic intensity and these exercises are especially recommended for patients who have difficulty in obtaining an orgasm and for impotence problems.

The Kegel exercises were originally designed to help women by restoring vaginal muscle tone after childbirth. The partners of such women also benefited from this improved vaginal tone.

The PC exercises help increase awareness of feelings in the genital area, and to increase pleasure during foreplay and sexual intercourse. Blood circulation in the genital area is increased and this increases sexual responsiveness. The exercises can also be used to enable patients to increase control over their orgasms.

The PC muscle can be contracted by pretending to stop a flow of urine. If this proves difficult, patients are asked to practise while actually urinating, repeating it several times and passing only a teaspoon of urine at a time.

Patients can check their progress by watching the PC muscle movement in a hand mirror. Women are instructed to lie down, place a finger in the vagina and contract the PC muscle, feeling the contraction around the finger. Men are asked to contract their PC muscle, at the same time placing a finger on each side of the penis. In this way they can see the muscle move the penis a little and feel the strength of the contraction. Patients are recommended to practise ten contractions on six different occasions each day – perhaps each time they have a drink or answer the telephone. They are asked to make each contraction last three seconds. This is the usual programme for the first week. During the second week 'fluttering' is described. By this method the PC muscle is contracted and released as rapidly as possible until control is gradually gained. This 'fluttering' is recommended to be carried out six times a day, and the number of contractions increased from ten to twenty. After this initial training the PC exercises can be combined with deep breathing. Patients are instructed to tighten their PC muscle while inhaling and to release the whole pelvic region as they exhale.

Another way of describing this is to ask the patient to pull up the entire pelvic area as though trying to suck up water into the genitals. It is sometimes easier to explain this to women patients by asking them to imagine they have a tampon at the opening of the vagina and that they are using the PC muscles to suck the tampon into the vagina. They are then requested to push out the imaginary water and to bear down as if they were making a bowel movement, but with more emphasis on the genital than the anal area, and to exhale. Bearing down can be held for about three seconds. Patients are instructed to try inhaling, sucking in, bearing down and exhaling ten times, then to twitch (or 'flutter') ten times, and finally to continue with the ordinary paced contractions, gradually increasing them to fifty a session. These 'bearing down' or relaxation of the pelvic region exercises are reputed to increase vasocongestion in the vagina, and should result in an increase in lubrication.

In this way patients learn to focus on vaginal sensations and feelings, and while these are taking place patients can try to enjoy some sexual fantasies and attempt to picture their partner.

Sometimes patients report that their muscles seem to get tired easily, and they are advised not to worry about this, for fatigue is a normal response for exercising any new muscle group. A rest between sets is recommended for a few seconds. Once good control is established ten to twenty-five contractions a day should be sufficient.

5 The basic steps of treatment for all dysfunctions

Sensate focusing

Once reassurance has been achieved, reorientation aims understood, basic relaxation techniques learned, the therapist can then introduce the couple to the sequential stages of treatment.

The couple should first be told that they are being given a new opportunity to get together physically and to explore their feelings and sensations in an undemanding way, and that to begin with sexual intercourse is forbidden. They should be reminded that they will be discussed in detail so that new tasks and modifications on their progress during each visit to the therapist. The success and difficulties that they may have encountered with the tasks will be discussed in detail so that new tasks and modifications may be agreed upon. Intelligent patients will soon get the idea of treatment and make their own suggestions and modifications within the broad principles of treatment.

The first task is called sensate focusing. This consists of mutual stroking, caressing, touching and massaging. It is vital to have a warm and comfortable place for this; it does not matter in the least whether this is the bedroom or the lounge, or even the kitchen. It might be a good idea to have a warm bath first, especially if one of the partners is tense or unrelaxed. It is important to give a lot of time to this task: each session should last approximately half an hour to one hour. And it should be carried out with the light on.

It should be explained that the partners are to explore new sensations, the sensations of stroking each other slowly and firmly; of light touch, soft kneading, gentle scratching and deep massage. They will experience sensations that they may have forgotten or possibly never experienced. This early massage should exclude all those parts of the body that are closely associated with sexual behaviour and hence with a sense of previous failure. The couple are asked at this stage to avoid touching the breasts, the clitoris, the vagina, the penis and the testicles. Patients should be encouraged to abandon themselves to the sensations rather than to strive to experience them. They should be encouraged to think of their exercises as fun sessions and to enjoy themselves.

It must first be agreed which partner should begin to massage the other, and the therapist will probably choose the more confident partner, but it is not of vital importance for there will be a change of roles during each session. Usually one partner should be asked to be responsible for inviting the other to participate in the activity, and on the next occasion the roles are reversed. Shared initiative in this type of activity is important, even if it is hard for a shy partner, otherwise one partner will be associated with dominance.

The actual technique should be explained in some detail, as the therapist cannot depend on the couple's imagination. The therapist should explain that at any time one person is active and the other passive. Partner A can massage the back, the neck, the buttocks and the legs of partner B, while partner B lies face downwards. This can last about ten minutes, after which partner B takes the active role for a similar spell.

Some suggestions need to be made about massage technique, but there are also some excellent books available. Massage should be given with the fingers and the hands. A deep soothing but gentle kneading massage of the soft parts of the body would be one way of explaining it. One should use a slow but rhythmic stroke as a degree of regularity is restful. The partner receiving the massage should respond with suggestions as to what he or she likes best – a more gentle stroke, a slower or quicker rhythm. Some people prefer a deep massage using the fingers, while others like a massage performed mainly with the finger tips. Patients should be asked to keep their finger nails fairly short, but they should try some gentle scratching and pinching in addition. The passive partner should always try to respond, either verbally or in some other way which gives obvious feedback: groans, grunts and sighs can carry messages equally well. This feedback is an essential part of the sensate focusing, as each partner should learn quickly which techniques will give the most pleasure to the other partner. It is part of therapy to encourage both verbal and non-verbal responses, particularly since many people who come for treatment are quite inhibited in expressing themselves in any sexual encounter, and will enjoy learning this new abandon, which can be very exciting.

When A has given B massage on the back and vice versa, A lies down on the back, and B massages A's front. This area includes the neck, shoulders, chest, arms, hands, stomach, legs and feet. The face may also be massaged with gentle finger-tip movements tracing out the lips, the eyes, the forehead and the nose, and sensitive areas will be discovered around the lips particularly. Firmer massage of the temples and forehead is sometimes very reassuring. After roles have been reversed the couple should be asked to lie together and cuddle one another.

Many therapists suggest the use of some body oil which can make the massage smoother and more sensual. The only disadvantage of such oils is that they may cause a mess; however, some mess must be accepted if the sexual partnership is to flourish, and a large bath-towel will usually help.

The patients will ask how often they should do the sensate focusing. The couple should be encouraged to have a session several times a week, if possible, but should avoid times when they feel tension or fatigue. Otherwise, it is only necessary to go to bed a little earlier, or perhaps during the day if it is possible.

During these sessions complete nudity is advised, and only where one partner is very embarrassed should clothing be allowed. Serious embarrassment over nudity may require graded steps to overcome it, and perhaps very dim lighting could be arranged at first.

During the initial treatment session the therapist may have concluded that sensate focusing was going to cause too much anxiety on its own without further preparation. In order to find out whether this is so, the therapist may ask the partners to touch each other during the session. The couple remain clothed and they are asked to relax, then to hold hands and then to touch each other on the arm. When it is clear that such touching produces too much anxiety the therapist may teach the anxious partner to relax more deeply by means of deep muscular relaxation. The couple may then be advised to have a relaxation session with some self-administered desensitisation before each massage encounter. (Muscular relaxation and desensitisation are explained under 'Fundamentals', section 2.) Often the more relaxed partner can help the tense partner to relax by making soothing remarks and suggestions of relaxation.

Where such touching or massage is done with the therapist present, it provides an opportunity for advice and encouragement. Often the male partner is rather too heavy-handed for the woman to enjoy, and the therapist should advise him to be more gentle. On the other hand, the woman might hardly touch her partner, who would prefer a heavier pressure. Here again the therapist can offer advice.

After a surprisingly small amount of practice, most couples find sensate focusing sessions very pleasurable. Very little is demanded of them by way of sexual response, but at the same time they experience the giving and getting of sensual pleasure. This pleasure has often not been experienced for some time as the couple have been concentrating on the sexual act itself, which has become associated with both anxiety and failure. Many people are very pleased to report sexual excitement during sensate focusing, when they had begun to believe that they had lost sexual feelings forever.

When this activity is successful it regularly leads to a greater degree of affection as well, which reinforces the new hope of success. Some couples report that they also have more respect for their partners. Sensate focusing forms the foundation for nearly all the later sessions the couple are asked to do at home. Mutual sessions should always commence with sensate focusing, which helps to relax the couple, before they continue with more demanding tasks.

The couple are asked to keep a careful note of their experiences so that when they next come for treatment any difficulties may be discussed. This report often illuminates the problem for the therapist still further, and he or she can then evolve strategies to overcome the difficulties with the help of the couple – who should be joining in the game of treating themselves with enthusiasm. When the therapist considers that the couple have made progress and are enjoying sensate focusing, usually after two treatment sessions, the next stage of focusing can be described.

If the patients have had little or no experience of masturbating they are next asked to move on to 'self-focusing', which is carried out by the individual patient without the presence of the partner until the patient wishes to invite the partner to watch. If the therapist considers one partner has negative feelings towards the other then self-focusing with positive conditioning and fantasy shaping is recommended. Patients who are happy about self-masturbation can go straight on to the genital sensate focusing stage.

Self focusing

There are some people who have never masturbated – people who have, for one reason or another, never learned to stimulate themselves sexually, whether to orgasm or not. They may have believed masturbation to be unhealthy or dirty and so have avoided even thinking about it. They may simply have been ignorant of the possibilities. Others may have tried self-stimulation, but perhaps found it unsatisfactory and not continued.

The patient who has never masturbated should learn to do this alone before attempting masturbation with the partner. Then it will be possible to direct the partner and be more confident of coming to orgasm in this way.

Male self focusing The majority of men have learned to masturbate, but for those who have not, the therapist must tell them how to proceed. The patient should explore his genitalia in private and find out which parts give him sexual feelings to whatever degree. The touching should include the testes and all parts of the penis. He should also touch the underside of the penis along the urethra towards the basal parts adjacent to the anus. The frenulum and glans are generally the most sensitive parts and are best stimulated gently until some degree of sexual excitement is present. The therapist may have to tell the patient how to move the foreskin backwards and forwards. In order to reach a climax the man can excite himself in whatever way he finds most stimulating. The commonest method is to grasp the erect penis fairly firmly with the fingers and thumb and rub it up and down its length in imitation of the thrusting of the penis in the vagina. If the penis is either naturally or artificially lubricated the hand may slip up and down over the glans, which is for some men very stimulating. Or the forefinger and thumb may encircle the circumcoronal sulcus between the glans and the shaft, which is a very sensitive area, with part of the hand pressing upon the frenulum or area around it to good advantage. The degree of force and vigour is a matter for experiment.

While masturbating in the most exciting way he can find, he should be encouraged to use any fantasy he may find stimulating; then, when ejaculation is inevitable, he should switch his imagination to an image of his partner, attempting to picture her as vividly as possible while the orgasm takes place.

Female self focusing   It is much more common for the therapist to meet women who have not masturbated. Some women who have never done so may resist the idea strongly. The therapist may have to use a lot of tact and sympathetic persuasion to get them to try this hitherto unacceptable practice. Learning self-masturbation is particularly useful for women who have not experienced orgasm, or who do so only rarely. If they can teach themselves to obtain orgasms during self-masturbation they can then get them during mutual masturbation and later during intercourse.

The American sex therapists Lobitz and LoPiccolo recommend a course of therapy which was originated mainly for anorgasmic women. As many women who find difficulty with orgasm are not either familiar with their bodies or at ease with its functions, they begin with some sessions of physical self-examination.

The woman should set aside some time when she will not be observed or distracted, making sure she is as warm and relaxed as possible. The first step is to undress in front of a mirror and examine her body carefully from as many angles as possible. In this way she can familiarise herself with her appearance and imagine herself as seen by her partner. This is probably especially useful to women who do not like to undress in front of their partners and who make love in the dark. Next she should take a hand mirror and, remaining as relaxed as possible, should slowly examine her genitals in detail, carefully noting the important parts: the labia, the clitoris, the clitoral hood, the urethral opening, the vaginal entrance and the anus. Now she can take some lubricant – baby oil, massage oils, KY jelly, or one of the many other lubricants sold for sexual purposes – and apply some to the clitoral-urethral-vaginal area. She should now lie back into a comfortable position and begin to rub her genitals gently, finding out if there is any special area which seems best. She may prefer to begin by stimulating her nipples or thighs and go on to her genitals afterwards. When she has found some means of giving herself pleasure, however small, from genital stimulation, she must gently persist, all the while relaxing and trying to enjoy herself. The most rewarding areas will usually be found around the clitoris, the clitoral hood and the urethral opening. The stimulation can go from one area to another to increase the variety.

The actual movements used will vary from one woman to another. Most women use either the index or middle finger or both. The movement can be a to-and-fro motion along the shaft of the clitoris, including the clitoral hood and glans when ready. Or the sensations may be found to be better alongside the clitoris. Alternatively, she can rub the area using a circular movement with the pads of both the index and middle fingers. It will not be long before the woman discovers for herself the preferred method.

During the first attempt very little may be attained, and the woman need not be disappointed when no orgasm happens after half an hour. If she is tired or not enjoying herself much, she should stop and try again at another session. The progress of learning to masturbate to orgasm can be seen as a series of lessons as in learning anything else. The therapist may tell the woman to persist with several sessions per week if possible.

If the woman is having difficulty in obtaining pleasure she may require help in learning relaxation. The therapist may also suggest that she tries some sexual fantasies to assist her arousal and, if she is willing, some erotic stories or erotic pictures.

During her practice sessions the woman should also exercise her pubococcygeus muscle in a rhythmic manner, which will help condition the muscular responses of orgasm itself. These exercises are described under 'relaxation and muscle training'.

For some women who have difficulty in getting aroused the vibrator is the answer. The therapist can suggest which one to buy, and tell her where to buy it, or if she is too shy, tell her where one may be ordered by post. The vibrator should be used against the part which seems to suit the woman best, which she must find by trial and error. If the vibrator is too strong, she could vibrate it against a thigh or finger resting on the clitoral area. Some vibrators are built to be inserted into the vagina like a dildo – some women like this, others find it less satisfactory than clitoral stimulation. If the vibrator is producing sexual excitement, she should vary the vibration with some finger stimulation of the same area; the excitement will transfer, and the finger movements can be made to vibrate like the machine. Women who use the vibrator should be warned not to do so in the bath for safety reasons, though it is a good idea to practise manual stimulation either in the bath or in a state of relaxation afterwards.

The woman may find that she is distracted by guilty thoughts or other thoughts which interfere with the sexual enjoyment. It is best to face such thoughts and try to think clearly and slowly about them. If they persist, the thoughts should be carefully noted and discussed with the therapist.

Some women find they can reach a pitch of excitement but cannot go that little bit further and have the orgasm. They seem able to get right to the point, but then something stops them. Most therapists believe that this final inability is due to a lack of relaxation and an inability to abandon oneself to the orgasm. The therapist should try to discover the reason. If it is necessary to teach some relaxation, then do. Some women may be trying too hard. Advise them to desist for a while and then begin again, if necessary many times. Other women who are very inhibited may be able to achieve orgasm by deliberately enacting an ecstatic experience: by breathing heavily, by groaning, crying out, by jerking or arching movements of the body, or by rhythmic contractions of the pubococcygeus muscle. Women who allow themselves to 'let go' in this way may well find that the next time they reach a plateau of excitement they will 'tip over' into orgasm.

The emphasis throughout is on the idea that learning orgasm is a gradual process for some, that it requires patience, relaxation, technique, a willingness to experiment with vibrators, and a willingness to learn ecstatic abandon.

Including the partner – positive conditioning Couples who have had sexual difficulties for some time may reach a stage when the partner no longer arouses them sufficiently. This is usually because of an accumulation of negative feelings – anger, resentment and distress – which have accompanied their anxious sexual encounters. It is a case of negative conditioning. The stage of self focusing is a good time to change this. Both men and women have been encouraged to use fantasy during self and mutual masturbation. Lobitz and LoPiccolo have suggested a very useful method to enhance the arousal and attachment between a couple. Initially the patient is encouraged to fantasise during masturbation, using any thoughts or scenes which they find stimulating. At the moment when orgasm is just about to happen, patients should switch from the fantasies that have been used, to a fantasy of their partner. They should envisage the partner as clearly and vividly as possible. An association is thus established between sexual pleasure and the partner. The patient is instructed to continue masturbating to orgasm, but on subsequent occasions to switch the fantasy to the partner at successively earlier and earlier stages during the act. In this way a progressively longer time is spent fantasising the partner during sexual arousal and the association between them is strengthened. This method can be used by both women and men and can also be used during mutual genital sensate focusing.

When the man or woman has made some progress with self focusing, the next stage is to invite the partner to watch. The stage after this is to arrange sessions which are done with the partner actively participating in a programme of mutual genital sensate focusing.

Genital sensate focusing
Basically this follows the programme suggested by Masters and Johnson but most clinics have variations of their own. It is a matter for each clinic to decide whether the genital manipulations should begin as mutual genital sensate focusing or as individual self focusing; it will depend on the masturbatory experience of the patients.

Assuming then that a session is to be mutual, the environment and occasion must again be arranged with care. The session should begin with a period of sensate focusing and then proceed to the genital stage. The woman may begin by stimulating her partner's nipples and breasts. Some men are surprised and even embarrassed by this, but in fact fifty per cent of males respond sexually to such stimulation. It may take the form of stroking, tickling or gentle pinching, or the whole breast area may be firmly rubbed. The man then takes his time to stimulate the breasts and nipples of his partner who can explain to him just how she likes this done; it is best to be quite gentle at first and to increase the stimulation as the excitement is produced. Each partner could spend five to ten minutes on this task.

When the next step of genital stimulation is being explained, the therapist should make certain again that the anatomy of the parts is understood. Models and diagrams are useful here. Usually it is advisable to show the couple a model or diagram of the female genitalia in the resting stage and then to show the same genitalia in a state of excitement.

The stimulation may begin with either sex, the couple deciding together who is to be stimulated first, but it is given one at a time and not together. This arrangement allows each partner to concentrate fully upon pleasuring and learning to pleasure the partner, who is relieved of any need to perform themselves. They have no task but to enjoy the stimulation and give some directions as to how it is best done.

Let us suppose that the woman is to be stimulated first. The man adopts a position with his back against some support – the back of the bed perhaps. He spreads his legs with a slight bend at the knee and the woman sits between them, leaning back against his chest – her legs also apart. The man can then easily touch both her breasts and her genitals, and the woman may look down and watch the stimulation, guiding the partner's hands as she wishes. She can indicate where to start, the most desirable motion, the speed and the weight to be employed. The man might begin by stimulating her breasts, nipples, stomach and thighs. He should use gentle tickling, stroking or kneading movements in long, even, rhythmic strokes. When some excitement and relaxation has been achieved he can, with the aid of a lubricant, begin to explore the genital region. A gradual but persistent invasion would be one technique which could lead to his hands exploring the vaginal opening, the labial surrounding, the urethral and clitoral areas. Gentle stroking with a circular or to-and-fro motion can be advised at the outset, with not too much pressure. The clitoral glans is the most sensitive area and should not be attacked directly, but left to a stage of considerable excitement, and in the meantime only gently brushed or touched. The clitoral shaft and hood may be rhythmically rubbed and stroked. In order to get exactly the right technique, the woman should guide the man's hand from time to time and also tell him from moment to moment how to proceed and where to touch. The man's other hand is free to caress his partner wherever she may please.

The genital stimulation may be varied at will. The man should not be afraid to stop for rests, especially where the woman may have maintained a plateau of excitement for some time, or where the orgasm just will not quite come. At one of the genital sensate focusing sessions it is a definite therapeutic recommendation for the man to attempt to vary the level of excitement which she shows. He can bring her to near orgasm, then allow the excitement to subside, then bring her on again and so on. The technique is known as 'teasing'. In such a situation also, it is quite permissible for the woman to enact or role-play orgastic excitement, since in doing so the vital inhibition may be released. There may come a stage when it seems appropriate to stop before orgasm is reached; this the couple must decide for themselves. They should continue the genital sensate focusing of the woman for a minimum of half an hour unless the stimulation causes anxiety or exhaustion. The therapist must stress that the orgasm is not the goal of the session but is a valuable bonus where it happens.

Next it is the turn of the man. Here the woman sits supported in a similar position to the man. The man faces his partner, puts his legs on either side of her and lies back with his genital region between her legs and so very accessible to her.

The woman may begin by stroking the thighs and accessible parts of the buttocks and anal region. She can begin with gentle tickling, stroking, pinching or scratching. As some excitement shows, the gentle manipulations can be made more vigorous with kneading and massage. When ready, the woman can begin gently to explore the testicles. She should ask just what part he likes touched and how. Next the penile shaft may be held, squeezed, and gently masturbated. The glans should not be touched directly yet, but if the man has a foreskin, the invested glans may be held and rubbed through the foreskin. The junction between the glans and shaft may be rubbed at this stage, but again not too firmly. The other hand may either hold the penile shaft or the underside of the penile base. Massage may be given both in front of the junction with the scrotum and behind. The underside of the penis, which appears as one of the three columns which compose the organ, runs backwards and may be felt extending almost to the anus before disappearing. The whole course of this column on the underside is sensitive, especially near the frenulum and towards the penile base. The woman should feel all these regions and ask what is pleasurable.

For the man who has had difficulty in relaxing during sex this is a good time to attempt to relax. He can be asked to try and relax his muscles and surrender himself to the sensations which he is experiencing. For some men it is stimulating to be allowed to fantasise at this time – to fantasise anything sexually exciting. However, if orgasm approaches he should switch his fantasy to his partner, again in order that orgasmic pleasure may be associated with her image. Sexual fantasy can be used by either man or woman while subject to sensate focusing. During this stimulation, part of the time may be given over to fantasy and part to pure enjoyment. Each person has to decide what is best for them.

When the excitement becomes more intense the glans, the frenulum and the circumcoronal sulcus can be stimulated directly. Some men produce a clear lubricant themselves, and this may be used, but if it is not sufficient the woman can use a lubricant over the sensitive end parts. If the man has a foreskin, this will have to be retracted, and the act of drawing back the foreskin and then pulling it forward again needs some skill. It is best done by means of an encircling finger and thumb and is much easier with lubrication. The act of pulling the foreskin backward and forward is in itself a means of exciting the glans and can bring some men to orgasm.

Again it must be stressed that neither orgasm nor erection is the goal of genital sensate focusing. The only intention is to give pleasure. If the man has been able to relax and enjoy this sensate focusing, it is likely that some excitement and erection will have occurred. In this case the woman may proceed to masturbate the penis manually by rubbing up and down the shaft and glans. Her fingers and thumb can encircle the shaft gripping it as tightly as he wishes. The up-and-down motion may include the glans, as if it were slipping in and out of a vaginal entrance. The finger and thumb may also nestle in the circumcoronal sulcus, making to-and-fro movements up against the junction of the glans and shaft. Many men find this very exciting. As with self masturbation the vigour and speed of the masturbation can be varied. Throughout the genital contact, the man must keep the woman continually informed about the best technique and his state of excitement.

For the man who has experienced impotence, the woman can use a further technique. The genital sensate focusing, let us say, produces an erection; she can stimulate it for a while, then allow the erection to die away. She may then again stimulate the penis to erection and repeat the cycle a number of times. This alternation of erection and softness can reassure the man that even if his erection subsides during sexual play it can be revived – he should cease to worry about it.

This technique is allied to 'teasing' which was explained in the section in which the woman was the subject. Teasing may also be done to the man to find out what he likes. Rest pauses of ten to fifteen minutes can also be taken, during which time the couple can relax and cuddle a bit – no active sexual behaviour is required. Such rest pauses are good where anxiety is considerable. Persistent anxiety can be very tiring.

When the genital sensate focusing does not result in orgasm the partners must not be allowed to worry; the task has as its aim the giving, receiving and experiencing of relaxed sexual pleasure. If this can be learned and performance goals for the moment set aside, the pleasure will be greatly enhanced. Erections and orgasms will follow. They do not have to come in the first few sessions.

Oral sex
This is an important stage in the treatment of sexual dysfunction, both in females and males. It is particularly useful in the treatment of premature ejaculation, impotence and orgasmic dysfunction.

There are many people who find the idea of oral sex repugnant. Not only are they ignorant of it, but also shy to experiment with it. The therapist must open the subject with some care and move on from it if resistance is too great. The couple can be reassured on various points. To begin with it is a widespread practice for both sexes, and those who do it are in no way depraved or indeed different from other people. Oral sex has been practised from ancient times, when it was wisely recommended for potency problems. For people who are interested in the history of sexual conduct, Vatsayana, the author of the *Kama Sutra*, refers approvingly to the pleasure of oral sex. There have, however, been societies, usually Christian and puritan, which have forbidden oral congress. In some states in the U.S.A. it is still an offence. But today such extreme attitudes are less common and since Kinsey's report, oral sex has become a commoner sexual pastime.

There is also the idea that oral sex is dirty or unhygienic. This idea is usually only a rationalisation of a deeper repugnance, and it can be pointed out that the mouth itself is in this way similar to the genital regions – both areas normally have many bacteria and other organisms living in them but these organisms do no harm as the healthy body has very adequate defences.

If the couple has never had oral sex, it is a good idea to suggest that they wash first, since this will diminish the strong genital tastes which they may find unpleasant. When a couple is used to oral contact and enjoys it, washing immediately before is unnecessary, providing they wash regularly in any case. It makes no sense to wash away odours which are sexually exciting.

For women who have doubts about oral sex there is the added anxiety that the man may ejaculate into her mouth. Indeed some women dislike the taste of semen. For women who have this anxiety there are various ways of managing. She can ask her man to withdraw when orgasm is imminent, or judge herself when she should do so. If she removes the glans from her mouth the moment the ejaculation begins, very little need enter her mouth, and any that does can be wiped off on a tissue without hurting her partner's feelings. When oral sex has become more of a pleasure and the woman has got more used to the taste of semen she may want to try an ejaculate in her mouth and try swallowing it. It can do no harm, and semen is in fact nutritious.

Males who feel ashamed or diffident about ejaculating during fellatio can withdraw a bit early and allow the remainder of the stimulation to be manual.

Those patients who do find the taste and smell of the genital regions unpleasant should be encouraged to change. The therapist can explain to them that when a person is in a state of low sexual arousal these odours may seem unpleasant, whereas in a state of sexual excitement the odours become stimulating and attractive. For this reason the couple can be advised only to make an oral–genital approach when they are well aroused. Another method of desensitisation is to suggest that they should gently smell their hands after periods of genital sensate focusing. Strong repugnance can be overcome by a somewhat frivolous ploy. Jam, jelly or honey is spread on each genital area and each partner takes it in turns to lick it off. It is but a small step to continue licking. There are also some fruit-flavoured lotions now available.

Women sometimes have the fear that the penile glans will not fit into their mouths or that when it is inside it will press into their throat causing gagging. The answer to this is that most women are able to do it without difficulty and they should try it gently at first with the assured cooperation of their partner. Gagging is a possibility, but it is possible to learn to control it. After all, the woman is in a position to withdraw the penis the moment a deep penetration is threatened.

Having dealt with these anxieties, the actual techniques can be discussed. Let us say the man is going to give his partner oral sex, that is cunnilingus. The couple should begin with some sensate and genital focusing until there is a pleasant degree of sexual arousal. The woman may then be in several possible positions, but the following one is excellent. The woman should lie on her back with her legs open. She may half turn sideways until one thigh is able to rest on the bed forming a pillow for the man's shoulder and head. The man can descend upon her, opening up her labia to expose the clitoral region, which he can then reach with his mouth and tongue. He should then kiss and lick this part, gently licking the clitoral shaft, hood and glans, which may be much more pleasant and arousing for the woman who is very sensitive than the touch of the drier and rougher fingers and fingernails. If the woman is pleasurably excited the man may lie his head down upon the pillow of her lower thigh and increase the speed and pressure of the stimulation with both the tongue and the lips. Cunnilingus can result in orgasm if the woman can relax sufficiently to be carried away, but orgasm, it must be emphasised, is not the object of the preliminary practice. While the man is performing the woman does nothing; her part is to enjoy it.

Cunnilingus is excellent for the anorgasmic woman, as it is for women with vaginismus. It should follow the two stages of sensate focusing.

Next it is the turn of the woman to give oral sex to her partner. This is called fellatio. The man can lie on his back with the woman kneeling or sitting beside him; she can then lean over and take the penis into her mouth. As in the position described for cunnilingus, the man can turn half sideways, allowing the woman to rest her head if she wants. To start with it is better, however, for the woman to lean over and leave her head free to move, thus enhancing her sense of control.

The penis may be taken gently into the open mouth, though it is pleasant to allow it to slide between the moistened lips. It is usually possible for the woman to take in the whole glans. She can then lick and suck the end piece, pushing it gently in and out of her mouth while encircling it with her lips. The circumcoronal sulcus and frenulum may be given a lot of attention. The woman should be careful with her teeth, but they can be used when sexual excitement is intense to rub gently against the penis. The glans may be allowed as far in as the woman can tolerate; for women who are practised, it can enter to the back of the throat. In the early stages of learning fellation the advantage of having the head free is clear; if the penis enters too far the woman can quickly withdraw. When a man is sexually excited he may be tempted to give a thrust which can cause gagging.

While the penis is in the mouth the shaft may be held in one hand and this can give extra stimulation when the to-and-fro movements allow the glans to slide outside the mouth. The penis which is not entirely erect can also be supported in this way.

Again, during the early sessions orgasm should not be strained for.

A prior agreement should have been reached regarding ejaculation, which can be dealt with as described above.

While the man is receiving fellatio he is not required to do anything other than relax and enjoy himself. He can be allowed to fantasise if he wishes, or to watch the activity, which can be very stimulating for him.

After some practise there is no reason why the couple should not attempt mutual oral–sexual contact. It is possible to do this in the position called *soixante neuf*, 69 (which describes the position the bodies adopt). The man and woman lie side by side but head to tail. The man's head being near the female vulva and the woman's head near the male genitals. Each partner can lie on their side, but some adjustments are required to allow the man to gain entry. This usually means the woman turning slightly on to her back and opening her legs.

There is also a position in which one person lies on their back and the other supports themselves on hands and knees, again head to tail. The difficulty here is that the one lying down may have to strain upwards to maintain contact pressure, thereby straining the neck, and as excitement mounts the one on the top may find his or her arm muscles collapsing.

Success with oral sex can allow the final stage of treatment to proceed. However, the fact that oral sex is used as a step towards intercourse need not invalidate it as an exciting means of obtaining orgasm in its own right, and as a means of obtaining regular sexual pleasure after the cure has been effected.

Positions
The 'woman above' position The best known and most commonly used position for sexual intercourse is the so-called

'missionary' position with the man lying on top of the woman. It is a position which gives the woman little freedom, which may be the reason for its popularity in a masculine dominated society. Women have mixed feelings about this position, and it does have some disadvantages. The woman's natural desire to move her pelvis during intercourse becomes difficult and the weight of some men is difficult to bear.

These disadvantages are overcome in the 'woman above' position, which men can also find enjoyable. Masters and Johnson called it the 'female superior position', which sounds somewhat formal, and recommended it as the first position to be tried when the stage of intercourse has been reached. They also recommended it should follow on from genital sensate focusing, but the sequence described in this book works in the same way except that it may be used to follow either oral sex or genital sensate focusing if the couple have been steadfastly resistant to the idea of oral sex.

In this position the woman kneels or sits astride her partner who lies flat on his back. She is instructed to mount him in this kneeling position, with her knees placed approximately in line with his nipples and parallel to his trunk. Both partners are face to face. The woman may take up any position from being quite upright to one in which she leans forward to lie on top of the man's chest. Genital contact can be maintained throughout. Initially the couple are instructed to try practising getting into this position and are asked not to attempt insertion. The practice can often be combined with some genital stimulation. If an orgasm takes place for either partner when practising this position and enjoying mutual masturbation, this is a bonus, but an orgasm should not be the goal. The goal is to relax and enjoy experimenting with the sensations obtained by practising the 'woman above' position.

This position is intimate, as the couple may kiss easily. The woman can kiss the man's lips and throat, ears or eyelids. The man can kiss his partner and caress her breasts or stroke the nape of her neck or buttocks. The couple can both see each other's facial expressions and this can be exciting. The only real disadvantage is that sometimes the man's movements are restricted, though if the woman leans forward and raises her bottom slightly the man can thrust from below, especially if he places his feet flat on the bed with his knees in the air.

The man is told that he may lie still and nothing is required of him. He should try to relax and enjoy himself. Above all he should not worry about his erection. The woman will judge when the erection is sufficient and when ready guide it into her. Once introduced the penis may be allowed to rest while the man enjoys the sensations of being inside. If the erection is sufficient the woman may commence up-and-down movements of her torso, allowing the penis to slide in and out. She may begin with small movements, especially is the penis is not entirely erect, but the movements may increase in amplitude as the excitement mounts. The couple should again not be aiming at orgasm, only at pleasure.

The woman is asked to think of the penis as hers to play with, feel, explore and enjoy. She is told that this is a particularly good position for clitoral stimulation and if she cannot achieve enough stimulation she, or her partner, can try some manual stimulation of the clitoris. As the angle of attack is awkward for the man, he may find it easier to use his thumb. But it is easy for the woman to stimulate herself in this position, and the man can enjoy watching her. She is asked to begin by moving, then to keep still and enjoy feeling her partner's movements. Partners are asked initially to alternate movements in this way. Later they are asked to move together simultaneously. Some women have been able to have an orgasm for the first time in this position, either with or without manual clitoral stimulation.

The depth of penetration may be controlled by the woman. When she sits bolt upright it is at its deepest, and when she leans right forward it is at its shallowest. There are patients who do not like the idea of deep penetration, and to be able to control this is reassuring. But when the woman is controlling the in-and-out movement she must adopt a position which is most comfortable for this. She will find it more difficult when bolt upright and easiest when she leans forward a bit.

As with oral sex, the 'woman above' position may later be incorporated into the ordinary sex life of the couple.

The 'feel free' position In the 'feel free' position the woman lies on her back with legs bent at the hips and knees and the legs moderately parted. The man lies on his side with the axis of his body at right angles to the axis of the woman's body. He inserts his body under the woman's raised legs which may then fall over him, her heels against his back. His genital region is then against hers, and he may bend his knees and hips for comfort.

The 'feel free' position is an important position for the therapy of orgasmic dysfunction. In this position the woman is free to enjoy some manual stimulation, provided by herself or her partner, and training instructions for orgasmic dysfunction can be practised.

When the woman has stimulated herself or been stimulated to a point just prior to orgasm the man can insert his penis and thrust vigorously as she comes to orgasm. At later stages in the treatment the man makes his entry and the masturbation is stopped progressively earlier.

The other treatment method is just as easy to carry out in the 'feel free' position and consists initially of penile entry followed by manual stimulation to orgasm. Little by little, the manual stimulation is stopped earlier, at first just prior to orgasm and then earlier and earlier until such manual stimulation is unnecessary.

If the couple prefer to combine both penile insertion and manual stimulation of the clitoris this is an easy and convenient position in which to undertake both types of stimulation.

Lateral face-to-back position   This is an easy position to get into and is preferred by many patients. The woman lies on her side facing away from her partner, then the man lies on his side facing her from behind. When the partners are in position the woman can raise her upper thigh slightly, reach down between her legs, take the penile head and guide it into position for penetration, allowing the man to take over. The amount by which the legs are bent at the hip and the knee are matters which must be worked out on the spot. Penetration is quite good and there is a certain amount of clitoral stimulation, but if this is inadequate it is possible for either partner to stimulate the clitoris, though it is much easier for the woman. Both partners can move freely and this is a good position in which to practise PC muscle contractions.

Lateral face-to-face position   Both partners lie on their sides facing each other with their legs stretched out. Penetration is slight and the position is intimate for kissing and caressing. Clitoral stimulation is slight and manual stimulation of the clitoris is difficult in this position. This could be a comfortable position for a woman who has had vaginismus or dyspareunia; it is not particularly good for anorgasmic women. It is probably not terribly good for impotent patients as penetration may not be easy.

The upright rear-entry position This is really very similar to the 'lateral face-to-back' position except that instead of lying the couple kneel. In order to adopt this position the woman kneels on all fours with her bottom in the air, her legs slightly apart and her torso sloping downwards towards the bed – her head and shoulder can rest on the bed. The man kneels and can either adopt a completely upright position or can double over the woman's back, though this will diminish penetration. Penetration is best begun from the upright position in which the angles made by the penis and the vagina are well aligned. From this position the man can watch the penis sliding in and out which is exciting for him. It is a position allowing deep penetration and one which emphasises masculine control.

Clitoral stimulation by the penis and pubis of the man is not very good. Manual clitoral stimulation is possible either for the woman or the man, though not easy. The man is able to caress the body, buttocks, breasts and thighs of his partner easily. The position does not allow much face-to-face intimacy.

Many couples enjoy the deep penetration provided by this position. The 'upright rear-entry' position is often recommended for use during pregnancy as the woman bears no weight in this position and her uterus sinks into the body cavity away from the thrust of the penis. The depth of penetration can be controlled by the man not going in the whole way if his partner dislikes this.

When the therapist suggests this position some patients are shocked that they should adopt a position used by animals. They have the idea that it is 'dirty' or defiling. Such couples need to be reassured that this position is both normal and natural, and the fact that animals employ it may be regarded as a recommendation. For couples who seem ready one could also say that in sex therapy our animal attitudes are in some ways to be encouraged, especially in those who are inclined to be refined and fastidious. Such attitudes may be a positive barrier to sexual enjoyment which in any case has an earthy quality.

This position is probably best for male problems of impotence or low sexual drive. Men who are under treatment for premature ejaculation should only employ the position when some control has been learned in the 'woman above' position. Where the man with this problem begins on this position he can employ the squeeze technique on himself and of course may control his thrusting and thus his stimulation. The position is not recommended for the early stages of treatment for female anorgasmia or vaginismus. For couples who are beginning to experiment for the pleasure alone, these positions are very worthwhile.

The position can be modified into one in which the man lies on top of his partner who is lying face downwards, and enters her from behind, though the penile/vaginal alignment will be improved if she put a pillow or pillows underneath her to raise the bottom.

Chair positions Many couples are very conventional when it comes to sexual intercourse. The limits of sexual behaviour are narrow and only a few positions are accepted as normal. This is an attitude the therapist tries to undermine. Therapy, and sex itself, should become a fun activity and an adventure. For this reason the therapist may recommend chair positions for those who are reasonably agile. These positions are for the later stages of treatment but can be sexually exciting. There are two basic conjunctions.

The woman facing the man The man sits upright on an armless chair, the woman sitting astride facing him, and lowering herself upon his penis when it is ready. The chair should be low enough for the woman to rest her feet on the floor for she is responsible for the thrusting movements. In the downstroke her weight is borne by the man's thighs. The man's movements are limited but he can clasp her buttocks and help raise her up and down. He could otherwise caress her body and breasts.

This is a very loving position as the couple can kiss and talk together, face to face. The position can be a very gentle position with penetration about two thirds of the way. If the woman leans back slightly the penetration can be deeper.

Clitoral contact is moderate in this chair position but it is possible for the woman to stimulate herself as well.

The position can be used in all disorders during the later part of treatment. It is especially good for impotence and vaginismus. The unusual and adventurous feelings which this position may bring about are most excellent in those couples who have a low drive associated with a limited range of sexual behaviour.

The woman facing away This can be seen as another variant of the rear-entry position. The man sits on the chair as before. The woman presents her bottom towards him and sits down upon his erect penis, guiding it into her with her hands between her slightly parted legs. She is thus sitting upon his knee, her back against his chest. The position is less intimate than the facing position and penetration is only about half-way though this can be increased if she leans forward.

Clitoral stimulation is rather poor though manual stimulation by either the man or the woman is easy. The man is well placed to caress her body and breasts. The woman can reach down and stimulate the testes, the entering penis and the area around the penile base on the underside. The woman has to perform the up-and-down movements which, as in the facing chair position, can be tiring if continued too long.

This second chair position has the same advantages as the first though it is less intimate, but the clitoral contact is poorer and the penetration not so deep. Despite this, it should be tried as some couples find it pleasurable and manual clitoral stimulation is easy.

The 'man above' position This is usually one of the last positions which a therapist will recommend to patients. Those who have failed to enjoy sex or who have failed in performance, have failed in this position. The position is associated with past failures. The woman who has vaginismus thinks of this position as the position in which she is at her most helpless. The majority of men who have experienced impotence or delayed ejaculation have experienced these failures in this position. Women with anorgasmia are unable to achieve any manual stimulation in this position. It is thus of no great value to them.

To women who feel the new currents of liberation within society, the position mirrors the passive and helpless attitudes which men have expected them to adopt. It is the position in which the man 'takes' the woman and does his pleasure upon her. For the woman who wants to experience some control over the sexual act, new positions are required. This position, known as the 'missionary position', also has the disadvantage that many people are bored with it, having practised it too often.

However, despite the many disadvantages the position is at least intimate. The couple can readily kiss and talk, bite or nibble.

The ear is very accessible for those who enjoy licking, kissing, nibbling or blowing in this region. There is intimate contact along the whole of the torso, extending downward to the stimulating contact between the male pubis and the female clitoral regions. The rubbing between the female and the male in this position may be sufficient clitoral stimulation for some women.

Penetration is about half-way, though this is not a serious disadvantage. If the man raises his torso and hips a little he may watch his insertion and thrusting movements if he wants. The man who is very heavy, and inconsiderate as well, may prove something of a burden during prolonged intercourse. Some of this pressure can be relieved by the man raising himself slightly upon his elbows and knees.

There are some variations which mainly concern the woman's legs.

(*i*) *With the woman's legs straight* In this position the man can either lie between her legs or he can have his knees resting outside hers. Clitoral stimulation is not so satisfactory but is still adequate. The depth of penetration is reduced. In all these positions it is sometimes better with the woman's buttocks resting on one or two pillows.

(*ii*) *The woman's knees are bent at about a right-angle* Clitoral stimulation is good. This is a somewhat easier position than with the legs straight.

(*iii*) *The woman's knees are drawn up* Here the penetration is at its deepest and this is the position in which weight is most readily borne. Clitoral stimulation is excellent by direct contact. The position is said to be good for securing pregnancy.

(*iv*) *The woman's knees are drawn right up and her feet are in the air or crossed over his back* This position is somewhat more acrobatic but has the same advantages as the third variant.

Other positions There are numerous other positions which can be adopted in sexual intercourse but none is especially useful in therapy. When the couple have reached the point of trying other positions for pleasure, therapy is really at an end. Patients will, of course, ask about other positions and there is no reason why they should not be tried if the couple is interested.

Some couples mention that they have seen pictures of couples having intercourse standing and would like to try this themselves, but this is a difficult position for insertion and also difficult if the man is taller than the woman – she can stand on her toes or wear platform soles but it is not usually much of a treat.

Other positions involve the woman lying on her back with her legs falling over the edge of the bed. The man kneels upright on the floor between her legs and is able to enter readily – penetration is good. It is a position of masculine control but finger stimulation of the clitoris is easy for the woman. The main difficulty with this position is that most beds are too high.

There is also the position in which the woman lies with her legs open on a table or desk, with her bottom drawn right to the edge of the table. The man approaches standing and enters. The woman's legs may then wrap themselves about his back. Again, there are often height difficulties; nevertheless both are adventurous and pleasant.

The 'woman above' position has a variant in which the woman faces the man's feet, not his head. The position can be uncomfortable for men and does not offer the same advantages as the facing position.

Couples who wish to experiment further should buy one of the many available manuals of positions, some of which are excellently illustrated with commentaries on the merits and demerits of each position.

6 Additional treatment for specific dysfunctions

Vaginismus

Before sensate focusing is suggested to the woman suffering from vaginismus, she is taught deep relaxation and asked to go through a desensitisation procedure involving graded dilators. This graded dilator method was first introduced by Haslam in 1965. At the start she is asked to relax in the bedroom and when she is ready she or her husband can insert the smallest, well-lubricated dilator into her vagina. The dilators come in a set, of which the lesser members are thin and rod-like, but becoming increasingly thicker and more penile.

Masters and Johnson included partner participation in the graded dilator insertion tasks. The female patient asks her partner to insert the smallest dilator in her vagina and leaves it in her vagina for a couple of hours before removing it. As the size increases she becomes reassured that she will be able to transfer this tolerance to the penis. Throughout, it is agreed that the woman has full control over the pace and details of treatment. She ends with the largest dilator inside her for several hours while she lies comfortably relaxed on the bed. She repeats this a second night.

The next stage is to ask her to try some self-focusing of the clitoris when alone. Next to try sensate focusing and genital sensate focusing with her partner, continuing with some oral sex. At each of these stages the largest dilator should be inserted at the end of the session.

Finally the 'woman above' position is reached. The dilator can be used first and then the woman can remove the dilator and try penetration of the penis. She has full responsibility for guiding the penis into her, at her own pace. She should not be pressurised by her partner. She controls the speed and depth of penetration. Because of her 'above' position she can at any moment retreat – she is in no way constrained – which is a great reassurance for her. For this reason the 'woman above' position is decidedly the best coital position for vaginismus, dyspareunia and for an unconsummated marriage. It reduces the woman's anxiety and when sexual intercourse is achieved in the 'woman above' position without difficulty, the couple can progress to other positions.

This graded dilation method produces good results and is more effective and humane than the surgical method employed in the past when the woman is anaesthetised and wakes to find the largest dilator inserted in her vagina. This traumatic method is often thought to produce an intensification of the trouble. Graded dilation can be combined with initial imaginal systematic desensitisation when the patient imagines the procedure first and later tries it out at home.

Helen Kaplan suggested that the method used should be individually tailored for each case: instead of dilators, a tampon or the fingers of the wife or husband can initially be used, combined with relaxation.

Most therapists report a high success rate for the graded dilator approach which may or may not be preceded by a course of desensitisation in the imagination. Using graded dilators combined with their standard method Masters and Johnson claim a hundred per cent success rate. The dilation procedure should be combined with whatever supporting treatment method the patient needs.

Orgasmic dysfunction
The programme for orgasmic dysfunction differs somewhat from the basic treatment. Many anorgasmic women are conditioned in the passive and servile female role of the recent past. Treatment should aim to liberate them into a new sexual attitude. Hitherto they may have been passive in sex; now they should attempt some initiative and find out what pleases them, which manipulations are the most exciting, and be able to ask for and receive these attentions. Some self focusing will help women to identify the pleasure points of their bodies.

The woman with orgasmic dysfunction will have to learn masturbation if she does not do it already. She must take some responsibility for her experience. She can no longer just 'lie back' and hope it will be all right. Many successful clinical approaches include 'attitude restructuring' and learning masturbation techniques. The Lobitz and LoPiccolo masturbation programme is especially effective for stages and techniques of masturbation and the success rate for the primary anorgasmic woman is a hundred per cent. This includes 'fantasy shaping' and the use of vibrators if necessary. The partner is gradually included in the programme and the woman can ask him to watch her masturbate when she is ready for this step. For women who are very anxious, systematic desensitisation in the imagination can be used before she goes home to practise a new step *in vivo*.

The therapist must teach the woman these things during discussion and recommend books for her to read. Her ability to fantasise should be developed and she should be encouraged to use fantasy during genital sensate focusing. Nancy Friday's books *My Secret Garden* and *Forbidden Flowers* will accustom her to the immense range and variety of female fantasy. The therapist should also suggest some erotic or 'blue' films. Lobitz and LoPiccolo reported that three of their primary anorgasmic women had their first orgasisms after they had happened to see a 'blue' film at their local cinema.

Occasionally one meets women who are unable to obtain orgasm during either genital or self focusing. One method which can be tried consists of exaggerating or acting out the desired elements. The woman is instructed to get as near to orgasm as possible then to pant, gasp, scream, contract the PC muscle convulsively and to attempt to lose control. The method may work by encouraging responses which are waiting to be emitted but for some reason are inhibited. Often for the first time these women are letting themselves go after years of self-control.

Training the PC muscle in 'fluttering' is reputed to be a helpful practice for most patients. Deep relaxation is also useful when patients complain that they are over-tense or anxious.

During the early stages of treatment, then, the therapist hopes that the patient will learn to achieve orgasm through clitoral and genital self-stimulation. She is then in the same position as a woman who complains that she can achieve orgasm in masturbation but not during intercourse. Orgasms should now be obtained during genital sensate focusing, producing a 'partner-induced orgasm'. This is part of the Masters and Johnson programme and was introduced several decades ago by Helena Wright. The orgasm can be induced manually or with a vibrator. Two methods may now be used in order to achieve orgasm during intercourse.

Method I For the first few occasions the orgasm, clitorally stimulated, may be allowed to begin before insertion. Next the insertion is timed to take place a little earlier. Several positions are suitable for this method and include the 'woman above' position, the 'lateral' positions and the 'feel free' position. Some vigorous thrusting will be taking place when orgasm occurs. Hopefully the thrusting will produce the orgasm. By stopping clitoral stimulation and replacing it with penile insertion and thrusting at successively earlier points, the woman can allow the orgasm to become dependent on vaginal sensations alone.

Method II In this method the penis is inserted early on. Clitoral stimulation takes place either with the finger or with a vibrator. Either the man or the woman may provide the clitoral stimulation. In the early sessions the clitoral stimulation continues to orgasm. Next the stimulation stops just short of orgasm which is allowed to occur by penile thrusting alone. The process continues by halting the clitoral stimulation earlier and earlier. On any occasion that the clitoral stimulation ceases too early and no subsequent orgasm results, clitoral stimulation may be started again, only to stop when penile/vaginal orgasm seems again to be a possibility. With some practice orgasm can be attained by penile/vaginal stimulation alone. Of course clitoral stimulation during intercourse may be continued as a means of obtaining sexual pleasure in its own right. The best positions for this method are the 'woman above', 'rear entry', 'lateral', 'feel free' and perhaps 'chair' positions.

Most therapists report better results for women with primary orgasmic dysfunction than for those with secondary anorgasmia. Masters and Johnson reported an eighty-three per cent success rate for primary anorgasmia compared with a seventy-seven per cent success rate for secondary anorgasmia. Lobitz and LoPiccolo confirmed this difference. In their 'masturbation and stimulation therapy approach' all their primary anorgasmic women improved, but only one third of their secondary anorgasmic women responded. Many of these latter women, however, had a poor marital relationship and this might explain this result.

Because of the great variety of treatment approaches the therapist may be in some doubt as to which approach to employ in a given patient. The anxiety relief method of relaxation and systematic desensitisation in imagination in the clinic, before practising the exercises *in vivo* at home, would be recommended for the anxious patient.

Several therapists have successfully used systematic desensitisation during treatment. A Dutch study by Walter Everard has shown that this method is far more effective if the woman is accompanied by her partner during the treatment sessions and they both sit and relax and imagine carrying out the exercise at home. Masters and Johnson found the presence of the partner to be an essential part of their treatment method, both during treatment sessions and during all the *in vivo* stages of their method of desensitisation.

One Irish study by Ethna O'Gorman shows that systematic desensitisation can be given in 'group' form: all the women share the same hierarchy of sex scenes about which they feel anxious, while their partners sit in a separate group and discuss problems.

In vivo methods of desensitisation are becoming increasingly popular, although Everard found no difference between Masters and Johnson therapy and systematic desensitisation in the treatment of orgasmic dysfunction. In the States Betty Dodson and others use group *in vivo* methods to teach sexual liberation to women who attend the group without their partners. In these groups they learn to compare and appreciate their genitals: this achieved, they proceed to group masturbation training. Such group methods should be allowed to spread to Europe.

Systematic desensitisation can be enhanced by the use of films or video-tapes depicting scenes of sexual foreplay and intercourse. American therapists have found that such material helped to improve patients' relationships with their partners.

The 'stimulation therapy' approach would be appropriate for the woman with a low sex drive. When slides or films are shown a 'modelling' effect takes place in which the woman sees another woman doing and enjoying a task she is afraid of. She becomes desensitised, reassured and can then enjoy the filmed activity and allow herself to become stimulated.

Studies measuring the effect of 'stimulation therapy' are few. Lobitz and LoPiccolo combined the method with other methods and reported good results. One American-controlled study by Robinson with no therapist contact showed that women who viewed video-tapes of sexual activity increased their own sexual activity and changed their previously unfavourable attitudes towards specific activities shown in the video-tapes.

One British study by Patricia Gillan has shown that erotic pictures, stories and tapes of the 'sound of sex' presented to women patients during treatment helped them to enjoy sex more and develop a better sexual relationship with their partners, compared with a control group which received relaxation training and 'pseudo therapy' or talked only about non-sexual topics. Most of these women only became 'orgasmic' after follow-up when they were given additional modified Masters and Johnson treatment combined with the Lobitz and LoPiccolo masturbation programme.

There is increasing evidence that erotic stimuli can be used in treatment to help disinhibit patients, reduce their anxiety and change their attitudes.

Impotence

The choice of treatment for impotence should be based on the symptoms reported by the patient. Is he reporting high anxiety over his sexual interactions or is he complaining of low sex drive when nothing seems to excite him? He could be suffering from a combination of these two problems. If the man is anxious treatment should be centred around 'anxiety relief' methods. If his sex drive is low, treatment can be based on increasing his sex drive by stimulating his senses. This latter form of treatment is 'stimulation therapy' and may be combined with anxiety relief methods in the treatment of the man who is both anxious and suffering from a low sex drive. The methods to be described are used to complement the basic treatment for sexual dysfunction, whatever type of impotence the man is suffering from.

One anxiety relief method for treating impotence could be called a 'distractor technique'. This consists of diverting the man's attention away from the erection to concentrate on the pleasure which can be obtained from being touched genitally. This distraction is obtained not by any trick but merely by suggesting that the man concentrates his attention elsewhere. It can be employed while the stop-start or teasing technique is used. In this the erection is produced by the partner's manual stimulation; after a good erection has been obtained the stimulation should cease – the erection will subside – a relaxed rest pause ensues – the stimulation is again taken up – the erection returns, and so on, over a few cycles. By this means the man may see that to lose the erection is no great disaster as it can be made to return. Another way of focusing attention away from the penis is to get the man to use his fingers, mouth, lips or tongue to pleasure his partner. His partner's pleasure can be a 'turn on' for him. If his attention is upon giving and receiving pleasure in areas away from the penis he will forget it for a while.

Genital stimulation may also be given to a man under circumstances that make intercourse impossible, and when his attention is partially distracted. Jack Annon has suggested some ideas: the woman can stimulate her partner's penis in the back of a car while riding home; under a rug on the beach; at a concert, film or play. The man knows that nothing is expected of him, that it is just a game. If he is able to erect under these circumstances it will help him to see that he is quite capable of erections when his performance anxiety is removed and his attention elsewhere. At first sight such suggestions may seem a little bizarre, especially to the conventional and well behaved, but they will also illustrate the idea that sex should not be confined to special times and places.

Relaxation is another well known 'distractor technique'. The man is asked to relax deeply during genital sensate focusing and other sexual tasks. He should concentrate on deep breathing and muscular relaxation rather than focusing attention on the erection.

Background noise can be used as a 'distractor technique' – 'white noise', or a constant drone of monotonous sound, like waves on the seashore, an electric fan, or a constant hum. There is an American record called 'Environments' which has ocean waves on one side and birds singing on the other. Other music can be used to stimulate couples when they are engaged in sexual pleasuring; the man with low sex drive might be aroused by accompanying music such as Indian evening ragas, African drumming, reggae, madrigals.

Fantasies may be used for both anxiety relief and stimulation. The man can think of any image he chooses and concentrate on this during the time he is being genitally touched. The therapist should give him permission to enjoy any fantasy he wishes, and if necessary reassure and desensitise him to any feelings of guilt or shame he may feel towards the fantasy. If the couple prefer, the partner could read some erotic stories or letters from magazines. If the man is more aroused by visual stimuli he could look at some pictures that he finds sexually arousing. Some of these erotic stimuli should help to increase arousal and each man should be encouraged to explore the full range of his erotic preferences.

The 'woman above' position is an important step for the treatment of impotence associated with anxiety and/or low sex drive. It should only be attempted when oral sex and genital sensate focusing have led to good erections. Now the woman can adopt the correct position and give the man some masturbatory stimulation which can last a considerable time. She may use the 'teasing technique' of allowing the erection to rise and fall. About two sessions should be given over to masturbation techniques before a session of insertion. The man must experience both as much reassurance and as much sexual excitement as possible in this position before insertion. Ejaculation is allowed to take place should it occur, but again it is not the prime aim.

There is a prior agreement that the woman will judge the moment for insertion. When she deems the man ready she will guide the penis into position and lower herself upon it, helping it inside. It is not necessary for the penis to be completely erect for insertion to be possible. Jack Annon recommends the use of the 'stuffing method', suggesting that the penis can be stuffed into the vagina when the man is only slightly aroused. This relieves anxiety associated with vaginal entry. Once inside movements may allow the erection to increase. The man should be encouraged to ignore the state of his erection and think only of his sensations. Sometimes when the erection is poor it is better for the couple to stay still and ensure that it remains inside while relaxing together; the erection will return, provided the man can avoid worry and relax or think of some arousing fantasies. In any case, where the sequence of genital sensate focusing and oral sex has been successful, erectile failure will not be very likely.

If after some thrusting with a reasonable erection the man finds that it begins to fail, the penis can be allowed to slip out, manual or oral stimulation can be substituted, and when the erection returns the penis can again be inserted.

Even where insertion and thrusting succeed the therapist must request patients not to strive towards orgasm and performance. The purpose of the initial penetration is to form the habit of a pleasurable erection free from pressure and anxiety. When this is attained orgasm will follow naturally.

The 'quiet vagina' technique can be recommended during the 'woman above' position stage. The couple remain still for twenty to thirty minutes without movement – other than that needed to maintain erection. It is a useful intermediary step between insertion and intercourse. The usual demands of performance and thrusting are eliminated and therefore there is no pressure on the man; he need only enjoy himself.

Other positions are recommended and have been described in the basic treatment. It should be stressed that the 'man above' position should usually be the last recommended position, because this is so often associated with high anxiety and bad habits.

Results of treatment for impotence have been promising. For men with secondary impotence Masters and Johnson had a seventy-three per cent success rate. With primary impotence the comparable rate was only fifty-nine per cent.

Success for 'anxiety relief' methods of treating impotence is high. The traditional method of systematic desensitisation in the imagination followed by *in vivo* practice, as developed by Wolpe and Lazarus, obtained an eighty per cent success rate. Friedman used a form of systematic desensitisation in which the relaxation was produced by intravenous drugs and seventy-three per cent of his patients improved.

The use of stimulation therapy is relatively new. Lobitz and LoPiccolo's technique of fantasy shaping and positive conditioning worked for four out of six impotent men. Patricia Gillan used stimulation therapy without including the Masters and Johnson approach and she found that sixty-six per cent of her impotent patients improved. Hartman and Fithian, two Californian sex therapists, showed couples films of sexual intercourse and used what they call a 'bio-psycho-social approach' backed by some of the Masters and Johnson techniques and they reported a comparable success rate to that of Masters and Johnson.

All these methods should be carefully studied. It is important to segregate patients with low sex drive and those with anxiety to provide more effective and speedy therapy.

Premature ejaculation

There are several ways of treating premature ejaculation. Many therapists now use the 'squeeze technique'. This is usually applied during genital sensate focusing. Immediately the man gets a fifty per cent erection his partner should 'squeeze' his penis by firmly placing her thumb on his frenulum and her first two fingers either side of the coronal sulcus: If the woman feels her right hand is not strong enough she can use both hands to supplement the grip. She should be reassured that she will not injure the penis when she applies 'the squeeze'. She can be shown a diagram or rubber model of the penis and practise the squeeze on the model in the presence of the therapist. If there is no available partner attending for treatment the man can be taught to squeeze himself.

After the penis has been firmly squeezed for a few seconds, the man loses his desire to ejaculate and experiences a partial loss of erection. After fifteen to thirty seconds his partner is asked to stimulate his penis again and when it is erect to apply the 'squeeze'. If the man feels he is anywhere near the stage of 'ejaculatory inevitability', he should indicate to his partner that she should squeeze him immediately. He can learn to judge his excitement and signal to his partner when he wishes the 'squeeze' to be applied. His partner can learn to judge for herself when he is becoming excited and apply the squeeze when she judges it to be necessary without being asked to do so.

It is possible for partners to enjoy fifteen to twenty minutes of sex play without ejaculation by using this technique during genital sensate focusing. At the end of a session partners are allowed to masturbate to a climax, with self-induced manual stimulation.

The next stage is to vary the stimulation technique by the partner stimulating the penis orally, using the fingers and thumb to apply the squeeze as before. This is a good intermediary step between manual and vaginal stimulation.

The 'woman above' position is recommended next while using the 'squeeze technique' as follows. Initially the partners are advised to try stimulating the penis without any insertion and to use the 'squeeze technique'. After this has been tried the penis may be inserted. Both partners are instructed to keep still so as to avoid overstimulating the penis.

The squeeze can be applied when necessary by the woman raising herself, slowly and gently, applying the squeeze and then remounting. This can be repeated several times. This stage is often tricky as ejaculation can occur when the woman raises herself. The secret is good practice and good communication.

The man is allowed to thrust a little during the next stage, as he will have learned some control of sexual excitement. If he feels he is going to lose control at any time he should ask for the squeeze technique to be applied. The woman is told to be prepared at any time to pull out gently and squeeze hard. If the woman feels her partner is becoming too aroused she can apply the squeeze without awaiting any verbal signal.

The couple can then go on practising the squeeze in the woman above position and usually achieve full intercourse and ejaculation after one month's practice. Each time they have sexual intercourse they are asked to practise the squeeze at least two or three times before penetration. After treatment is finished they are advised to employ the squeeze at least once a week for the six months which follow treatment. Masters and Johnson recommend that when the woman is menstruating is a good time to have a practice session. The couple should then have a fifteen to twenty minute session devoted specifically to manual stimulation of the penis, applying the squeeze several times.

The squeeze can be learned by the man who has no regular

partner, and when sexual intercourse becomes possible, the upright rear entry position is the best. This position leaves the hands free to manipulate the penis. The squeeze can be applied either before entry or in the middle of intercourse by a quick withdrawal, squeeze and reinsertion.

Another technique used in the treatment of premature ejaculation is based on the Semans' 'stop and start method' and recommended by Helen Kaplan. The woman stops the stimulation of her partner's penis when he signals her to do so. Kaplan advises the man to focus his attention on the erotic sensations he feels when his penis is stimulated and instructs his partner to stop stimulating him when he feels he is approaching ejaculation. He then notices and learns that the sensation disappears in a few seconds. When his excitement has subsided, the stimulation may recommence. He is allowed to ejaculate after four periods of stimulation. By this time he has learned to recognise the intense sensation that occurs just prior to ejaculation and he has also learned to communicate to his partner to stop stimulating him at that point. After some control has been learned the procedure can be repeated, increasing the intensity of sensation by lubricating the penis to approximate vaginal sensation. This method is practised in three to six sessions. The patient usually reports spontaneously that he feels he has increased his ejaculatory control. At the end of each session the woman should enjoy a manual or oral climax by clitoral stimulation.

The 'woman above' position is then recommended. It is a good position as it allows the woman to shove while the man controls her pelvic thrusting with his hands. Again the 'stop-start' method is employed. During a 'stop' the woman keeps still and the penis remains motionless in the vagina. If the Kaplan method is used coital orgasm is allowed after four practice sessions.

Jack Annon suggests yet a third method. In this the man ejaculates as quickly as normal. He then rests a while and resumes sexual play. Many men with premature ejaculation have a short refractory phase and can resume sexual play quickly with a good erection. The second ejaculation will be found to be somewhat delayed compared with the first. This delay can allow normal intercourse to take place.

There is no controlled trial to test the superiority of one technique over the other. Masters and Johnson reported a ninety-seven per cent success rate (with a five-year follow-up) for the squeeze technique. Kaplan prefers the stop-start technique and also reports a high success rate. It is probable that all three methods are effective as premature ejaculation is usually a fairly easy dysfunction to treat. The Annon method should only be used, however, where it is quickly found that a good erection returns early after a first ejaculation. It is a method only for males with a high sex drive.

Delayed ejaculation

Delayed ejaculation is a difficult condition to treat as the man has often arrived at this point after many years of increasing stimulation. He is like an addict who requires greater and greater stimulation. He is often a man who views sex in a rather mechanical and unemotional manner. The orgasm is like an unpalatable concession. Such men need to be taught to 'give in' to their bodies, not to dominate them. Relaxation sessions should be given in which the man surrenders to sensation, and when he has learned this, he can likewise surrender to sensation during genital sensate focusing. As in the basic treatment orgasm is not the early goal and must be firmly avoided. Relaxation and surrender must be learned first. Eventually the intensity of stimulation may be built up, the man relaxing all the while and allowing his body to take control. Orgasm must be forgotten. It will follow in good time. The stage of genital sensate focusing may be a long stage in those conditions. Careful stimulation techniques must be used. A lubricant is essential. The man must abstain from self masturbation between the sessions, and enough time between sessions must be given to allow sexual excitement to be considerable at each session. Of course, when a session does not lead to orgasm the next session may follow very soon afterwards. Stimulation therapy in the form of erotic pictures or stories is usually helpful at this early stage of treatment.

The manner of penile stimulation is important. On each occasion there should be lengthy periods of quite gentle stimulation before vigorous masturbation, either of the shaft or the glans, is given. The latter type of stimulation produces a tense response if given too early or continued unremittingly. It is a type of stimulation which has been associated in the past with frenzied striving. It is better to leave it until late in the course of treatment, when the man has learned to surrender his dominant desire for control.

A vibrator may be used during the stage of genital sensate focusing as a new kind of stimulation may hasten ejaculation. Its use should be quickly abandoned unless quite successful.

When orgasm is being obtained rather more easily the couple may go on to intercourse using the 'woman above' position. The man lies on his back in a restful manner while the woman gives him either manual or oral stimulation. This, of course, will have been practised before, and should have reached a stage in which there is excellent excitement and orgasm outside the vagina. While giving the stimulation the woman kneels alongside her partner in whatever position pleases her, and leans over his genital region.

Let us suppose the decision has been made to allow intercourse. By now the man will have a good idea when the orgasm is imminent. When he believes himself close he signals this to his partner, who, kneeling beside him, is in a good position to throw one leg over to his other side, form the kneeling 'woman above' position astride her partner, and lower herself on to his penis, allowing entry. She should then commence vigorous thrusting to stimulate him as much as possible. This stimulation may bring the already excited man to orgasm, which of course is the desired result. If this succeeds the couple can continue like this but mounting a little earlier on each subsequent occasion. Hopefully the man will learn to overcome his retarded ejaculation in this way. They can then try other positions or adopt the 'woman above' as part of their normal repertoire.

If the initial attempt, despite vigorous thrusting by the woman, fails to produce an ejaculation, she should dismount and again, by manual or oral stimulation, bring the man to an even nearer point; when orgasm is practically upon him, as before, she should quickly mount and begin thrusting. If the moment is well judged orgasm must follow.

The advantage of this method is the ease with which the woman can shift from manual or oral stimulation directly and speedily into coitus.

This method has been successful in the Masters and Johnson report on their programme statistics. Some clinics have unofficially reported a higher success rate when oral sex and/or a vibrator are included in therapy. It must be stressed that this condition is unusual.

7 How is success measured? What are the results?

The main problem of measuring success in treatment is to establish what criteria should be used. The usual criterion is the frequency of sexual intercourse, before and after treatment. Whereas this is a satisfactory measure for men it is not so for women. While even a slight degree of impotence is a serious barrier to sexual intercourse, quite a considerable degree of fear and dysfunction in the female does not prevent sexual intercourse either before or after treatment.

The achievement of orgasm is a good measure of change for women, but it fails for men, as some men can ejaculate even while flaccid. In any case not all women wish to have an orgasm during sexual intercourse; some prefer to masturbate before or after sexual intercourse, especially if the vaginal stimulation of intercourse is insufficient.

One of the most rigorous studies of change during sex therapy is by Lobitz and LoPiccolo. Their S.I.I. (Sexual Interaction Inventory) measures sexual behaviour, according to self-reported ratings which are made before and after treatment so that a comparison can be made. Before treatment each patient is asked two things. They are asked firstly what they would like to happen in their sex lives; and secondly what actually does happen. As part of these questions they are asked to assess the desirability of certain activities, seen from their point of view and also from the point of view of their partner. The activities are put as written questions in the form of a questionnaire which covers such items as kissing, oral sex, sexual intercourse, foreplay and orgasm. A comparison can then be made between what happens and what is desired, for each partner, before and after treatment. The congruence of their goals is also available.

Naturally any questionnaire presupposes that it will cover all the likely sexual areas which are desired. In so far as no questionnaire can do so, the method is less than perfect. Unfortunately some kind of standard way of asking the questions has to be used, since otherwise the assessments would be too subjective.

It is also desirable to be able to compare the results of different clinics and different methods. At the moment many clinics use their own questionnaires or rating scales. Thus the assessment

211

rules differ between the clinics, making comparisons difficult. There is a move in Europe to standardise such assessment methods. A questionnaire has been devised in Amsterdam called the General Assessment Scale. The questionnaire measures sexual behaviour and satisfaction and may be given before and after treatment. Part of the scale measures the non-sexual interaction between the partners which is of course very important also. At present the scale is being used at treatment centres in the U.K., the Netherlands and Germany.

The minimum requirements for adequate reporting of results should really be stated. The clinic must say how the patients were selected. If some of the people were rejected as unsuitable, why was this? For if a clinic selects only the most promising cases success rates will of course be high. The readers of any report should also know what would have happened to the patients if the treatment had not been given. Might they have got better spontaneously, or found another partner? One way of dealing with this difficulty is to have an untreated group to act as a control group. Another way is for the control group to receive a different form of treatment whose efficacy, compared with no treatment, is known. In the absence of controls one can not be certain that treatment is better than nothing, or a holiday, for instance.

The clinic should have a good measure of the sexual situation before and after treatment which is the same in application and content for all patients. The clinic must describe in detail the nature and degree of the sexual dysfunctions which are being treated. Some follow-up is desirable: assessment of the situation some months or years after treatment has ended and of whether there has been any falling off in results. Finally, the treatment itself must be described very comprehensively, and the number of 'drop-outs' in the middle of treatment listed. These should be counted as failures, or clinics give a spurious idea of their success.

Most of the reported results of sex therapy do not measure up to these standards. This is not to say that they are valueless, only that they are not as good as they might be. Some results are little better than advertisements, others approach the moderate excellence of consumer reports. Therefore, one has to be critical. The skill lies in being able to apportion the credence to be given to the results. Here, the number of rules that they have observed is crucial and success rates given as percentage figures can only be taken as a rough guide unless most of the rules have been followed. Inter-method and inter-clinic comparisons can only be made when the experimenters have observed the same rules.

Having made the rules of the game clear it is only fair to say that sex therapy is in its infancy but it will not be long before the process of comparison and evaluation will define more accurately the best methods which are available in particular disorders. Until then we must make do with rather approximate results.

The 'pure' Masters and Johnson method, as reported by them, has a high success rate for the patients they treated. It is effective for most dysfunctions. Admittedly no controls were used and defaulters (patients who failed to complete the treatment course) are not counted. Masters and Johnson were very strict in their selection of patients, avoiding severe psychiatric cases. They also found that patients who came from other cities improved more than patients attending from their own home town of St Louis. Similar results have been reported, using the pure Masters and Johnson approach, by Lorna and Philip Sarrel from Yale, U.S.A. Their therapy includes intensive treatment lasting a fortnight, given by two co-therapists, and also a shorter modified treatment.

It is encouraging that other sex clinics, even using drastically modified Masters and Johnson techniques, are reporting good results. Sometimes only one therapist can treat the couple; often the time interval between therapy sessions is two weeks; often the 'psycho-sexual clinic' is part of a state health service out-patients department where there is a shortage of time – perhaps only half an hour allowed for the treatment session. Again, European clinic patients have no 'time contract' for their therapy, whereas the Masters and Johnson patients are all given a fortnight's deadline and were thus highly motivated to get better in a short period of time.

Some clinics have combined a modified Masters and Johnson approach with traditional psychotherapy. Kaplan, in the U.S.A., reports good results but is unclear about her criteria of success. British clinics at Sheffield and Bradford report a good success rate combining techniques.

The Maudsley Hospital and Rochford General Hospital psycho-sexual clinics in England also use a modified Masters and Johnson technique combined with the treatment method outlined in this book: a permissive atmosphere; the use of relevant desensitisation; and the recommendation of erotica. Pleasure sheets are given to the patients which list erotic literature, art, films and magazines. At the Maudsley, if defaulters are omitted, the success rate shows a seventy-three per cent improvement, and at Rochford seventy-one per cent. At both centres treatment in groups, with both partners attending the sessions, for ejaculatory problems and female low sex drive problems, have so far proved even more effective.

Controlled trials in London and Rochford are at present being conducted to measure the efficacy of combining a Masters and Johnson modified therapy with the use of sex education and stimulation therapy. Research at Rochford is also being carried out to see whether it is necessary to present homework tasks or exercises in a graded sequence. What happens if the 'woman above' position is suggested at the beginning of treatment? A further controlled trial is being carried out at the Maudsley to see whether one therapist is equally effective as two co-therapists. Over the next decade or so these and similar questions will be clarified, though some variety of approach will doubtless remain.

Behavioural techniques are likely to remain highly important in sex therapy and it is hoped that therapists will be aided by this approach in improving people's sex lives and increasing human happiness.

Recommended books

1 Therapy

ANNON, JACK *The Behavioural Treatment of Sexual Problems* (Honolulu, 1975: Kapiolani Health Services, Honolulu, Hawaii 96814) Good descriptions of sex therapy, especially 'distractor techniques' in the treatment of impotence. Useful chapters on learning theory, although too many references are quoted and this could be off-putting. Good bibliography on counselling techniques and interviewing skills, and also on behavioural principles and their application.

BELLIVEAU, FRED and RICHTER, LIN *Understanding Human Sexual Inadequacy* (London, 1971: Hodder [paperback]) An easy to read down-to-earth explanation of Masters and Johnson's method of therapy. A historical background of sexology is also provided.

CHARTHAM, ROBERT *The Sensuous Couple* (London, 1971: Ballantine) Useful suggestions for couples to try out sensuous activities in different settings with sensitivity exercises. Good ideas on techniques, on oral sex and sharing fantasies. Direct approach, very readable.

DOWNING, GEORGE *The Massage Book* (New York, 1972: Random House) Excellent straightforward instructions on how to massage yourself, your animals and your lover. The book includes Essalen-style massage techniques and goes further into other types of massage and meditation. Recommended for therapists and their patients.

HARTMAN, W. E. and FITHIAN, M. A. *Treatment of Sexual Dysfunction* (Long Beach, 1972: Center for Marital and Sexual Studies, 5199 East Pacific Coast Highway, Long Beach, California 90804) This is one of the few books to include a 'stimulation approach' to therapy, like the use of video-tapes of sexual intercourse. Therapy also has a bio-psycho-social foundation. Poor drawings, but easy to read.

215

KAPLAN, HELEN *The New Sex Therapy* (New York, 1974: Quadrangle) For advanced reading, very lengthy and compendious. There is an especially good section of the treatment of anorgasmia. There is no systematic control of treatment which is a combination of behaviour therapy and psychotherapy. Good illustrations.

KNOX, D. *Marriage Happiness. A Behavioural Approach to Counselling* (Champaign, Illinois, 1971: Research Press) A straightforward account of behavioural principles and reinforcement in a marriage relationship.

LIBERMAN, R. P., KING, L. W., DERISI, W. J. and McCANN, M. *Personal Effectiveness* (New York, 1975: Research Press) Shows the importance of social skills training and communication in the context of social relationships. Practical examples.

MASTERS, WILLIAM H. and JOHNSON, VIRGINIA E. *Human Sexual Inadequacy* (London, 1970: Churchill Livingstone) For advanced reading. This classic includes good basic therapy descriptions with useful case histories. Poor drawings include a left-handed demonstration of the 'squeeze technique'.

2 Sex education

BANCROFT, JOHN *Deviant Sexual Behaviour* (Oxford, 1975: Oxford University Press) A well written book, more for the advanced reader, by a British psychiatrist. There is a clear account of treatment and research in the field of deviations which include: paedophilia, fetishism, exhibitionism, sadism and homosexuality.

BELL, ROBERT and GORDON, MICHAEL *Social Dimensions of Human Sexuality* (Boston, 1972: Little, Brown) A sensible account of the social and behavioural aspects of premarital, marital and extramarital sexuality.

BRECHER, RUTH and EDWARD *An Analysis of Human Sexual Response* (London, 1969: Panther) This is a simple explanation of *Human Sexual Responses* by Masters and Johnson, and a lot easier to read. There are additional sections which give a clear account of the 'clitoral versus vaginal orgasm' controversy and also practical application of sex research. A balanced view is given as this book ends with a paper by a psychoanalyst who attacks this type of research. The claim that Masters and Johnson have mechanised and dehumanised sex whilst overemphasising the importance of the female orgasm is unsupported.

CAUTHERY, PHILIP and COLE, MARTIN *The Fundamentals of Sex* (London, 1971: W. H. Allen) Clearly written and probably the best text book on sex education in Britain. It is mainly devoted to a biological approach. Their account of the human male and female is comprehensive. The chapter on sexual intercourse is excellent and includes some well chosen photographs. There is a sensible account of v.D. One chapter which discusses normality starts with a witty account of what exactly is legal; this is followed by a good account of deviations.

COMFORT, ALEX *The Joy of Sex* (New York, 1972: Simon and Schuster) A superb middle of the road guide to normal sexual behaviour in the 1970s. The best book for encouraging the average person to enjoy and experiment with sex. Caution is stressed. Enjoyable and useful illustrations; good for stimulation therapy. Highly recommended for everyone, including patients.

FORD, C. S. and BEACH, F. A. *Patterns of Sexual Behaviour* (New York, 1951: Harper and Row) This book is the best convenient source of information on the sexual habits of different human and other animal species. It places man's sexual behaviour in the context of sexual behaviour within the animal kingdom. Easy to read.

MASTERS, WILLIAM H. and JOHNSON, VIRGINIA E. *Human Sexual Response* (Boston, 1966: Little, Brown) For advanced reading. This classic is an account of excellent research on the phases of sexual response. Good description of the function of the clitoris. Includes useful chapters on ageing males and females and their sexual responses.

3 Female sexuality

BARBACH, LONNIE GARFIELD *For Yourself. The Fulfilment of Female Sexuality* (New York, 1975: Doubleday) Probably the best book on female sexuality. Includes sensible chapters on sex and orgasm, partners, bringing up children sexually, sex and pregnancy, menopause and ageing. Lively sections on opportunities for women to experiment with and enjoy masturbation and pornography. This is a worthwhile liberation book and should be useful for European anorgasmic women (Barbach refers to these as pre-orgasmic) as well as their American sisters.

BOSTON WOMEN'S COLLECTIVE *Our Bodies, Ourselves* (New York, 1973: Simon and Schuster) A classic feminist health book for women. Easy to follow, covering areas on contraception, reproduction, being gay, nutrition, V.D., self-defence and rape. A useful family reference book, direct with no frills.

CHARTHAM, ROBERT *What Turns Women On* (New York, 1974: Ballantine Books) A frank account by a British writer about the sensory experiences of women. Easy to read sections on erotic literature, visual stimulation, women's initial reactions to pornography, music, and sexual fantasies. The chapter on touch and sexual arousal is sensual and well described.

FRIDAY, NANCY *My Secret Garden* (London, 1975: Virago/Quartet) American women responded to advertisements in various magazines to send in their sexual fantasies to Nancy Friday. The result is a highly recommended collection of erotic material which is suitable for stimulation therapy. Wide range of exciting fantasies from lesbian activities to rape.

HOLLANDER, XAVIERA *The Happy Hooker* (London, 1975: Tandem) This autobiography of a madame is honest and entertaining and is rather like an updated version of *Fanny Hill*. Erotic descriptions of bisexuality, orgies, sado-masochism, bondage are included; in fact almost nothing is left out.

'J' *The Sensuous Woman* (London, 1971: Mayflower) Rather a coy approach to female sexual fulfilment, but some of the recommended exercises might be helpful for some patients. Some of her suggestions might please the male partner more than the female.

KINSEY, A. C., POMEROY, W. B., MARTIN, C. E. and GEBHARD, P. H. *Sexual Behaviour in the Human Female* (Philadelphia, 1953: W. B. Saunders) This classic study of American female sexual behaviour is good for facts but heavy to read. There is information on male and female attitudes to pornography, visual stimuli, etc.

MARTIN, DELL and LYNN, PHYLLIS *Lesbian Women* (New York, 1972: Bantam) This is a book by lesbians about themselves and other lesbian women they have known. Direct and easy to read. They have been active in the lesbian movement for twenty years.

4 Male sexuality

ANONYMOUS *My Secret Life* (New York, 1966: Grove Press) A randy account of a man's sexual adventures in Victorian England. Bawdy and erotic, with an almost unbelievable amount of bisexual energy spent. Good for patients to read as part of stimulation therapy.

HOFFMAN, MARTIN *The Gay World* (New York, 1968 : Basic Books)
One of the best and most readable books about the lives of homosexual men. Sensitively described by an American Psychiatrist who participated in this scientific study of gay men in a community in San Francisco. Gives a fair account of prevailing social attitudes.

KINSEY, A. C., POMEROY, W. B. and MARTIN, C. E. *Sexual Behaviour in the Human Male* (Philadelphia, 1948 : W. B. Saunders) This classic on American sexual behaviour of the male should be used as a reference book only and need not be 'read'.

LEWIS, STEPHEN *Male Sexual Fantasies* (New York, 1974 : Ace Books, 1120 Avenue of the Americas, New York 10036) Erotic collection of male fantasies, good reading for stimulation therapy, recommended for patients.

'M' *The Sensuous Man* (New York, 1971 : Lyle Stuart) Good for male patients or men who need permission to enjoy themselves. Sometimes a bit joky, but on the whole the suggestions are useful and practical.

SCOTT, VALERIE X. *Surrogate Wife* (New York, 1971 : Dell) Written by a surrogate female partner reputed to be helping cases referred by Masters and Johnson, when accepted for treatment without a female partner. A good account of nine men with sexual dysfunctions including one homosexual hunchback who initially refuses to wash.

Where to get sex therapy in the U.K.

1 Referral by outside source needed (*free treatment*)

Hospital treatment on the N.H.S. is free, but it might be necessary to remain a long time on a waiting list (some centres have a year's waiting list). Some G.P.s treat their own patients who have relatively simple problems and refer the more severe cases elsewhere. In order to be assessed for hospital sex therapy either a referral from a G.P. or from within the hospital is necessary.

A sex clinic in a hospital is sometimes referred to as a 'marital clinic' or 'psycho-sexual clinic'. The practical problem for most hospitals is which department the clinic should be housed in. It is usually run as the out-patient clinic of the psychiatry or obstetrics and gynaecology department. The clinic is usually held once or twice a week. There is no clinic which provides the traditional Masters and Johnson therapy, where patients are seen on a daily basis for a fortnight.

Most clinics in the U.K. are flexible when it comes to a modified Masters and Johnson method, which might include co-therapists or one therapist, but the usual rule is that couples should attend for 'conjoint therapy'. Some clinics will treat individuals on their own, or group treatment (good for moral support) might be available.

The Family Planning Association has a list of all G.P.s who have attended the F.P.A. seminars on psychosexual problems.

The following is a list of N.H.S. sources for sex therapy in the U.K. Referrals must be made through a G.P. or a hospital consultant.

Wherever possible we have indicated the name of the individual responsible.

Beckenham
Beckenham Hospital
BECKENHAM
Kent   01 650 0125

220

Birmingham
Hollymoor Hospital
Northfield
BIRMINGHAM   021 475 7421

University of Birmingham
Department of Psychiatry
Queen Elizabeth Hospital
BIRMINGHAM   021 472 1301

Blackburn
Queen's Park Hospital
BLACKBURN
Lancashire   0254 55222

Bradford
Department of Psychiatry
Bradford University
BRADFORD
West Yorkshire   0274 498121

Cardiff
Cardiff Royal Infirmary
Newport Road
CARDIFF   0222 33101

Coulsdon
Netherne Hospital
COULSDON   Downland
Surrey   56700   Mrs Sarojini Asirdas

Doncaster
Doncaster Royal Infirmary
DONCASTER
Yorkshire   0302 66666   Dr M. Davis

Fareham
Knowle Hospital
FAREHAM   Wickham
Hampshire   832271   Dr M. Perring

Leicester
Carlton Hayes Hospital
Narborough   Narborough   Dr Anne
LEICESTER   2225   Kolaszynska-Carr

Where to get sex therapy in the U.K.

London

Charing Cross Hospital
Fulham Palace Road
SW6   01 748 2050

Claybury Hospital
WOODFORD
Essex   01 504 7171   Dr D. Irwin

The Cassel Hospital
Ham Common
Ham
RICHMOND
Surrey   01 940 8181

Guy's Hospital Medical
    School
St Thomas Street
SE1   01 407 7600   Prof. J. P. Watson

Institute of Psychiatry
De Crespigny Park
SE5   01 703 5411

The London Hospital
Whitechapel
E1   01 247 5454

Maudsley Hospital
Denmark Hill
SE5   01 703 6333   Dr M. Crowe

Middlesex Hospital
Mortimer Street
W1   01 636 8333

Queen Charlotte's
    Maternity Hospital
Goldhawk Road
W6   01 748 4666

St George's Hospital
    Medical School
Department of Adult
    Psychiatry
Clare House
Blackshaw Road
SW17   01 672 1024   Dr R. S. Kalucy

St Olave's Psychiatric
  Hospital
Lower Road
SE16   01 237 8275

St Thomas's Hospital
Bromfelde Road
SW4   01 928 9292

University College Hospital
Gower Street
WC1   01 387 9300

Westminster Hospital
Dean Ryle Street
Horseferry Road
SW1   01 828 9811

Manchester
Department of Psychiatry
Withington Hospital
West Didsbury
MANCHESTER   061 445 8111   **Dr H. R. Beech**

Psychiatric Unit
University of Manchester
Oxford Road
MANCHESTER   061 272 2762

Plymouth
Freedom Fields Hospital
PLYMOUTH
Devon   0752 68080

Moorhaven Hospital
PLYMOUTH
Devon   075 54 2411

Rochford
Rochford General Hospital
ROCHFORD   Rochford
Essex   544471   **Dr A. Jack**

St Albans
Hill End Hospital   St Albans
ST ALBANS   55555

Where to get sex therapy in the U.K.

Sheffield
Psychiatric Department
Hallamshire Hospital
Glossop Road
SHEFFIELD   0742 303901   Dr W. L. Tonge

Sidcup
Queen Mary's Hospital
SIDCUP
Kent   01 302 2678

2 Self-referral (*usually free treatment*)

Some patients are too embarrassed to tell their G.P. that they have
a sexual problem. There are some centres where a person can
drop in for an assessment and be recommended a suitable treatment
centre.

The Brook Advisory Centres
233 Tottenham Court Road
LONDON W1   01 580 2991 or 01 323 1522

This centre was set up in 1964 as a registered charity. Consultation,
contraceptive supplies and pregnancy tests are all free at centres
in Birmingham, Edinburgh and London, although no one is refused
help in the other centres through lack of money. The centre is mainly
for young people who need advice. The centre refers people to N.H.S.
sex clinics in hospitals if they consider this to be necessary.

The Forum Personal Adviser
2 Bramber Road
LONDON W14 9PB   01 358 6181

This service was started in 1970. Initially people are asked to complete an application form and, on the basis of the information they
provide, the Secretary to the Adviser arranges an appointment with
a suitable therapist (usually qualified in psychology or medicine).
Each person is given a consultation lasting a full hour, in private.
Some therapists suggest attendance for another couple of occasions.
The aims of this service are to impart knowledge, reassurance
and guidance. The centre is attended by an almost equal number
of men and women, together or single, with sexual or marital problems. People are referred to other centres.

224

Grapevine
296 Holloway Road
LONDON N7   01 607 0935

People are offered advice on a suitable place to go for treatment
and are also given information about sexual education and problems. There is a 'phone in' service.

The National Marriage Guidance Council
is considering the development of services for sexual difficulties
in addition to its marital counselling work. Enquiries about the
existence of local facilities should be addressed to the Head of
Counselling, The National Marriage Guidance Council, Herbert
Gray College, Little Church Street, RUGBY.

The Family Planning Association
27 Mortimer Road
LONDON W1   01 636 7866

Psychosexual sessions are held in some of the birth control clinics
run by the F.P.A. Some of these clinics are being taken over by
the N.H.S. and are free, but other clinics charge for consultations.
An average of six sessions is required. Couples are encouraged
to attend, but F.P.A. clinics are mainly attended by women who
cannot bring a partner, or have none. The therapists are usually
women doctors who belong to the F.P.A. Institute of Psychosexual
Medicine. A physical examination is always given. A permissive
and reassuring attitude is the aim during therapy.

Family Planning Association Clinics
The following is a list of those F.P.A. clinics which give advice on
sexual problems. Many of these clinics are being taken over by the
Area Health Authorities who are also starting new clinics specialising in sexual problems. Appointments should be made by telephone
or in writing.

Central London
Raymede Health Centre
Telford Road
W10   01 960 0942

Finsbury Health Centre
Pine Street
EC1   01 837 6363

Shepherd's Bush F.P.A. **Clinic**
160 Shepherd's Bush Road
W6   01 602 2723

London Area
Brentford Health Centre
Albany Road
High Street
BRENTFORD
Middlesex   01 570 2805

The Caryl Thomas Clinic
Headstone Drive
HARROW WEAL
Middlesex   01 863 7004

F.P.A. Clinic
133 Wood Street
BARNET
Hertfordshire   01 449 5345

F.P.A. Clinic
49 Eastern Road
ROMFORD
Essex   Romford 44702

F.P.A. Clinic
20 Seymour Road
HAMPTON WICK
Middlesex   01 674 3502

F.P.A. Clinic
33 St James's Road
CROYDON
Surrey   01 684 4594

F.P.A. Clinic
Bedonwell School Health Centre
Bendonwell Road
BELVEDERE   01 310 6014

Marital and Child Welfare Clinic
Station Approach
WELLING
Kent   01 854 1825

Hillingdon Ante-natal Clinic
Duchess of Kent Maternity Wing
Hillingdon Hospital
HILLINGDON   01 997 9521

226

Cranbourne Health Centre
Mutton Lane
POTTER'S BAR
Hertfordshire   Hatfield 65983

Health Centre
High Street
HODDESDON
Hertfordshire   Hoddesdon 6351

County Health Services Clinic
Coval Lane
CHELMSFORD
Essex   Chelmsford 51671

F.P.A. Clinic
The Forum
Walton Road
MOLESLEY
Surrey   01 674 3502

F.P.A. Clinic
2a Guildford Road
WOKING
Surrey   Woking 4160

Health Centre St Johns
Hermitage Road
WOKING
Surrey   Woking 4160

Birmingham
F.P.A. Clinic
14 Frederick Road
Edgbaston
BIRMINGHAM   021 454 2865

Chorley
The School Clinic
Collison Avenue
Devonshire Road
CHORLEY
Lancashire   Chorley 2709

Eastborne
The Clinic
Avenue House
The Avenue
EASTBOURNE
Sussex   Eastbourne 24177

227

Where to get sex therapy in the U.K.

Exmouth
Exmouth F.P.A. Clinic
Devon County Clinic
89 Withycombe Village Road
EXMOUTH
Devon   Exmouth 2610

Gillingham
Medway Towns F.P.A. Clinic
Cambridge House
4 Mansion Row
Brompton
GILLINGHAM
Kent   Medway 43759

Glasgow
F.P.A. Clinic
2 Claremont Terrace
GLASGOW   041 339 6821

Grimsby
Grimsby F.P.A. Clinic
Health Centre
Milton Road
Nunsthorpe
GRIMSBY   Grimsby 79426

Leeds
Leeds F.P.A.
Burmantofts Health Centre
1 Beckett Street
LEEDS   0532 42290

Liverpool
F.P.A. Clinic
9 Gambier Terrace
LIVERPOOL   051 709 3968

Manchester
F.P.A. Clinic
Palatine Centre
63/5 Palatine Road
Withington
MANCHESTER   061 434 3555

228

Norwich
F.P.A. Clinic
18 Kingsley Road
NORWICH   0603 21872

Nottingham
F.P.A. Clinic
14 Regent Street
NOTTINGHAM   0602 40431

St Albans
St Albans F.P.A.
Hill End Hospital
ST ALBANS
Hertfordshire   St Albans 51153

Shrewsbury
The Health Centre
Wellington
TELFORD   0743 222518

Stockport
Stockport Hospital F.P.A.
Ante-natal Clinic
Steeping Hill Hospital
Bramhall Moor Lane
Hazel Grove
STOCKPORT   061 483 1010

Tunbridge Wells
Tunbridge Wells F.P.A. Clinic
21 Dudley Road
TUNBRIDGE WELLS
Kent   0892 30002

3 Private treatment

Private treatment fees range from £5 to £30 a session, depending on whether there is one therapist or two co-therapists. Some therapists charge according to a patient's means. Treatment can be more intensive as some clinics are prepared to treat patients twice a week or more frequently.

The N.M.G.C. will provide a list of private therapists. Some of the therapists are G.P.s, psychiatrists or psychologists. The F.P.A. lists all doctors trained in psychosomatic gynaecology, so all these therapists are medically qualified.

Where to get sex therapy in the U.K.

Most of the private therapists are in London. It is usually necessary to be referred by a G.P. Waiting lists exist, but they are usually shorter than N.H.S. waiting lists.

Private therapists see couples or single patients. There is only one centre surrogate therapy is provided (substitute husband or wife therapy) and that is at the Institute for Sex Education and Research in Birmingham. There is a waiting list of about a year for male patients but females are usually treated promptly.

London

Mrs M. Ballard
37 Kyrle Road
SW11   01 228 1948

Dr P. Gillan
7 Upper Harley Street
NW1   01 486 1348

Ms Katharine Hopkinson
38 Bouverie Road
N16   01 800 6871

The Margaret Pyke Centre
27 Mortimer Street
W1   01 580 3077

Centre for Behavioural Psychotherapy
38 Weymouth Street
W1   01 935 6379

Centre for Bio-Energy
22 Montague Street
W1   01 402 9475

Birmingham

Institute for Sex Education and Research
38 School Road
Mosley
BIRMINGHAM   021 449 0892

Note Members of the British Medical Association have been advised by the General Medical Council that if they allow their names to appear in a list of this sort it may be regarded as advertising, which is forbidden to members of the B.M.A. This ruling has severely restricted the number of private consultants we have been able to list.

Index

Since many subjects occur *passim*, entries refer only to the most important passages. **Bold figures** indicate a definition or description.